The Eagle and the Waterpots

A Commentary on the gospel of John

Les Wheeldon

ISBN: 9798360139133

DEDICATION

I dedicate this book to my wife Vicki, who has been a shining example to me of the love of God through her faithful abiding in Christ.

ACKNOWLEDGMENTS

I acknowledge with grateful thanks the help and encouragement of my wife Vicki, Graham Cline, Mary Seaton, John Shaw, Larry Hill, Hugh Burney and countless others. I also owe a great debt to the writings of G Campbell Morgan.

Foreword

Back in the days of CD's, I recall receiving a set of Les Wheeldon's talks on John's Gospel, entitled "The Six Waterpots".

Having read and studied over the years quite a number of commentaries and books on this magnificent gospel, I casually left the CDs in my car to listen to at leisure at a later date. However, after hearing the first disc I intuitively realised I had discovered treasure. These talks opened up to me new angles of truth and insight I had never seen before. So now at last, we have it in book form with added depth and even a study guide.

With incisive perception, Les brings fresh insight and revelation to the various parabolic miracles and events contained in this wonderful gospel. As you read "The Eagle and the Waterpots", I trust doors of fresh understanding and illumination will be opened to you.

Larry Hill, Dublin.

Preface

The gospel of John is arguably the greatest piece of literature ever penned. It was written under the inspiration of the Holy Spirit and has a power to reach the heart in a way that only the Bible can. I have loved reading it and preaching from it. It has been a doorway to discover the wonder of Jesus, to love Him more and surrender my life to Him. I pray that my commentary may aid some to make the same life-changing discovery.

Les Wheeldon

CONTENTS

John's gospel and the flying eagle

John's gospel stands out as one of the most sublime pieces of writing ever penned. The reader is struck by the form, the order and the beauty of the prose and also of the truth that is set out here. While we must not worship the words of the gospel, one is deeply aware of the seal of the divine on its pages. John's gospel is beautiful, because of the majesty of the One who is described. The gospel was written by John to inspire faith in Christ (John 20:31) and as faith in Christ rises in the heart through the reading of this little book, so the hand of Christ reaches out and touches the reader. Christ is real, and has given us this book so that we may know Him and experience Him beyond the page.

The flying eagle

If you swapped your eyes for an eagle's, you would be able to see an ant crawling on the ground from the roof of a 10-storey building. You could make out the expressions on basketball players' faces from the worst seats in the arena. Objects directly in your line of sight would appear magnified, and everything would be brilliantly coloured, rendered in an inconceivable array of shades. Studies suggest that some eagles can spot an animal the size of a rabbit up to two miles away.

The more scientists learn about eagle vision, the more amazing it seems. Thanks to developing technologies, some aspects of their eyesight may eventually be achievable through optical enhancement. Other aspects, we can only imagine.

In part, eagles have excellent vision because their eyes, which are very large in proportion to their heads, are densely packed with sensory cells. While humans typically have 200,000 light-sensitive cells per square millimetre of retina, eagles may have 1 million — five times more. Similarly, while humans have only one fovea, a funnel-shaped part of the retina where vision is sharpest, eagles have two. Finally, where people see just three basic colours, eagles see five, enabling them to pick out even well-camouflaged prey.

The gospel of the flying eagle

There are many themes in this book, but the greatest is the theme of the inner life of Christ, which can be likened to a flying eagle. The first three gospels describe the life of Christ mainly from the position of a witness of the outward events, not the inner thoughts and motives. Matthew, Mark and Luke observe the facts: the birth, the miracles, the words, and finally the death and resurrection of Jesus Christ. There are glimpses in those gospels of the inner life of Christ. But it is in John's writings that the Holy Spirit takes us behind the scenes to see inside Jesus. This is one of the great keys to the book, and draws the reader to marvel, but also to believe that they, too, can be renewed in the image of Jesus and partake of the same life, and thereby the same inner life.

This same pattern of describing people and events from different standpoints is repeated in the Bible's record of the early church. The book of Acts describes the church from the outside. Thus, the word "love" is not actually found on the pages of that book, but it is love that filled those first believers, and love that was worked out in their everyday lives in the early church.[1] It is the apostle Paul who takes us behind the scenes to see the inner life of the Christian (Romans) and of the church (Ephesians).

God gives a perfect account of the most important events of history by giving us a sight of the same thing from different perspectives. God does this in His word on many occasions, which is why there are two accounts of the creation, and two accounts of the history of the kings of Israel. In the creation account in Genesis chapter 1 – 2:3, God takes the reader into outer space to see the creative activity from a viewing platform seated beside Almighty God. Then in chapter 2:4, the reader is taken down onto the earth to see God create the first man and the first woman. It is by this method that God allows the reader to fully perceive and appreciate the wonder of creation, or, in the case of Jesus, the wonder of the person of the Son of God. We should not be surprised that there are four gospels; we should rather be surprised that there are **only** four gospels. It is John who reminds us that if the world were filled from end to end with books about Christ, yet there would still be more to say about Jesus the Son of God (John 21:25).

While the eagle is nowhere mentioned in John's book, it has often been associated with this gospel. The Renaissance painters depicted John with an eagle and the other gospel writers were each associated with the other living beings described in John's Revelation (4:7).[2] Matthew was often associated with the lion

---

[1] The word love occurs once as an adjective in the book of Acts: *"Our beloved Barnabas and Paul."* (Acts 15:25 NKJV)

[2] There are many examples to choose from including: Rubens picture of the four evangelists in Schloss Sans Souci, Berlin c. 1614; see also the Book of Kells in Trinity College Dublin which has an illumination of the four evangelists with their symbols c. 800. Jerome AD 342-420 (the translator of the Bible into

(king), Mark with the calf (servant sacrifice), and Luke with the man (humanity). The "flying eagle" is revealed in John, as Christ is seen from the standpoint of One who dwells with the Father. He has a soaring Spirit, and comes to every situation from the standpoint of the Father's love and from eternity. This cannot be attained by meditation alone, but by a living fellowship with God in Christ.

It should come as no surprise to us that to the church are given two wings as of a great eagle, (Rev 12:14). These are given so that she might escape the onslaught of the devil against her. On occasions, the church has relied too much on other means such as the power of intellect, to fight the darkness of unbelief. Philosophy and education may improve the mind, and prosperity may improve our physical living conditions, but to soar on eagle's wings will keep us safe from the attacks of the powers of darkness and empower us to break their hold on the minds of people. This gospel then has a message that will be a key to all who would know the secret of victory over sin and darkness.

Seeing Him who is invisible.

"You are from beneath, I am from above." John 8:23.

Jesus is here describing the eagle's perspective. He had a life rooted in God, in the courts of divine life. The point here is that Christ, as a man, had an inner life that waited in perfect stillness on His Father and on His will. Such a life is not dominated by the events that spill out into our circumstances one after another. While so many are dominated by the tyranny of unfolding problems, Christ is settled in the eternal, with a clear undisturbed view of His Father.

Latin – the Vulgate) associated John with the flying eagle in his commentary on Matthew. Augustine of Hippo (AD 354 – 430) made the same link in his harmony of the gospels.

Born from above (John 3:7)

The question is how to rise to these heights? The answer of Christ is that it is humanly impossible, but God has the answer through the gift of the Holy Spirit. By the Spirit we are born from above, and this means that the Christian has roots which reach into the presence of God on high. Christ Himself is the Son of the Most-High God (Mark 5:7) and was conceived through the Holy Spirit, *"the power of the Highest"* (Luke 1:35).

Pilate claimed authority over Christ, claiming to have power to crucify or release Him (John 19:10). Christ was racked with pain at this moment from the terrible scourging He had received (John 19:1) and His ears were filled with the mockery of the soldiers (John 19:3) and the demands of the chief priests (John 19:6). But despite all these threats and all this pain and anguish, there was an incredible calm and authority in Christ. He looked beyond Pilate to see what was above him. *"You could have no power at all against Me unless it had been given you from above."* (John 19:11). Jesus was looking at the Mount Everest of God (a coincidentally fitting name for the world's highest mountain). In the foreground He could see the pale, weak figure of Pilate who was wagging his finger at Jesus as if he were greater than the mountain. Pilate was like an ant on the slopes of the world's highest mountain. This is the eagle's perspective, and this must be our perspective too.

Above the storms and clouds.

Christ walked on water in John 6:19. He walked through the storm, against the wind, over a sea that was boiling with ceaseless turmoil. The point is not that we should also walk physically on water, but that we should walk through the far worse turmoil of life and the attacks of the wicked one. The surface on which we walk through life is not solid ground - it moves beneath our feet. There are frequent references to Christ in a

5

boat in a storm. In Mark 4:37, the writer describes a sea in which it is impossible for the normal person to lie still, let alone sleep. The waves were violent and the description was that of a severe storm which would have left the disciples battered and bruised by the frequent knocks against the side of the boat. But through it all, Christ slept on a pillow. Truly He was from above. It is not merely that He was so different, but that He also invites us to partake of the same life and faith which is rooted in a peace that passes understanding. Jesus was not mocking the disciples when He said: *"Why are ye so fearful? How is that you have no faith?"* (Mark 4:40). He was challenging them to realise that they did not have to live as a prey to circumstances, but could rise above the storms of life.

Surrendered to the Father's will

The inner life of Christ was one of complete surrender to the will of the Father. Christ claimed to have a life of surrender in the area of personal initiative. *"Most assuredly, I say to you, the Son can do nothing of Himself, but what He sees the Father do; for whatever He does, the Son also does in like manner."* (John 5:19). This is not passivity; it is the complete focus of the will in surrender to the Father. The lazy man will delight in the concept of a totally passive will, but this is not what Jesus was speaking of. Jesus was ablaze with love and devotion, but that love and devotion were not directed to acting according to natural light, or to carnal enthusiasm. This devotion was directed to the stilling of all other powers to the sole purpose of the enthroning of the Father's will. This is perfect activity, since it is the direction of the whole being towards the true purpose of our existence, which is God Himself.

The will is the power to focus our being on one thing; it is the use we make of our powers. The whole personality active is the will. This means that when we direct our lives to the pursuit of selfish pleasure, we are engaging our wills. The passive life is by definition listless and despondent. Christ focused His heart and mind in complete concentration and the application of Himself to the Father's will.

Jesus claimed that He saw the Father do things (John 5:19) and that He heard the Father speak (John 5:30). This was the fruit of waiting on God. As Christ dwelt above, His inner eye and ear were opened to perceive God. This was the basis of a faith ministry that could see maimed limbs restored and the decomposed body of Lazarus restored to life. This was also the life that stood before the Sanhedrin, Pilate, baying crowds and finally, before His executioners and not seeing the hand of man but the hand of God.

This then, is the perspective of John's Book. Christ came from above and became a man. As a man, He then developed a human life that dwelt above and came to every situation from the perspective of eternity. He was the Creator and the Giver of life itself. Above all, He was from the Father's heart, the perfect revelation of God. God was clearly seen and understood without shadow or veil through the person of the Son. He was and is flawless, perfect and sinless. He is alone able to bear absolute power over the universe on His shoulders, because He has no wrong thoughts, no carnal or selfish ambition. He is God: Love perfectly expressed to human beings.

.

JOHN 1

THE WORD BECAME FLESH

The inner life of Christ – the Prologue
(John 1:1-18)

1 In the beginning was the Word, and the Word was with God, and the Word was God. 2 The same was in the beginning with God. 3 All things were made through him. Without him, nothing was made that has been made. 4 In him was life, and the life was the light of men. 5 The light shines in the darkness, and the darkness hasn't overcome it. 6 There came a man, sent from God, whose name was John. 7 The same came as a witness, that he might testify about the light, that all might believe through him. 8 He was not the light, but was sent that he might testify about the light. 9 The true light that enlightens everyone was coming into the world.

10 He was in the world, and the world was made through him, and the world didn't recognise him. 11 He came to his own, and those who were his own didn't receive him. 12 But as many as received him, to them he gave the right to become God's children, to those who believe in his name: 13 who were born not of blood, nor of the will of the flesh, nor of the will of man, but of God. 14 The Word became flesh, and lived among us. We saw his glory, such glory as of the one and only Son of the Father, full of grace and truth. 15 John testified about him. He cried out, saying, "This was he of whom I said, 'He who comes after me has surpassed me, for he was before me.'" 16 From his fullness we all received grace upon grace. 17 For the law was given through Moses. Grace and truth were realised through Jesus Christ. 18 No one has seen God at any time. The one and only Son, who is in the bosom of the Father, has declared him.

John's gospel opens with the prologue (John 1:1-18). It takes us up above history to the earliest point in time that can be described or conceived. This is the deep, focal point of Christ's being and the true perspective of faith. The opening words *"In the beginning"* take us to the earliest point mentioned anywhere in the Bible. Genesis 1:1 opens with similar words and reaches back to the creation of the world. 1 John 1:1 is similar to John 1:1 but reaches back only to the incarnation. But here in John 1:1, the inner life of Christ is described in its complete, original simplicity.

The beginning here is not the starting point of creation or of Christ's earthly sojourn; it is the condition that exists in God beyond time. The beginning then is not merely in time, but in position. This is the fountain head of God and of all that is. The Hebrew word for "beginning" contains the word "head" ("rosh") and indicates that the beginning is the head of all things. The Greek word "arche" contains the concept of "rule" and indicates that it is the origin of all government and power. "In the beginning" then, is not merely a point in time, it is a place in spiritual order. We are to come to the beginning, and as we do so, we approach the unspoilt life of God Himself.

To imagine this state and condition we have to imagine a place before all things existed. In the beginning, there were no cars, no houses, no trees, no planets and no stars. Above all there was no sin and no devil. There was only God. In the beginning was Christ alongside and in relationship with His Father. There is in that relationship a profound stillness, a rest, an awed peace of being. This is the air on which the eagle soars. The seraphim around the throne of God were created for this place. Since the day of their creation they have covered their faces in rapt wonderment at what they see. Think of one of them visiting our planet and attending our meetings. They might rightly wonder if they are servants of the same God. Yet these same creatures, attendant on the man Jesus Christ, would have sensed the unspoilt wonder of eternal rest in His heart and mind, and the perfect rest and poise of His being.

That Christ is at home in these places may seem obvious, since He is in truth the place itself. It is He who is the light that shines (John 1:4-5 and 8:12) and the life that sustains (Col 1:17). Whatever else may ever be said about prayer and our relationship with God, it is essential that our hearts enter into quiet waiting on God, or we will never understand the breath-taking wonder of His being.

Christ is the light of the world. Physical sunlight produces green life in plants, and sustains life in that realm. Sunlight produces vitamin D and is vital for healthy bodies. Sunlight warms the earth and keeps conditions right for all life. All these are mere physical effects. Christ is uncreated light. He shines through the heart and imparts life to those who receive the light of His penetrating presence. He is the light that improves our heart states as we wait before Him. He awakens hope and washes our beings free from unbelief and all negative things. As we wait on God we are transformed into His image (2 Cor 3:18). Here is the key to life in the Spirit: dwelling in an unclouded relationship with God. This is precisely the inner life of Christ: the Son with the Father (John 1:18).

John's "logos"

The prologue is full of astonishing implications that slowly dawn upon the reader. John was supremely aware of Jesus Christ and the meaning of His life in a way that makes all things secondary to this marvellous person. Read the prologue exchanging the word "logos" with the word "love":

"In the beginning was Love, and Love was with God and Love was God. Love was in the beginning with God. All things were made by Love and without

Love was nothing made that was made. In Love was Life and the Life was the Light of men. .... Love was in the world, and the world was made through Love, and the world did not know Love. Love came to His own and His own did not receive Him, but as many as received Love, to them He gave the right to become the children of God, to those who believe in His name." John 1:1-12.

This is a valuable exercise, because it brings home to the reader the wonder of the Person described. Nevertheless, although Jesus is Love, as God is Love, yet all "love" is not Jesus. Human love and affection, even the affection of animals reflect the love of God but they are not God. The value of this exercise is only to help the reader to realise the implication of saying that the logos is the key to everything. Jesus made everything, and He made everything with loving motives. He came to the world as an expression of eternal Love.

The most startling declaration of John 1:1 is that Jesus is the "logos". The Greek word "logos" was filled with associations just as the words "Iwo Jima" or "Dunkirk" do not evoke merely geographical associations. Greek philosophers who lived before John, had used the word to indicate "the key to everything."

To the first-century readers of the gospel, they would have thought of different concepts associated with the "logos". Greek philosophers such as Heraclitus (540 - 475 BC), Plato (427 - 347 BC), and Aristotle (384 - 322 BC) used "logos" to mean the underlying key to the universe, the secret that explains everything. To them it might have been a force, or a mathematical equation, but not a person. To Philo (20BC- 50AD) there was a religious aspect to the "logos", but not a personal one. Similarly, Albert Einstein in the twentieth century spent his life searching for the one mathematical formula that lies at the centre of all science. This is what the Greeks called "logos".

11

John takes up this word with all these associations and declares that the key to all things, physical and spiritual, was Jesus, who has existed from eternity with God His Father. The key to the universe is not physics, nor mathematics ($E=mc2$), nor biology. Jesus, the Love of God incarnate, is the key to the universe. The universe only makes sense because of Jesus, who reveals the heart of God and hence the meaning of everything.

There are four aspects of the character of Christ that emerge in John's description of Jesus as the "logos". They are:

    (i)   Deity
    (ii)   Personality
    (iii)   Creator
    (iv)   Incarnation.

(i) Deity: "Logos" in relationship with God

The opening words of John's gospel:

"In the beginning was the Word, and the Word was with God and the Word was God" (John 1:1).

"In the beginning" directs us to ponder Christ's pre-existence, (as Paul said later: "He is before all things", Colossians 1:17). By this phrase John declared the divinity of Jesus Christ, and His equality with God. He is the only true concept of God. In other words: Jesus Christ is God.

Nothing greater can ever be said about Christ than that He is God. The word "God" encapsulates infinity, omnipresence, omniscience and omnipotence. If Christ be God, then He is the Almighty One, and there is no limit to His knowledge, wisdom, holiness and power. If Christ be less than God, then He is an influence, and has resources. But Jesus Christ is infinite God. This simple fact communicates the tranquillity of absolute lordship and authority. Christ is the centre of all things.

(ii) Personality: the "logos" not a force, or a principle but a person, the Son of the Father

The phrase "with God" is from a preposition meaning "facing", describing relationship. In John 1:18 the language of Sonship is used. The "logos" is a person - *"the only begotten Son who is in the bosom of the Father"* (John 1:18). He is expressive of the personal love of God: *"He came unto His own"* (1:11). Jesus is a person full of grace, truth and glory: *"we beheld his glory, the glory as of the only begotten of the Father, full of grace and truth"* (John 1:14). It is of the nature of humanity to make all things impersonal. Many think of God as "power", such as electricity. But God is not impersonal, and every depersonalization of truth is deceiving. Power in ministry is potentially attractive and might even be inebriating. But to love power and influence is to be deceived. Jesus brings us to the true centre of power, which is Himself.

(iii) Creator: "logos" in relationship with the physical universe

Psalm 33:6 declares that the heavens were made by the word of God. In John's prologue this statement is further defined, in that Jesus, the "logos", is the Creator, through whom all things were made. This is a further statement of deity, namely that Jesus is the Creator God. All things were made by Jesus. Jesus, who walked the earth, was and is the Almighty God who created the boundless universe. This startling contrast makes us realise that true glory is not in size but in character. The infinite variety and beauty of the creation declares the greater wonder and immeasurable intelligence of the person who made it.

(iv) Incarnation: the relationship of "logos" to humanity

The statements of John's prologue are full of profound mystery, and none so great as the phrase in verse 14: *"the Word became flesh"*. This was not preceded by any statement of a Greek or Jewish philosopher. It directly contradicted the teaching of the Gnostics who had difficulty with the concept of Christ being man as well as God. This phrase declared that the physical universe is not inherently evil. It also declared the mystery that, though the "logos" was not a man in His pre-existence, yet He became a man for the purposes of redemption. The idea of redemption is introduced when John said we can become God's children by receiving the "logos". The phrases *"He was in the world"* (1:10) and *"He came to His own"* (1:11) both describe aspects of the incarnation. They describe the purpose, namely to bring light, life and new birth to a fallen humanity. Underlying this truth of the incarnation is the love of God. God loved the world and sent His Son, the "logos", to become a human being, to bring light, grace and truth. Contained in this introduction is the inevitability of the cross, through the conflict between light and darkness, and the fact that the "logos" came to His own, and His own did not receive Him.

Conclusion

The term "logos" was taken up by the Holy Spirit, through the apostle John. He took up a term that was full of associations, both for Jews and Greeks. John identifies Jesus as the "logos", different to the "logos" of philosophers, but the fulfilment of the Hebrew Old Testament hope of a Messiah. Christ is the living Word, God's agent of creation, God's only Son and God Himself, who became flesh, to bring the full divine self-disclosure to the human race. John describes in words the mystery of the incarnation, and the mystery of the person of Christ. His use of "logos" is central in conveying the transcendent nature of the person of Christ.

The role of John the Baptist (John 1:19-34)

[19] This is John's testimony, when the Jews sent priests and Levites from Jerusalem to ask him, "Who are you?"
[20] He declared, and didn't deny, but he declared, "I am not the Christ".
[21] They asked him, "What then? Are you Elijah?"
He said, "I am not."
"Are you the prophet?"
He answered, "No."
[22] They said therefore to him, "Who are you? Give us an answer to take back to those who sent us. What do you say about yourself?"
[23] He said, "I am the voice of one crying in the wilderness, 'Make straight the way of the Lord, as Isaiah the prophet said."
[24] The ones who had been sent were from the Pharisees. [25] They asked him, "Why then do you baptise, if you are not the Christ, nor Elijah, nor the prophet?"
[26] John answered them, "I baptise in water, but among you stands one whom you don't know. [27] He is the one who comes after me, who is preferred before me, whose sandal strap I'm not worthy to loosen." [28] These things were done in Bethany beyond the Jordan, where John was baptizing.
[29] The next day, he saw Jesus coming to him, and said, "Behold, the Lamb of God, who takes away the sin of the world! [30] This is he of whom I said, 'After me comes a man who is preferred before me, for he was before me.' [31] I didn't know him, but for this reason I came baptizing in water: that he would be revealed to Israel." [32] John testified, saying, "I have seen the Spirit descending like a dove out of heaven, and it remained on him. [33] I didn't recognise him, but he who sent me to baptise in water said to me, 'On whomever you will see the Spirit descending and remaining on him is he who baptises in the Holy Spirit.' [34] I have seen, and have testified that this is the Son of God."

John the Baptist did not know who Jesus was and stated this clearly: "I did not know Him." (John 1:31). The greatness of the person of Christ was such that the responsibility of identifying Him was too much for any one individual. God Himself spoke from heaven at the baptism of John to announce that Jesus was His Son (Matthew 3:17). Thus, John received and preached that Jesus was the Son of God (John 1:34). God also gave to John the revelation that Jesus was the redeeming Lamb of God bearing away the sin of the world (John 1:29).

John was challenged by the Pharisees concerning his own identity, and on that count, he had no doubts: he knew that he was merely a voice (1:23). He used the remarkable phrase: *"I am not"* (1:20 and 21) which was in stark contrast to the bold assertion of Jesus: *"I am"* (8:58). It was echoed later by Peter who denied he was a disciple with the same words: *"I am not"* (18:17). This describes the human condition, indicating that there is a profound lack, an inner emptiness, a void that can be summed up as **non-life**. Jesus Christ has life, and He alone. What people often consider "life" is excitement, experience, etc. But what the Bible describes as life is selfless love, fellowship with God, the ability to enter the unseen world of the Spirit. Human life is locked in earthbound dimensions, but Christ is Himself another realm, another kingdom. That kingdom is what makes sense of everything that is visible. Without that "life", the pleasures of earth run out as stale bread, and rotten fruit. John the Baptist and Peter the apostle made no claim to be anything at all compared to Christ.

John further identified Jesus as the baptiser in the Spirit (1:33). This is the unique greatness of Christ: to impart a life that is of a different order. It is the uniquely distinctive ministry of Jesus, to take dead, empty men and women, and to impart His life to them.

The flying eagle and the first disciples (John 1:35-51)

35 Again, the next day, John was standing with two of his disciples, 36 and he looked at Jesus as he walked, and said, "Behold, the Lamb of God!" 37 The two disciples heard him speak, and they followed Jesus. 38 Jesus turned and saw them following, and said to them, "What are you looking for?"

They said to him, "Rabbi" (which is to say, being interpreted, Teacher), "where are you staying?"
39 He said to them, "Come, and see."
They came and saw where he was staying, and they stayed with him that day. It was about the tenth hour. 40 One of the two who heard John and followed him was Andrew, Simon Peter's brother. 41 He first found his own brother, Simon, and said to him, "We have found the Messiah!" (Which is, being interpreted, Christ). 42 He brought him to Jesus. Jesus looked at him, and said, "You are Simon the son of Jonah. You shall be called Cephas" (which is by interpretation, Peter). 43 On the next day, he was determined to go out into Galilee, and he found Philip. Jesus said to him, "Follow me." 44 Now Philip was from Bethsaida, of the city of Andrew and Peter. 45 Philip found Nathanael, and said to him, "We have found him, of whom Moses in the law, and the prophets, wrote: Jesus of Nazareth, the son of Joseph."
46 Nathanael said to him, "Can any good thing come out of Nazareth?"
Philip said to him, "Come and see."
47 Jesus saw Nathanael coming to him, and said about him, "Behold, an Israelite indeed, in whom is no deceit!"
48 Nathanael said to him, "How do you know me?"
Jesus answered him, "Before Philip called you, when you were under the fig tree, I saw you."
49 Nathanael answered him, "Rabbi, you are the Son of God! You are King of Israel!"
50 Jesus answered him, "Because I told you, 'I saw you underneath the fig tree,' do you believe? You will see greater things than these!" 51 He said to him, "Most certainly, I tell you all, hereafter you will see heaven opened, and the angels of God ascending and descending on the Son of Man."

John passed on his disciples to Jesus (1:36-7). They were drawn to see the simplest aspect of Jesus' life: *"Where do you live?"* This is because Jesus is essentially uncomplicated. His life is not filled with intricate mysteries that baffle and confuse with long technical words and explanations. It is the mystery of depth combined with simplicity. Commonplace life is endued with meaning because of Christ. He lifts the simplest actions to the outworking of a magnificent life. Christ is the cure for the cynical heart. He fills the everyday moments of earth with joy.

The most powerful Christian testimony is in the tiny details of lives that are fulfilled and meaningful. Many people live lives seeking to escape from the emptiness of the day. The person who knows Christ is filled with contentment and a sense of purpose that make ordinary moments to be the outworking of a joy that is not dependent on circumstances, but on an inner poise and relationship. The disciples sat with Jesus and were quietly convinced that they were with a person unlike any they had ever met before. Jesus spoke to them words that indicated a destiny and a purpose far beyond what any person may dream for their lives. We may entertain fantasies of special holidays, houses, events etc. but Jesus gave Peter a new name, and declared that this was to be his destiny, to be a solid person, reliable and faithful. Peter was none of these things, but from the moment he met Christ, the solidity of rock entered into his soul. This was to be his ultimate calling and that of all who believe in Jesus Christ.

Nathaniel also was given a sense of purpose by the sense of insight that came through the word of Jesus, that He had seen him under the fig tree (1:48). It was such a small detail, but it was the bearing of light to the ordinary details of life that was so powerful. Caring for a child, helping another human being, serving others with selfless love: all of these things involve the most ordinary of human activity but they are filled with meaning by the touch of the presence of Christ. He notices us. He loves us.

This first chapter shows the reader that Christ brings the divine revelation of the heart of God down to the simplest level. He brings God to ordinary men. The eagle soared above the world of man, and then came and lived in an ordinary room and welcomed them to stay with Him for the day. What did they discuss all day? What plans did they make? All such questions reveal the restless heart of man, who fills all his days with movement without ultimate purpose. The disciples sat with Jesus and found there in Him the purpose that took the hurry out of their souls, and made them change every priority they had ever entertained. By simply meeting Jesus, they had come home.

JOHN 2

THE SIX WATERPOTS OF STONE

The wedding in Cana (John 2:1-12)

2 *The third day, there was a wedding in Cana of Galilee. Jesus' mother was there.* *² Jesus also was invited, with his disciples, to the wedding.* *³ When the wine ran out, Jesus' mother said to him, "They have no wine."* *⁴ Jesus said to her, "Woman, what does that have to do with you and me? My hour has not yet come."* *⁵ His mother said to the servants, "Whatever he says to you, do it."* *⁶ Now there were six waterpots of stone set there after the Jews' way of purifying, containing two or three metretes apiece.* *⁷ Jesus said to them, "Fill the waterpots with water." So they filled them up to the brim.* *⁸ He said to them, "Now draw some out, and take it to the ruler of the feast." So they took it.* *⁹ When the ruler of the feast tasted the water now become wine, and didn't know where it came from (but the servants who had drawn the water knew), the ruler of the feast called the bridegroom* *¹⁰ and said to him, "Everyone serves the good wine first, and when the guests have drunk freely, then that which is worse. You have kept the good wine until now!"* *¹¹ This beginning of his signs Jesus did in Cana of Galilee, and revealed his glory; and his disciples believed in him.* *¹² After this, he went down to Capernaum, he, and his mother, his brothers, and his disciples; and they stayed there a few days.*

The ministry of Jesus began at a wedding and it will end at a wedding (Revelation 21:2). At the wedding in Cana the bride and groom were not named, but in the background stood Jesus the bridegroom with His disciples the bride. The facts are simple: the wine ran out and the party was about to be spoilt. This indicates the emptiness of life without Christ, and most importantly without the fullness of His life through the power of the Holy Spirit. This is equally true whether it be the emptiness of immoral people who follow their lusts, or the emptiness of religious careers without the reality of Christ within.

Jesus' mother was somehow aware that her son had the answer, and informed Him of the need. Mary had never seen Jesus perform a miracle. True, she had personally witnessed the staggering miracle of the incarnation in her own body. But she did not yet know what extraordinary power was about to be revealed. Nevertheless, Mary realised that if only her son was placed in charge, He would sort everything out. Whoever makes Jesus Lord of their life will immediately find that He is the answer to their deepest need.

Jesus was troubled and linked the need for wine with His hour: the cross. His mother was gently rebuked with the reminder that she was not in charge, but she was not offended, but rather acknowledged His lordship, and sent the servants directly to Him. There were six waterpots (six is the number of man – created on the sixth day). All were empty, each containing about twenty to thirty gallons, making each pot to be approximately the size of a human being. Jesus commanded them to be filled with water, and then commanded the servants to serve it to the master of the feast. The water was turned to wine, and the master of the feast declared it to be the best wine, unconsciously declaring that the new covenant will be better than all the covenants that preceded it.

Six waterpots of stone

The first great theme of John's gospel is the inner life of Christ. The second great theme of John's gospel is the impact of Christ on the human race. Here in chapter 2,

Jesus oversaw the filling of six waterpots of stone and the transformation of the water into wine. In the subsequent chapters Christ came to six men and women with an impact that is equally breath-taking: Nicodemus (chapter 3), the woman of Samaria (chapter 4), the lame man at the pool of Bethesda (chapter 5), the woman taken in adultery (chapter 8), the blind man (chapter 9) and Lazarus (chapter 11). This is the structure of the whole of the gospel as Christ encountered six individuals and transformed their lives. While this structure is not explicit (in that John does not number them 1 to 6) it is nevertheless part of the majesty of the gospel that it has this beauty and order within it. It is not the order of the logician who seeks to explain everything by points and sub points. It is rather the beauty of the flower or of the eye, which touches something in our souls and at the same time is pleasing to our sense of order and form.

These six waterpots describe the needs of the human race from the morally upright Pharisee (Nicodemus) to the failed life of the divorced woman in chapter 4 and the immoral woman taken in adultery in chapter 8. It moves from the need of the cripple and the blind man to the impossible bondage of physical death in Lazarus. All were on the same level of need as far as Jesus was concerned. People might judge Nicodemus to be a much better human being, but in the eyes of Christ he was as dead as Lazarus and as much in need of the mercy and power of God as the adulteress. Since Christ did not come for the righteous but to bring sinners to repentance, it is imperative that we rightly assess our tremendous need of His love and power. If a person should ever think that he or she does not need Christ in a particular area of their lives, then they may well find themselves to be abandoned and helpless in that area until they confess their sin and need.

The water and the wine

The events at the wedding introduce two more great themes of the gospel: the water and the wine. The water is a symbol of the Holy Spirit, and the wine is a symbol of the life of Christ and of His blood. The striking thing about this event is the fact that water was transformed into wine. The symbols are perfect. Man is empty, he is lifeless at best, and evil at worst. He needs to be filled with life, but he also needs to be transformed. Here is the perfect description of the new covenant in His blood: God will give to a person such a gift – the fulness of the Holy Spirit, and this gift will produce the life and nature of Christ. In God's new covenant people, the water will be turned to wine.

This is in direct contrast to the old covenant, where the Holy Spirit rested on people but did not transform them. Samson was moved by the Spirit, but had a fundamental flaw in his moral character. He never turned the water into wine. Fallen humanity and God do not mix, they do not flow together, they do not cooperate and combine. If only a method could be found that changed water to wine then all would be solved. From the purely physical standpoint, if a scientist could make a machine that had an inflow of water at one end, and an outflow of wine at the other (and not just wine, but the best wine ever), he would become a celebrity overnight.

Such a machine exists, but it is not man made. The slopes of Israel are covered with these machines, and they are of course vines. The vine absorbs water from the ground, and turns it into sweetest grapes, which are then harvested and turned into wine. This theme is introduced at the wedding of Cana in Galilee, and is completed at the Passover feast in chapter 15 when Jesus declared He is the true vine. The vine is Christ but is also a picture of the believer. The vine is not a strong tree but has limp branches that cannot support themselves. They need a piece of wood to support them. So too Christ, as a vine, leant on the wooden cross to bear fruit, and produced the best wine. The believer too must learn that this gospel is not about being mere vessels that contain power. It is rather about being partners with God in the whole expression of God's love and life. As Christ came to reveal the Godhead, so too believers, by laying down their lives, bear fruit in their turn and manifest the Godhead. This great work of the new covenant is the theme of the gospel.

The first miracle

At the wedding in Cana in Galilee Jesus did His first miracle. It was a first for Him and for His mother and His followers. His mother had known Him for all these thirty years and had observed the beauty and wonder of His life. But now something new was to happen. Mary did not know what it would be, but she was the one who triggered the miracle by telling the servants that He had the answer: *"Whatever He says to you do it."* Perhaps there had been little moments of crisis in the home and she had discovered that He was always there with serenity of heart and mind to still the storms of life. But nevertheless, this was a new beginning.

Since the dawn of time, God is, and has always been the God of miracles, from creation and through all His redemptive dealings with the human race. As believers we are familiar with the miracles of Jesus in the gospels, just as Mary was familiar with the miracles in Israel's history. But still there is a beginning of miracles in every individual's life. What was the first miracle in your life? The miracle of Cana was the transformation of water into wine, and the only miracle that is guaranteed to us all, is precisely that.

He will change the nature and atmosphere of our hearts and we will know the rich quality of life that comes from knowing Him. Mary understood more than all the people at the wedding that if the problem were laid at the feet of Jesus, all would be well. That is precisely what we must do. Put Him in charge of our lives and our eyes will open wide in wonder at the matchless flavour of His presence.

The three stages of the miracle

There were three stages to this first miracle and we do well to notice their order and their scope:

Stage one: make Jesus Lord. Obey Him, lay the matter at His feet. Don't try and imagine what He will do, simply spread it before Him, make it His problem and let it cease to be yours.

Stage two: let Him fill you with His Spirit, His presence, His love. When Christ fills us with His Spirit, we receive power to live, power to pray and power to overcome temptation, but this is still only the potential for a miraculous life.

Stage three: pour out the wine. It is this third stage that we most often miss. We have felt the burden of need, there is a drought in our lives, we are dry and empty and we have been driven to fall at His feet by the pressure of that need. Then we have been touched, changed and refreshed by His grace. But though we know all this, there is another stage: that beautiful water of the Holy Spirit must deeply transform us so that we do not know the Spirit only as an addition to our lives, but as the very source. We need to have the beauty of love in the very fibre of our being. That miracle will only take place when we are poured out. The flow of the Holy Spirit will only be released as we love others and direct our lives to loving and serving others. Only then does the Christian life become the sweetest most miraculous wine of all.

The first person to receive the poured-out wine was the ruler of the feast. From this we learn that the first person we minister to is always the ruler of the feast in heaven – the Father. We are saved to worship Him. Just as Jesus always lived for His Father, so too believers must direct all their service to the One that Jesus lived to please.

The temple is cleansed (John 2:13-25)

¹³ *The Passover of the Jews was at hand, and Jesus went up to Jerusalem.* ¹⁴ *He found in the temple those who sold oxen, sheep, and doves, and the changers of money sitting.* ¹⁵ *He made a whip of cords, and threw all out of the temple, both the sheep and the oxen; and he poured out the changers' money and overthrew their tables.* ¹⁶ *To those who sold the doves, he said, "Take these things out of here! Don't make my Father's house a marketplace!"* ¹⁷ *His disciples remembered that it was written, "Zeal for your house will eat me up."*

¹⁸ *The Jews therefore answered him, "What sign do you show us, seeing that you do these things?"*

¹⁹ *Jesus answered them, "Destroy this temple, and in three days I will raise it up."*

²⁰ *The Jews therefore said, "It took forty-six years to build this temple! Will you raise it up in three days?"* ²¹ *But he spoke of the temple of his body.* ²² *When therefore he was raised from the dead, his disciples remembered that he said this, and they believed the Scripture, and the word which Jesus had said.*

Chapter 2 concludes with the first cleansing of the temple during the feast of Passover (John 2:23). The accounts indicate that after His temptation Jesus did not immediately begin to preach. He waited till John was imprisoned (compare Mark 1:14 with John 3:24). It was in these weeks that Jesus attended the wedding, cleansed the temple, made His great declaration to Nicodemus, and spoke with the woman of Samaria. By these things he placed His whole ministry in the context of joyous celebration and promise. It is right to remember this context of a wedding feast and to grasp that the gospel is essentially a banquet prepared for the human race. John the Baptist described the voice of Jesus as the voice of a bridegroom (John 3:29) and this colours all His acts and words.

The visit to the temple was deliberate and was prophesied by Malachi: "*The Lord whom you seek, will suddenly come to His temple*" (Malachi 3:1). Jesus was a regular visitor to the temple and often walked in the outer courts of the temple area, never entering the holy places where the priests ministered. Jesus was a branch from Jesse's stem and was from the tribe of Judah, not Levi and never entered the holy inner sanctuary of the temple. Jesus walked in the courts where traders sold animals that had been approved for sacrifice. There, too, worshippers had to change Roman coins into the temple currency so that their offering was clean. The practice was defiled by greed, and controlled by the Sadducees, the dominant party in the Sanhedrin, who occupied the chief office of High Priest, and made vast wealth through the temple trade. Jesus was filled with indignation at what He saw, and calmly and deliberately made a whip of cords (John 2:15). Then, with fearful authority, He drove all the traders out of the temple area.

Christ wants the hearts of His people to be clean, and He cleansed the temple as a symbol of this fact. The tragedy was that at some point the trade resumed. Whether one lone trader led the way, or whether the High Priest encouraged their return, the fact is that three years later, Christ had to cleanse the temple a second time (Mark 11:15). The lesson here is that Christ will deliver a soul from uncleanness, and sometimes He may have to do it twice. The deliverance of a soul must be accompanied by a deep resolve never to return to defiling thoughts and habits. Without such a resolve, the deliverance will prove to be in vain. This does not mean that we are kept by the power of our human will. It means that we must allow the Holy Spirit to fill us with determination to be holy in our walk with Jesus.

Christ then made the great declaration: *"Destroy this temple, and in three days I will raise it up again."* (John 2:19). He was prophesying His crucifixion and resurrection, and there is incredible sadness in this declaration. *"Destroy this temple"* was the description of what would later happen. The human race took that precious life and stamped it out. They not only killed Jesus, they used all their power and skill to defile and maim Him. As much as it lay within human power, the executioners of Jesus "destroyed" Him. Thank God that Christ, by the surrender of Himself to the cross, *"destroyed the works of the devil"*. (1 John 3:8). Christ did not just weaken the works of the devil, He destroyed them, but the price was high and the battle fierce. The magnificence and perfection of the victory is declared in the wonder of the resurrection. Christ restored the human race and recreated humanity to be a new dwelling place for God in three days.

The weak hearts of human beings

23 Now when he was in Jerusalem at the Passover, during the feast, many believed in his name, observing his signs which he did. 24 But Jesus didn't entrust himself to them, because he knew everyone, 25 and because he didn't need for anyone to testify concerning man; for he himself knew what was in man.

The last three verses of chapter 2 reveal Jesus' perception of the state of heart of those who were beginning to believe in Him. He could not commit Himself to these believers, because there were deep flaws that could only be removed by the work of the cross. The great events of chapter 2 were prophetic, and the fulfilment of this prophecy had to await three more years for the events of Calvary and the day of Pentecost.

So the second chapter ends, with the continuing theme of each individual as a vessel. A human being is a waterpot, designed to be indwelt of the spiritual water of life, the Holy Spirit. Each one of us is a house designed to be the home of God, but defiled and in need of cleansing.

JOHN 3

THE FIRST WATERPOT: NICODEMUS

3 Now there was a man of the Pharisees named Nicodemus, a ruler of the Jews. **2** The same came to him by night, and said to him, "Rabbi, we know that you are a teacher come from God, for no-one can do these signs that you do, unless God is with him."

3 Jesus answered him, "Most certainly, I tell you, unless one is born anew, he can't see God's Kingdom."

4 Nicodemus said to him, "How can a man be born when he is old? Can he enter a second time into his mother's womb, and be born?"

5 Jesus answered, "Most certainly I tell you, unless one is born of water and spirit, he can't enter into God's Kingdom. **6** That which is born of the flesh is flesh. That which is born of the Spirit is spirit. **7** Don't marvel that I said to you, 'You must be born anew.' **8** The wind blows where it wants to, and you hear its sound, but don't know where it comes from and where it is going. So is everyone who is born of the Spirit."

9 Nicodemus answered him, "How can these things be?"

10 Jesus answered him, "Are you the teacher of Israel, and don't understand these things? **11** Most certainly I tell you, we speak that which we know, and testify of that which we have seen, and you don't receive our witness. **12** If I told you earthly things and you don't believe, how will you believe if I tell you heavenly things? **13** No-one has ascended into heaven but he who descended out of heaven, the Son of Man, who is in heaven. **14** As Moses lifted up the serpent in the wilderness, even so must the Son of Man be lifted up, **15** that whoever believes in him should not perish, but have eternal life. **16** For God so loved the world, that he gave his one and only Son, that *whoever believes in him should not perish, but have eternal life. [17] For God didn't send his Son into the world to judge the world, but that the world should be saved through him. [18] He who believes in him is not judged. He who doesn't believe has been judged already, because he has not believed in the name of the one and only Son of God. [19] This is the judgment, that the light has come into the world, and men loved the darkness rather than the light; for their works were evil. [20] For everyone who does evil hates the light, and doesn't come to the light, lest his works would be exposed. [21] But he who does the truth comes to the light, that his works may be revealed, that they have been done in God."*

The material unique to John's gospel

John's gospel differs from the other three, in that events in Jerusalem are described that are not mentioned in the accounts of Matthew, Mark and Luke. This is particularly striking in the first four chapters, because at this point in John's gospel, Jesus had not yet begun His public ministry. Jesus began to teach, preach and do miracles sometime after the events described at the end of chapter 3.

Within a few weeks Jesus was presenting the great manifesto of the kingdom in the Sermon on the Mount (Matthew chapters 5-7). But before all of that Jesus gave this foundational revelation of the new birth. It is the foundation of all His teaching and without it the human heart must falter at the impossibly high standard of moral and spiritual life that He taught as normal for His kingdom. Nicodemus refers to the "signs" (John 3:2) that Jesus had done, and so it can be concluded that His healing ministry had already begun, though there is no record of specific healings in the first two chapters.

It is also of importance that this conversation took place during the feast of the Passover. There are three Passovers mentioned in John 2:23, 6:4 and 12:1. There is no coincidence here, and the association with deliverance from Egypt is obvious. Here in chapter 3 that deliverance is through new birth, in chapter 6 it is through eating the lamb, and in chapter 12 it is the Passover at which Jesus was crucified and became the sacrifice for sin that made salvation possible.

It is in this conversation with Nicodemus that Jesus declared the heart of the new covenant, and in language that was so simple and clear. He chose to unveil this truth to the man who at first might seem to be the one who least needed it. Nicodemus was *"the teacher of Israel"* according to Jesus, meaning that he was the most authoritative Bible teacher of his day. He was a ruler of the Jews, indicating that he was a member of the Sanhedrin, a fact that was confirmed later when Nicodemus was present during political discussions about Jesus at the highest level (John 7:50). His name has two possible meanings: "Conqueror of the people" from the Greek and "Innocent Blood" from the Hebrew. While this is not of vital importance, it is striking that Nicodemus presents the case of human innocence. He came meekly to Jesus in brokenness and humility seeking to understand the truth of God that Jesus was bringing. Nicodemus was not an adulterer, nor a thief or a murderer. He had no disease or demonic problem that made him a needy man. Nicodemus presents the best that the human race can be, and this is not meant ironically. Nicodemus was a genuine seeker of God, and the best that the old covenant could produce. There were others like him, such as Hannah and Simeon, Mary and Joseph, Zacharias and Elizabeth to name but a few.

The story probably began with Nicodemus observing Jesus in the temple from a distance, and being deeply touched and stirred by what he heard and saw. Then late one night, he set out from his house in Jerusalem and asked where he could find Jesus. He did not want anyone to see where he was going, and so he walked through the narrow backstreets of Jerusalem until he found the house where Jesus was staying. He was probably welcomed into a large room where Jesus was residing with some disciples. It may be assumed that Nicodemus and Jesus talked in a corner of the room and were probably overheard by John as they talked.

31

Nicodemus began the conversation using the collective "we know", as a smoke screen to hide his own inner turmoil. He asserted *"we know you are a teacher come from God"* and this was his first mistake. Jesus was not a teacher come from God. He was God.

Humanity's problem: its nature

Jesus gave the astonishing reply to Nicodemus that *"unless one is born from above, he cannot see the kingdom of God."* The statement was given without preparation or introduction. Nicodemus' reply shows a man who was struggling to keep up. He gave the obvious response, that it is too awesome an assertion that a human being can experience a second birth. An adult cannot be reduced to the proportions of a new-born baby. Can he?

Jesus then explained that this is not a second, natural birth. He was referring to a miracle that takes place in the spirit of a person, in the realm of his or her nature. *"That which is born of the (nature of) flesh is flesh, that which is born of the (nature of) Spirit is spirit."* By this masterful phrase, Jesus taught that a person's problem does not lie in the realm of his intentions, or of his education: humanity's problem is their nature. The best anyone has within them is distorted by the nature of sin.

John's gospel gives illumination on the deepest mysteries of human life, and one of them is the mystery of iniquity, the fact of sin. Sin is a terrible affliction and the cause of all the evils that are seen in human society. Sins abounds all around, and even a single, daily local newspaper contains enough evidence of this awful evil that is polluting and spoiling human life. But Nicodemus' name would never have appeared in the tabloids reporting cases before the criminal courts, or in the gossip columns describing the latest scandals. Nicodemus' name would have been mentioned in the section reserved for honoured citizens. But Jesus was declaring that the most honourable of men must be born again. The most principled of individuals is afflicted with the terrible disease of a sinful nature. Sin then is not measurable in terms of criminality or anti-social conduct. It is a bias, a leaning away from God. Sin is a tendency of the human heart, to drift away from God and to go one's own way. In terms of the next five waterpots, sin is seen to be spiritually crippling (John 5), capable of terrible moral failure (John 4 and 8), inwardly blind (John 9), and finally: spiritually dead (John 11).

God's solution: a new nature!

The problem of a man or woman is their nature, and God's solution is to go back to the deepest level of a person's existence which is their birth. God gives to us the miracle of a renewed nature through the activity of the Holy Spirit, making and renewing us from the deepest level of our unconscious being. This miracle of God is begun through an encounter with Christ in salvation, when the Holy Spirit awakens our dead spirit to the reality of God. It is taken a stage further when a person is baptised with the Holy Spirit, allowing the Holy Spirit to renew and take possession of all that they are, as God imparts the full power of victory over sin. This miracle is perfected at the resurrection of the dead, when all possibility of sin is removed forever. God requires us to turn to Christ in faith, believing Him to be the Son of God, and yielding in complete surrender to Him. He on His part, undertakes to forgive all sins, and to impart the power and life that are in Christ Himself.

The mark of a new nature is that a person is motivated and influenced by the invisible power of the Holy Spirit. Formerly a person was carried along by the prevailing current and tide of human frailty and spiritual darkness. Now we can swim against the tide. Jesus said you can hear the sound of the wind, but cannot tell where it is going or where it is blowing from. So is the person born of the Spirit. Imagine a clump of trees growing near the ocean. The offshore winds have blown on these trees since they were tiny saplings and as a result, they are bent under the force of the prevailing wind. Now imagine one tree which contradicts the prevailing wind and grows against it. That tree is subject to an invisible wind that no-one else can see. So is the Christian. They are driven by a nature and a pressure that only they can feel. For this reason, they are so often isolated in their moral stance, and in their choices. They are led by the Holy Spirit, and obedient to the laws of the kingdom of God written upon the heart.

The further mark of a renewed nature is that such a person can see and enter the kingdom of God. In one way this phrase seems to indicate the fact of salvation, but the phrase *"see the kingdom of God"* demonstrates that it is much more to do with the power to discern and recognise the hand of God. A person with a renewed nature is aware of the unseen world of the Spirit of God. Just as a someone may stand by the seashore and be unable to enter the realm of the sea, so human beings are all their lives millimetres away from the kingdom of God, but so often never realise this fact. The person with a renewed nature is not always aware of the kingdom with the same clarity. But it is this awareness of the eternal kingdom and the realm where God dwells, that makes a believer different. We begin by believing, but then progress to inner assurance or knowledge. Often such moments will be while worshipping, or reading the Bible.

The regenerated believer has seen the kingdom of God and from time to time he consciously enters into the world of the Spirit. A believer lives then in two worlds. Christ Himself was the perfect example of this. His Spirit was in heaven while His body was on earth (John 3:13). Believers are seated in heavenly places while still living ordinary lives here on earth (Ephesians 2:6). All of this would be mere believism or theory if we never experienced any of it. Believers are set apart because they are inwardly united with God. Through the Holy Spirit they have access to experience the wonders of that kingdom.

God's method: the cross.

Nicodemus asked the obvious question: how? Jesus gave the ultimate answer and described the cross. He linked the cross with the lifting up of the serpent in the wilderness. In Numbers 21:5-9, the people of Israel were once more being judged for their carnal behaviour. Their sin on that occasion was to complain about the repetitious diet of heavenly manna. It is astonishing that the sin of moaning provoked such displeasure in God. God taught the people that their complaints were like the venom of poisonous snakes and He sent fiery serpents among the people. Many were bitten and many died. Moses was given a means of salvation and was instructed to make a bronze serpent and to put it on a pole and lift it up to be visible from all corners of the camp. Any afflicted soul had merely to lift up his eyes and look in faith at the lifeless snake and he was immediately healed. Jesus said that in the same way, He the Son of Man must be lifted up (John 3:14) on a piece of wood, and that everyone who looks in faith at Him and His sacrifice will experience the power of God to save from the venom of sin. New birth takes place in the soul that looks in faith at Christ and Him crucified.

Jesus then described the cross to Nicodemus in words that have become perhaps the most familiar words in the whole Bible, in John 3:16. These words spoken by Jesus have strange tenses. One might expect Jesus to say "God so loves the world" and that "He will give His Son". God's love is surely constant, and when Jesus spoke to Nicodemus the cross was in the future. But Jesus was referring to the cross in the consciousness of the divine origin of that event. Jesus was describing not just the future event, but the agreement made between Father and Son at the outset of creation, before the foundation of the world.

"God so loved the world" is a description of God's relationship with the human race. "The world" does not, of course, refer to the physical planet on which we live.

It refers to the collective human race, to every person who will ever be born. We think of the human race in its historical stages. Human beings think of the human race as a vague, indeterminate random number of people. No-one knows how many there will be. But to God the number is known. When He created the angels, He made them as a fixed number on one particular day; in the same way He made the planets and the stars. But when He made the human race, He made them in such a way, that they would experience family. Humans come into the world in consecutive turns. In the original plan of God before the disaster of sin, the human race would have grown till the genealogical tree was complete and with no-one dying. Through sin and death humans are born and then after a short life they die and disappear from the stage of life. If death had not come into the world, the number of people on earth would be growing till it reached completion. On the day of judgment all human beings who have ever lived will be raised from the dead and stand before God. On that day we will see "the world" that God so loved. God saw the complete human race from the beginning and He loved what He saw.

The little word "so" is a Greek word that can be translated "in this manner". "That He gave His only begotten Son" is therefore the measure of that love. This refers to the fact that God knew in His wisdom that there was a risk involved in creating mankind. That risk was the mystery of free will. People argue about free will, but the greatness of human beings lies in their ability to think and act as moral beings. In this we are made in the image of God. God foresaw that sin was possible and therefore He planned a provision for sin in case it should occur. From before the foundation of the world, God loved every human being and gave His Son to redeem each one. The cross is God's provision for everyone who is born in this world, to experience the saving power of God.

Nicodemus was the first waterpot, and his life received a direction and a devotion that made him swim against the tide among the evil intrigues of the Sanhedrin. In chapter 7:50 he is seen attempting to stem the tide of religious evil that would drive the rulers of Israel to crucify their Messiah. Nicodemus was obviously touched at the deepest level of his being by the love of God. Though we know little about him beyond the brief references in this gospel, he received Christ as a true ruler of Israel should, and became one of the many waterpots to be filled and transformed with the divine gift of life.

John the Baptist's closing testimony.

22 After these things, Jesus came with his disciples into the land of Judea. He stayed there with them and baptised. 23 John also was baptizing in Enon near Salim, because there was much water there. They came, and were baptised; 24 for John was not yet thrown into prison. 25 Therefore a dispute arose on the part of John's disciples with some Jews about purification. 26 They came to John and said to him, "Rabbi, he who was with you beyond the Jordan, to whom you have testified, behold, he baptises, and everyone is coming to him."

27 John answered, "A man can receive nothing unless it has been given him from heaven. 28 You yourselves testify that I said, 'I am not the Christ,' but, 'I have been sent before him.' 29 He who has the bride is the bridegroom; but the friend of the bridegroom, who stands and hears him, rejoices greatly because of the bridegroom's voice. This, my joy, therefore is made full. 30 He must increase, but I must decrease.

John then turns in the rest of the third chapter to the ministry of John the Baptist, which had passed its zenith and was now drawing to its close. John was tempted by the Jews to be jealous of Jesus, by informing him that Jesus was experiencing greater success. John exhibited the supreme consciousness of the greatness of Jesus, and a pure delight that Jesus is exalted. He repeated that his ministry was to be:

- a forerunner, and not a replacement of Christ (3:28).
- self-effacing so that Christ may be glorified (3:30).
- full of the awareness of the uniqueness of

Christ, beloved of the Father (3:35), with the authority of heaven itself (3:31).

- conscious of Christ's role as the heavenly bridegroom of the redeemed human race (3:29).

John the Baptist's ministry may not have been with all the power of the apostles in the book of Acts, but it bears the same marks as the ministry of Paul, who later described his consciousness of being nothing in himself, (1 Corinthians 3:7), and that Christ was the focus of his preaching (1 Corinthians 2:2) and the bridegroom of His people the church (2 Corinthians 11:2). Ministers will be tempted to be jealous of other ministers. The answer to such temptations is to be conscious that true ministry is to connect people to God through Christ, and not to take glory that belongs to Him alone.

"He must increase, but I must decrease." (John 3:30). With these words John expressed the passion of all who grasp the greatness of Jesus Christ. The mark of all who are led of the Spirit is their thirst to show the life of another. Later Paul said the same thing when he exploded with the joyous confession: *"it is no longer I who live, but Christ lives in me"* (Galatians 2:20).

John's grasp of the greatness of Jesus

31 He who comes from above is above all. He who is from the earth belongs to the earth and speaks of the earth. He who comes from heaven is above all. 32 What he has seen and heard, of that he testifies; and no-one receives his witness. 33 He who has received his witness has set his seal to this, that God is true. 34 For he whom God has sent speaks the words of God; for God gives the Spirit without measure. 35 The Father loves the Son, and has given all things into his hand. 36 One who believes in the Son has eternal life, but one who disobeys the Son won't see life, but the wrath of God remains on him."

In the last verses of chapter 3 John the Baptist's assessment of Jesus continues with four great declarations about Him. (Since there are no quotation marks in the original Greek text, it is not possible to know whether these comments are a quotation of John the Baptist or the apostle John's commentary).

1. Jesus Christ was from above and is above all. His testimony is of things from above, concerning the true nature of God. Those who receive the testimony of Jesus certify (literally "set their seal") that God is true.
2. When a man is sent by God, he is backed up one hundred per cent by God. The Holy Spirit works with such a man without measure, and such a man speaks God's words.
3. The Father loves the Son and has given the Son the pre-eminent position in all things.
4. He who believes in Jesus Christ has eternal life.

These words affirm the message of the whole gospel that Jesus Christ is the cornerstone of all things for the human race. He was sent from God and therefore each one of us will be judged by our reaction to the words and the person of Jesus.

John also affirmed the central truth of the gospel that God the Father loves His Son. This was the supreme consciousness of Jesus and the explanation for His life, His power, His peace and His joy. They are likewise to be the consciousness of all the followers of Christ: that they are loved of God.

John also explained the mystery of one who is sent by God. This also is an underlying theme of the gospel. Being "sent" is not merely to be the beginning of our ministry at a point in time. It is to be the character of our ministry. Ministers are to dwell above in fellowship with the Father and the Son and to be constantly coming from that place. It is from there that they are to minister in word and deed to the needs of the human race. It is only as ministers follow Jesus' example and dwell in intimate communion with Him that they can maintain their consciousness of a divine calling and thus speak the words of God with effectual power.

JOHN 4

THE SECOND WATERPOT: THE WOMAN OF SAMARIA

4 *Therefore when the Lord knew that the Pharisees had heard that Jesus was making and baptizing more disciples than John* ² *(although Jesus himself didn't baptise, but his disciples),* ³ *he left Judea and departed into Galilee.* ⁴ *He needed to pass through Samaria.* ⁵ *So he came to a city of Samaria, called Sychar, near the parcel of ground that Jacob gave to his son, Joseph.* ⁶ *Jacob's well was there. Jesus therefore, being tired from his journey, sat down by the well. It was about the sixth hour.* ⁷ *A woman of Samaria came to draw water. Jesus said to her, "Give me a drink."* ⁸ *For his disciples had gone away into the city to buy food.*

⁹ *The Samaritan woman therefore said to him, "How is it that you, being a Jew, ask for a drink from me, a Samaritan woman?" (For Jews have no dealings with Samaritans).*

¹⁰ *Jesus answered her, "If you knew the gift of God, and who it is who says to you, 'Give me a drink,' you would have asked him, and he would have given you living water."*

¹¹ *The woman said to him, "Sir, you have nothing to draw with, and the well is deep. So where do you get that living water?* ¹² *Are you greater than our father, Jacob, who gave us the well and drank from it himself, as did his children and his livestock?"*

¹³ *Jesus answered her, "Everyone who drinks of this water will thirst again,* ¹⁴ *but whoever drinks of the water that I will give him will never thirst again; but the water that I will give him will become in him a well of water springing up to eternal life."*

¹⁵ The woman said to him, "Sir, give me this water, so that I don't get thirsty, neither come all the way here to draw."

¹⁶ Jesus said to her, "Go, call your husband, and come here."

¹⁷ The woman answered, "I have no husband."

Jesus said to her, "You said well, 'I have no husband,' ¹⁸ for you have had five husbands; and he whom you now have is not your husband. This you have said truly."

¹⁹ The woman said to him, "Sir, I perceive that you are a prophet. ²⁰ Our fathers worshiped in this mountain, and you Jews say that in Jerusalem is the place where people ought to worship."

²¹ Jesus said to her, "Woman, believe me, the hour comes, when neither in this mountain, nor in Jerusalem, will you worship the Father. ²² You worship that which you don't know. We worship that which we know; for salvation is from the Jews. ²³ But the hour comes, and now is, when the true worshipers will worship the Father in spirit and truth, for the Father seeks such to be his worshipers. ²⁴ God is spirit, and those who worship him must worship in spirit and truth."

²⁵ The woman said to him, "I know that Messiah comes, he who is called Christ. When he has come, he will declare to us all things."

²⁶ Jesus said to her, "I am he, the one who speaks to you." ²⁷ At this, his disciples came. They marvelled that he was speaking with a woman; yet no-one said, "What are you looking for?" or, "Why do you speak with her?" ²⁸ So the woman left her waterpot, went away into the city, and said to the people, ²⁹ "Come, see a man who told me everything that I did. Can this be the Christ?"

³⁰ They went out of the city, and were coming to him. ³¹ In the meanwhile, the disciples urged him, saying, "Rabbi, eat."

³² But he said to them, "I have food to eat that you don't know about."

³³ The disciples therefore said to one another, "Has anyone brought him something to eat?"

³⁴ Jesus said to them, "My food is to do the will of him who sent me and to accomplish his work. ³⁵ Don't you say, 'There are yet four months until the harvest?' Behold, I tell you, lift up your eyes and look at the fields, that they are white for harvest already. ³⁶ He who reaps receives wages and gathers fruit to eternal life; that both he who sows and he who reaps may rejoice together. ³⁷ For in this the saying is true, 'One sows, and another reaps.' ³⁸ I sent you to reap that for which you haven't laboured. Others have laboured, and you have entered into their labour."

[39] From that city many of the Samaritans believed in him because of the word of the woman, who testified, "He told me everything that I did." [40] So when the Samaritans came to him, they begged him to stay with them. He stayed there two days. [41] Many more believed because of his word. [42] They said to the woman, "Now we believe, not because of your speaking; for we have heard for ourselves, and know that this is indeed the Christ, the Saviour of the world."

The fourth chapter begins with the statement that Jesus was compelled to pass through Samaria. This was not a geographical necessity, since the quickest route from Jerusalem to Galilee was through the Jordan valley, not through the hills of Samaria. This was the necessity of love, under the guidance of the Holy Spirit. Jesus was constrained to make a detour through the city of Shechem, the modern city of Nablus, where Jacob's well can be seen to this day. This was a Samaritan area. The Samaritans were the hybrid remnants of the ten tribes of the northern kingdom, which fell in 722 BC. The Assyrian conquerors took the majority of the population into captivity and many of those who remained, intermarried. The Samaritans were despised by the Jews who saw them as a spiritually-failed people group. This assessment was accurate, which makes the grace of God all the more remarkable. Jesus made a point of visiting Samaria, to reach out to this woman and through her to the whole Samaritan nation. Later, Jesus commanded the apostles to preach first in Jerusalem, then Judea followed by Samaria. This indicates that though the ten tribes failed so deeply to keep God's covenant, God remained faithful to His covenant promise, and sent His Son and His apostles to bring them into His wonderful grace. Truly God loves all, including those who fail. His heart is moved with love and mercy to the disqualified.

The woman of Samaria herself was a moral failure. Jesus reminded her of this when He asked her to call her husband. He knew by revelation that she had been married five times already, and the man she was living with was not her husband. She was living in fornication. The fact that she had had five husbands is not explained any further (John 4:18). It probably meant that she had been married and divorced five times, or perhaps that she had had five casual relationships. Whatever the details of her life, this single fact represented a chasm of personal failure and hurt. Assuming she had married as a young woman, she would have had all the hope of youth, combined with the uncertainty of an arranged marriage. But her first marriage failed. At some point either she had left her husband, but more likely in the male dominated culture of the time, she had been dismissed by her husband. Then, as now, the words that are exchanged are the same: "I don't love you", or worse: "I hate you". Failed relationships produce self-loathing, bitterness and hopelessness. It is probable that she came to the well alone at midday to avoid the stares and rejection of the other women.

When she came to the well, she would have been disheartened to see a man at the well and a Jew at that. But then the man spoke, and His words somehow touched her very deeply. The words were simple: "Give Me a drink", but what cannot be conveyed is the voice of Jesus. God's word is life-giving, but His word must be spoken with the right tones or it can slay. Paul said "the letter kills" (2 Corinthians 3:6) meaning that the Bible can be quoted without imparting the Spirit of God. Jesus spoke these simple words, and through them conveyed the humility and purity of God.

It is easy to forget that whoever saw or heard Jesus was confronted with God incarnate. It is amazing that so few fell down before His mere presence. This was because He was veiled and the startling realization of who He was had to be revealed in stages. God speaks with an attitude of respect to sinners. God is never cynical nor can He despise people. He honoured this woman with a humble request for help. It is clear from her reaction that she was completely disarmed by His words, because they conveyed nothing of racial prejudice or male chauvinism. Here was a man of a totally different kind to those she had met before, and she expressed her shock and amazement in response:

"How is it that You, being a Jew, ask a drink of me, a Samaritan woman?" (John 4:9).

The answer of Jesus is of fundamental importance in defining His mission, and the whole significance of the New Testament:

> *"Jesus answered and said to her, "If you knew the gift of God, and who it is who says to you, 'Give Me a drink,' you would have asked Him, and He would have given you living water" (John 4:10).*

He told her that she needed to know two things, and that knowing these two things would lead to her praying a prayer that would change the whole tenor and direction of her life. These are the two things that lie at the centre of John's own gospel, and should lie at the centre of the church's message to a lost world. These two great revelations were (1) the identity of Jesus and (2) the nature of God's gift to sinners.

The identity of Jesus.

Jesus said that if she knew His identity, she would ask Him for living water. Her response was to confuse the physical and the spiritual, assuming that He meant water from the well. At the same time, she was aware that this was no ordinary man, and she gave voice to this dawning awareness by saying: *"Are you greater than our father Jacob?"* The Samaritan woman was awed by a sense of His greatness. This was in itself remarkable since Jesus had none of the trappings that kings and presidents associate with greatness. In fact, few today would believe that greatness is even possible, and some even delight in the weaknesses and failings of leaders. Politicians are treated with scorn and disbelief, to the point that few believe that any public official is sincere. But Jesus was without gold, or special robes, and even his motley retinue of fishermen had abandoned Him to satisfy their need of food (John 4:8).

Yet the woman sensed His greatness, and it was not

by His outward dress that she was impressed. It was the presence of Jesus that touched and convinced her of the truth of Christ. The woman felt the sinless holiness and moral purity of God. The word "feel" is disturbing to many, but it was not an emotional experience, but rather a sensing in the soul of the presence of God. Somewhere in the heart and the conscience is an awareness, a knowledge of things that cannot be explained. Human beings sense the presence of evil, and yet cannot explain how. Human beings are sentient creatures. They are not a combination of pure logic residing in mere physical matter. People feel happy or sad about their life, sometimes in a totally illogical manner. The truth is that the senses of the body and mind reach out hungrily for satisfaction, through food, drink, visual or intellectual stimulus, through books and films. But underlying all these levels of human thirst, there is a spiritual thirst for the living God. This woman knew that she was in the presence of a man of God, who was greater than the spiritual giants in the history of Israel.

Jesus said *"if you knew who is speaking to you"* and by this, conveyed the truth that we must first have a right understanding of who He is. John, the writer of the gospel, says *"these things are written that you may believe that Jesus is the Christ, the Son of God, and that believing you may have life in His name"*, (John 20:31). The woman of Samaria became convinced of His identity by this brief encounter and became the first woman to confess Him as the Messiah (John 4:29). Jesus exhibited supernatural knowledge of her past and this no doubt confirmed her conviction. Nevertheless, the speed with which she was transformed was remarkable, and indicates the power of the person of Jesus. Truly, He is almighty God in human form. The woman's faith is astonishing given the circumstances in which the revelation was given. Today, the equivalent would be a revelation being given at the kitchen sink in a back street slum in Calcutta. It demanded courage to step out and confess that God almighty had visited the earth in the form of His Son, the Messiah, and sent Him to her

45

backyard. Yet this is exactly where God feels most at home. The incarnation is in keeping with everything that is revealed about God. He loves the poor and disadvantaged. He identifies with them and sends His servants to minister to them.

The Gift of God

The second revelation was concerning the gift of God. Jesus called this gift "living water" (John 4:10). The phrase itself was arresting, since physical water is inanimate, and lifeless. By these words, Jesus indicated that the gift of God is a living Person, with a will, a distinctive understanding and ministry. He was ascribing personality to the Holy Spirit. No-one converses with water, nor with power such as electricity. But the Holy Spirit is a living, speaking, listening personality, and this is the revelation given through the phrase "living water".

The metaphor of water to describe the Holy Spirit indicated that He can be received in much the same way that human beings drink physical water. The difference that Jesus pointed out was that once a person has received "the gift of the Holy Spirit" (Acts 2:38 and 10:45), he or she will never thirst again but that the water will be rising in their heart *"springing up unto everlasting life"* (John 4:13-14). These words indicated the distinctive character of this gift. It is not merely a blessing or a momentary touch from God. It is the gift of God's own Spirit. God Himself is the gift. This sets the gift of God apart from the ministry of power or miracles. Clearly it is possible to cooperate with the Spirit to do great works and yet not receive the gift in the way that Jesus describes. This whole dimension of the gift is explored later in the upper room in chapter 14 of John, where the whole mystery of "indwelling" is introduced. God can live in us, and this indwelling is through the reception of the gift of God Himself.

The mark of the gift is then a soaring spirit that rises and worships. The gift of God is an inner fountain that rises under a pressure and a force that carries the believer into the realm of worship. Not that worship is an impersonal force that carries the worshipper away without the participation of his mind and will. The Holy Spirit reveals God to our inner man, and worship is the reaction of the soul to the sight of God. There is no other way to worship God than to worship Him in the dimension of the Holy Spirit. It is precisely in this inner activity that the soul is satisfied. Before a person receives the Holy Spirit, they thirst for the living God without knowing why. Many have said that there is a God shaped hole in the heart of man. This is one way of describing the desolation that grips the human heart and undermines all the pleasures of life. To live without God is like a thirsty man lost in the midst of a desert. His tongue is black and his throat parched. When he finds an oasis, he is driven beyond normal behaviour by extreme thirst to quench his thirst for survival. It is this desperate thirst that Jesus says will be stilled by the gift of God. Never again will the soul feel that lostness of inner despair and desolation. True, there is a normal hunger and thirst that daily needs fresh food, and in the same way the soul yearns continually for daily fellowship with God. But the misery of a life estranged from God is gone forever.

Some have speculated whether the question of the woman regarding worship was a deliberate distraction to deflect Jesus from probing further into her past. This may be the case, or it may be that she was giving expression to her longing to find the place of true worship, and her dissatisfaction with the outward forms of religious observance in Samaria and Jerusalem. Jesus took up the question of the woman, and assured her that special buildings and places will become irrelevant once the Holy Spirit has come. Then the believers themselves will be the location of worship, as they pour out their heart in spirit and truth. The word "truth" can be translated "reality", and this is the case here, that the Holy Spirit brings spiritual reality to the human soul.

The time had not yet come for the woman to receive this gift in its fullness. John makes it clear later that the Holy Spirit was not given until after Calvary (John 7:39). But the woman unquestionably tasted of the gift by meeting with Christ and knowing His saving grace and acceptance, and the encounter transformed her forever. Her prayer for living water would be answered more fully later, probably in Acts 8 when the Holy Spirit was poured out in Samaria. But for now, the woman was changed. Her hope was renewed and symbolically she left her waterpot, and rushed to share the news of what had happened to her. Her manner and even her changed appearance would have convinced the town of the reality of her words, and the whole town came out to see who this person was that had brought about such a deep transformation. Many believed, and Jesus taught them for two days (John 4:40). They were filled with joy to have the presence of Messiah among them.

The disciples are very much in the background in John's gospel. It is clear that they were not yet partakers of the same loving heart that motivated Jesus. They followed their rumbling stomachs to search for food in the Samaritan town, and they seem to have made the Samaritan woman feel unwanted, since it is on their return that she abruptly left. John says that the disciples "marvelled" that Jesus was speaking with her. Whether racial or male prejudice is not spelt out, but they did not have the grace of Christ in their attitude. How easily disciples can communicate their prejudice to sinners and drive them away.

Jesus said to the disciples that the fields were white and ready for harvest, but the disciples were not in a position to reap the harvest because of their prejudices. They were not in step with Jesus. They were not listening to the Holy Spirit and they were not equipped to hear the words of knowledge that would unlock hearts as Jesus had done. The whole event should lead us to gently seek the grace of the Lord to bring us into line with His great agenda of reaching a lost world with the love of God.

The second miracle/sign: the healing of the nobleman's son

[43] *After the two days he went out from there and went into Galilee.* [44] *For Jesus himself testified that a prophet has no honour in his own country.* [45] *So when he came into Galilee, the Galileans received him, having seen all the things that he did in Jerusalem at the feast, for they also went to the feast.* [46] *Jesus came therefore again to Cana of Galilee, where he made the water into wine. There was a certain nobleman whose son was sick at Capernaum.* [47] *When he heard that Jesus had come out of Judea into Galilee, he went to him, and begged him that he would come down and heal his son, for he was at the point of death.* [48] *Jesus therefore said to him, "Unless you see signs and wonders, you will in no way believe."*

[49] *The nobleman said to him, "Sir, come down before my child dies."* [50] *Jesus said to him, "Go your way. Your son lives." The man believed the word that Jesus spoke to him, and he went his way.* [51] *As he was now going down, his servants met him and reported, saying "Your child lives!"* [52] *So he inquired of them the hour when he began to get better. They said therefore to him, "Yesterday at the seventh hour, the fever left him."* [53] *So the father knew that it was at that hour in which Jesus said to him, "Your son lives." He believed, as did his whole house.* [54] *This is again the second sign that Jesus did, having come out of Judea into Galilee.*

In John's gospel there are eight "I am" statements and eight signs. Here in chapter 4, Jesus left Samaria and turned again to Galilee. There he performed what John calls the second sign (John 4:54). This was a simple miracle and of the eight signs it has the simplest meaning. The nobleman was anxious about his son. He loved his son and had set out on a quest to find Jesus with a deep love for him. When Jesus said to him *"Your son lives"*, the statement was full of meaning, in that it expressed the deep love of God the Father for His son. Later, the Father observed the death of His Son, and raised Him from the dead. As the nobleman lived for his son, so God the Father lives for Jesus. It is of the greatest comfort to any believer that God has linked the future of the believer with that of the beloved son. The word "Father" occurs 134 times in John compared with 61 in Matthew, 19 in Mark and 48 in Luke. The Father is a central figure in John's gospel, and is the motivating force in the life of Jesus. This is revealed in a short aside by Jesus in John 14:31, when Jesus declares that He is going to the cross so that the world might know that He loves the Father. The explanation for the inner life of Christ is this great loving heart of the Father for His Son and the Son for His Father.

This sign also reveals the measureless power of Jesus Christ. It is remarkable that Jesus did not go to the house of the nobleman. He simply spoke the command and the boy was healed at the very moment He spoke the words. Jesus' authority is not limited by geography. This is part of the declaration by John that Jesus is divine and holding absolute authority.

JOHN 5

THE THIRD WATERPOT: THE MAN BY THE POOL OF BETHESDA

5 *After these things, there was a feast of the Jews, and Jesus went up to Jerusalem.* ² *Now in Jerusalem by the sheep gate, there is a pool, which is called in Hebrew, "Bethesda", having five porches.* ³ *In these lay a great multitude of those who were sick, blind, lame, or paralyzed, waiting for the moving of the water;* ⁴ *for an angel went down at certain times into the pool and stirred up the water. Whoever stepped in first after the stirring of the water was healed of whatever disease he had.* ⁵ *A certain man was there who had been sick for thirty-eight years.* ⁶ *When Jesus saw him lying there, and knew that he had been sick for a long time, he asked him, "Do you want to be made well?"*

⁷ *The sick man answered him, "Sir, I have no-one to put me into the pool when the water is stirred up, but while I'm coming, another steps down before me."*

⁸ *Jesus said to him, "Arise, take up your mat, and walk."*

⁹ *Immediately, the man was made well, and took up his mat and walked.*

Now it was the Sabbath on that day. ¹⁰ *So the Jews said to him who was cured, "It is the Sabbath. It is not lawful for you to carry the mat."*

¹¹ *He answered them, "He who made me well said to me, 'Take up your mat and walk.'"*

¹² *Then they asked him, "Who is the man who said to you, 'Take up your mat and walk'?"*

¹³ *But he who was healed didn't know who it was, for Jesus had withdrawn, a crowd being in the place.*

51

14 Afterward Jesus found him in the temple, and said to him, "Behold, you are made well. Sin no more, so that nothing worse happens to you."

The fifth chapter opens with the scene by the pool of Bethesda during an unnamed feast of the Jews. There were always crowds in the five porches of Bethesda, hoping for a miracle. History books tell us that some three hundred people could be found there on any day of the year, but that the number frequently swelled to two or three thousand during the feasts of Israel. They came to wait beside the stagnant pool in the hope that they would witness a visitation by an angel. John states the simple fact that from time to time, God sent an angel to stir the water (John 5:4). It seems that the angel was invisible and that all that the people saw was the moving of the water. As soon as this occurred, there was a rush to get in the water, for whoever entered first was immediately healed.

The scene was itself a parable of the nation of Israel in the old covenant. The five porches suggest the covering of the Pentateuch, forming a house of mercy (the literal translation of Bethesda). The pool itself was stagnant and unmoving, quite unlike the living water promised in chapter 4. The fact that the angel stirred the water emphasised the need for the water to be moving for it to be living and to have effective influence. The Holy Spirit is never stagnant and John's gospel points the reader to the focus of the Spirit's moving, which is centred on the person of Christ Himself. In the New Testament, no-one was baptised in lakes such as the Sea of Galilee, but rather in flowing rivers like the Jordan. (This does not make it wrong to baptise in a lake, but the image of living water is remarkably consistent in the Scriptures).

The lame man had been by the pool for 38 years, and this number is found in Deuteronomy 2:14 referring to the years of Israel's wandering. The man is a picture of Israel: weak, diseased, unable to walk and needing a revival. The history of Israel was one of frequent divine visitations to stir a backsliding and disobedient nation. These visitations were often through the ministry of angels. The law itself came through the hand of angels (Galatians 3:19, Acts 7:53). Often a period of revival was marked by an angelic visitation as in the birth of Samson (Judges 13), or the call of Gideon (Judges 6:11). These periods of revival stirred the nation for a while but were followed by seasons of decline.

This picture of Israel can also be applied to the church, with its constant cry for a revival to come and refresh the state of the people of God. While a genuine cry for revival is pleasing to God and often leads to blessing, yet it is a grievous matter for the church to be so often in a state of backsliding and spiritual weakness, that such appeals have to be made so frequently. Moreover, it cannot be right that the church should spend years praying for revival when the promise of God's blessing through His Son is so clear, and that promise is the focus of this chapter.

Jesus stepped into the midst of this sea of human need, and addressed the man who was the symbol of backsliding Israel or of a lifeless church. He spoke directly to the man's will and desire, which is the womb of God's moving in a human being. James speaks negatively about desire in the context of temptation to sin. He says that when *"desire has conceived, it gives birth to sin,"* (James 1:15). The positive side of desire is that when a soul truly longs for God, desire brings forth faith through the received word of God (James 1:18, John 1:12).

Jesus asked the man *"Do you want to be made well?"* This was a shocking question, since it might be assumed that the man obviously wanted to be well, or why would he be by the pool? And who ever wanted to be ill? However, on closer examination, the question goes to the heart of a person's condition. Some hide behind their sickness to avoid the challenges of life. So when war comes, some will secretly be glad if they are disqualified from fighting through age, or colour blindness or some such condition. The fact of health implies responsibility towards others, who are less fortunate. Some souls are so lonely and cut off, that they love the attention they receive when ill. Pastors, psychiatrists and doctors are all aware that some of the people who seek help are looking for a comforting word of encouragement and love. Their need is much deeper than their physical condition.

If the question is then interpreted spiritually, it becomes even more searching. How deeply do believers long for freedom from the clinging spirit of the world, from the lusts of the flesh, from the poison of selfishness? When a person prays for spiritual health or even revival, God has the right to ask us: "Are you serious? Do you really want to be in spiritual revival?" The implication is that we must be prepared for God to take us at our word and then require from us the responsible attitude of a revived state of heart.

The man answered that he had no-one to help him. This cry is the sad reality of so many. There is no-one with any wisdom or experience, or clarity of spiritual walk to be able to help others. The general tone of this congregation by the stagnant pool was "every man for himself". But Jesus cut through all the reasons why the man could not be healed, including the waiting for the moving of the water and the lack of someone to help. With majesty and authority, Jesus commanded the man to do the impossible: ""Rise, take up your bed and walk". And immediately the man was made well, took up his bed, and walked." (John 5:8-9). There must be a realization of the constancy of Christ and His matchless, unfading authority and power. Out of Christ flow rivers of living water, and all a soul needs to do is to come to Him and be completely refreshed. God was declaring to Israel that the focus of His moving had changed from the hand of angels to His Son. His Son is not only available in seasons of revival. He can be reached by the believing heart at any moment.

Focus for a moment on the obvious: the man was healed. After 38 years of pain and paralysis, the pain stopped. He must have walked like one in a dream, and then came the rush of joy. God had stepped down into his circumstances and made him well. One of the great questions that arises from this event is: "does God always heal?" The miraculous intervention of God in our lives is a mystery and healing is certainly not as common as we would wish. So no, God does not always heal, and physical healing is not under our absolute authority. We may ask, but must leave the outcome in God's hands.

Nor is healing in our bodies sufficient of itself to change our lives. God longs to heal the deep wounds of our spirit, and put right the things that are wrong with our character. We may confidently expect God to intervene in our lives, because He loves us and wants to do us good. But our greatest need is for spiritual healing and there can be no doubt that God has a divine miracle for us all. Jesus made this promise universal when He said: *"Come to Me, ALL you who labour and are heavy laden, and I will give you rest."* Matthew 11:28.

Imagine now the man walking through the streets of Jerusalem with a broad smile on his face, testing his new found ability to walk, and even perhaps a skip or two. Then he met some religious leaders. They focussed on the man's transgression of the Sabbath by carrying his mat. His answer was to explain that he had just been healed, and in the process had been commanded to carry the mat. These religious critics were completely blind to the wonder of the miracle and resorted to the smoke-screen of their religious rules. Here as so often in the gospel of John, the chief enemies of Jesus are not governments or immoral sinners, but religious people who believed that they were superior by their legalistic practices. Remarkably, the man did not even know the name of the One who had healed him. (Evidently there is no formula or form of words that will guarantee a miracle). Today one might imagine the reaction of the church elders if they hear that God has used another ministry to heal one of their church members. There can arise a temptation to criticise others whom God uses, and often we may be tempted to find reasons why God cannot use that ministry. It surely could not be right for someone to be healed and then not even know who healed him. In the rest of the chapter, Jesus engaged with the Pharisees, seeking to win them from their sins of pride and envy.

Jesus then sought out the man and gave him a solemn warning. He commanded the man to *"sin no more, lest a worse thing come upon you."* (John 5:14). This word indicated the fundamental need of the human heart for power to overcome sinful habits. Jesus was not asking the man to be perfectly sinless from that moment on. But he was warning him, that if he returned to the sin that had troubled him in the past, his sickness would return. The link between sickness and sin is obvious. Worry, depression, bitterness, envy, all cause stresses and strains on the body, which are reflected in blood pressure, stomach ulcers, insomnia etc. For this reason, when a person refuses to forgive, they will cause huge damage to themselves. Sexual sin will cause guilt and shame, and the result may well be that the person feels lost and abandoned. Forgiveness and power to change our lives are the essential need of every human heart, and the foundation of all lasting healing. Jesus taught the man that he must receive power to change his conduct if he were to experience permanent healing. God's first touch in our lives is given to awaken living faith. If we will look up to Him, He has a second touch which will make us whole.

The lesson here is of vital importance. There is no blessing that will remove all moral responsibility. All without exception must build a relationship with God. People argue whether we are saved by a first or a second blessing. The answer is that we are saved as soon as we are reconciled with God through the forgiveness of sins. But salvation is not a "thing"; it is the beginning of a relationship. A saved man is changing because he is walking with God. Some may seem to walk faster than others, but in the end, each must be attentive to walking with God, not to serving some ideal or exalting an experience.

The healed man now knew who had healed him and he told the Jews (John 5:15). It is tempting to ask whether the man did this out of resentment at the warning word from Jesus, or perhaps to introduce his fellow Jews to the wonder of Jesus. There is no way of knowing, for the man simply dropped from the scene and is never mentioned again. The focus changed to the conflict between Jesus and the Pharisees about His identity.

The five witnesses to the identity of Christ.

[15] *The man went away, and told the Jews that it was Jesus who had made him well.* [16] *For this cause the Jews persecuted Jesus, and sought to kill him, because he did these things on the Sabbath.* [17] *But Jesus answered them, "My Father is still working, so I am working, too."* [18] *For this cause therefore the Jews sought all the more to kill him, because he not only broke the Sabbath, but also called God his own Father, making himself equal with God.* [19] *Jesus therefore answered them, "Most certainly, I tell you, the Son can do nothing of himself, but what he sees the Father doing. For whatever things he does, these the Son also does likewise.* [20] *For the Father has affection for the Son, and shows him all things that he himself does. He will show him greater works than these, that you may marvel.* [21] *For as the Father raises the dead and gives them life, even so the Son also gives life to whom he desires.* [22] *For the Father judges no-one, but he has given all judgment to the Son,* [23] *that all may honour the Son, even as they honour the Father. He who doesn't honour the Son doesn't honour the Father who sent him.*

[24] *"Most certainly I tell you, he who hears my word and believes him who sent me has eternal life, and doesn't come into judgment, but has passed out of death into life.* [25] *Most certainly I tell you, the hour comes, and now is, when the dead will hear the Son of God's voice; and those who hear will live.* [26] *For as the Father has life in himself, even so he gave to the Son also to have life in himself.* [27] *He also gave him authority to execute judgment, because he is a son of man.* [28] *Don't marvel at this, for the hour comes in which all who are in the tombs will hear his voice,* [29] *and will come out;*

those who have done good, to the resurrection of life; and those who have done evil, to the resurrection of judgment. ³⁰ I can of myself do nothing. As I hear, I judge, and my judgment is righteous; because I don't seek my own will, but the will of my Father who sent me.

³¹ "If I testify about myself, my witness is not valid. ³² It is another who testifies about me. I know that the testimony which he testifies about me is true. ³³ You have sent to John, and he has testified to the truth. ³⁴ But the testimony which I receive is not from man. However, I say these things that you may be saved. ³⁵ He was the burning and shining lamp, and you were willing to rejoice for a while in his light. ³⁶ But the testimony which I have is greater than that of John, for the works which the Father gave me to accomplish, the very works that I do, testify about me, that the Father has sent me. ³⁷ The Father himself, who sent me, has testified about me. You have neither heard his voice at any time, nor seen his form. ³⁸ You don't have his word living in you, because you don't believe him whom he sent.

³⁹ "You search the Scriptures, because you think that in them you have eternal life; and these are they which testify about me. ⁴⁰ Yet you will not come to me, that you may have life. ⁴¹ I don't receive glory from men. ⁴² But I know you, that you don't have God's love in yourselves. ⁴³ I have come in my Father's name, and you don't receive me. If another comes in his own name, you will receive him. ⁴⁴ How can you believe, who receive glory from one another, and you don't seek the glory that comes from the only God?

⁴⁵ "Don't think that I will accuse you to the Father. There is one who accuses you, even Moses, on whom you have set your hope. ⁴⁶ For if you believed Moses, you would believe me; for he wrote about me. ⁴⁷ But if you don't believe his writings, how will you believe my words?"

John records this dialogue between Jesus and the religious leaders, and by it he established the five-fold foundation for the identity of Jesus. Jesus raised the temperature of the encounter by the simple claim that God was His Father, and that the two of them had started working again (5:17). This was a double provocation, because Jesus asserted that He was the Son of God. He also indicated that the seventh day of rest, when God finished creating the world, was now over. God was on the move again. God was working and the Creator was now about to do something that would be the jewel of all His creative activity for all eternity. That creative act would be underlined in chapter 19:30, when He would declare that "*it was finished*", echoing the declaration of Genesis 2:1.

Jesus then plainly told the Jewish leaders that He, the Son of God, was in direct, unbroken relationship with the Father (5:19). This was because He was the object of the Father's love (5:20). He and the Father shared the power to give life (5:21). The Father had made Jesus the judge of the entire human race, and had made honouring Jesus the responsibility of all (5:22-23). It is Jesus who will raise the dead and will decide the destiny of all (5:28-29). These claims were absolute and left no room for negotiation. The claims of Jesus are not that He has a useful message to contribute some new ideas to the human race. His claim is that He is God the Son, holding all power over the eternal future of every individual who has ever lived. He then proceeded to explain why no-one has any excuse for rejecting Him.

1. The witness of John the Baptist (5:33).

The arrival of John the Baptist was a fulfilment of Isaiah 40:3 and Malachi 4:5. John the Baptist shook Israel by his preaching, and pointed unequivocally to Jesus as the Messiah. The multitudes had hailed John as a prophet, and the nation was poised with excitement at the imminent arrival of the longed-for Saviour of Israel.

2. The witness of the works of Jesus (5:36).

Jesus' miracles fulfilled many Old Testament prophecies such as Isaiah 35:5, which declared that Messiah will open the eyes of the blind and heal the lame. The miraculous power of Jesus was manifest in His three years of ministry, then through the ministry of the apostles in the book of Acts. But most importantly, His ministry has never ceased. It is not in the scope of this book to give even a short list of current miracles, but there can be no doubt that every year thousands of people claim a miraculous healing through the touch of Jesus Christ. Sceptics ask for proof, and this is not always easy to provide. But there are two answers to this request for proof. Firstly, the idea that Christians are given wholly to lying on such a scale is itself a monstrous claim. Secondly, on many occasions there are x rays, scans and other documents that prove a miraculous healing.

3.   The witness of the Father (5:37).

At first sight this claim seems to be illogical, since Jesus seems to be claiming that He and God agree who He is. That cannot be His meaning, since it all depends on His claims. Jesus was instead claiming that there is a separate, distinct witness to the identity of Jesus in the hearts of all who hear the gospel. Jesus was teaching that this is not mere instinctive knowledge, but that it is the activity of the Father, convincing us that Jesus is the Son of God. This is the claim that there is an inward pressure that we will have to resist, if we are to reject Jesus as Messiah. Jesus made this claim on more than one occasion.   He told the Jews at the Feast of Tabernacles in chapter 7:28 that they knew who He was and where He was from.

4.   The witness of the Scriptures (5:39).

There is in America a rock with the Declaration of Independence inscribed upon it. But if a person steps back from the rock, he will see that the writing is also aligned to form the silhouette of the head of George Washington. Reading the Bible is exactly the same. As we step back from the Bible, we see the outline of Jesus in all the Scriptures. Jesus' life is prophesied in two ways: firstly, through direct specific prophecies which indicate His place of birth, His lineage, the details of His death, the pattern of His ministry, and His world-wide influence.   Secondly, His life is prophesied through what the Bible itself calls types, or pictures. This method is much more subtle and is the most amazing dimension of the Bible's means of communication. It is a secret code, but not a code that needs computers or knowledge of the original languages. It is a hidden code, and yet it is in plain sight and it is constantly yielding more insights about Jesus to the reader. There are countless examples, which have been well documented. One example will suffice to indicate the wonderful detail of the Scriptures.

Joseph dreamed that one day all his brothers would bow down and worship him. Yet they rejected him and sold him into slavery for 20 pieces of silver. In Egypt he was falsely accused and condemned to the lowest prison. There he interpreted 2 dreams of the chief butler and the baker of Pharaoh. He dreamt that in 3 days the baker would be hung on a tree, and the butler would be raised to stand at Pharaoh's side. The elements were the bread and wine which speak of the death and resurrection of Jesus Christ. Joseph himself was then raised from the lowest dungeon to the highest throne, from where he ruled the world. He saved the world from severe famine by giving bread to all the surrounding nations. Multitudes came to him, and finally his brothers came and repented of their betrayal of him, and bowed before him. This story is full of details which unconsciously, and yet unmistakably parallel the life of Jesus.

5. The witness of Moses.

This fifth witness is an extension of the fourth witness, in that Moses' writings obviously form part of the Scriptures. But the mention of Moses is significant, because Moses was the great lawgiver of Israel, the one who had been used by God to shape the nation. He was their greatest prophet, and the Sadducees even believed that the five books of Moses were the only authoritatively inspired books.

Jesus was here directly claiming to be the fulfilment of a prophecy by Moses, that Messiah would be a prophet like him, who would replace him and become the foundation of Israel (Deuteronomy 18:15, 18,19).

Chapter 5 is about the third waterpot, which is identified with Israel. The nation needed a visitation, and its greatest hour had come. But only a despised remnant was prepared to welcome their Messiah. But for those who received Him, He gave the matchless power of a totally new and triumphant life.

JOHN 6

THE KINGDOM, THE BREAD AND THE WINE

John 6 After these things, Jesus went away to the other side of the sea of Galilee, which is also called the Sea of Tiberias. ² A great multitude followed him, because they saw his signs which he did on those who were sick. ³ Jesus went up into the mountain, and he sat there with his disciples. ⁴ Now the Passover, the feast of the Jews, was at hand. ⁵ Jesus therefore lifting up his eyes, and seeing that a great multitude was coming to him, said to Philip, "Where are we to buy bread, that these may eat?" ⁶ He said this to test him, for he himself knew what he would do.

⁷ Philip answered him, "Two hundred denarii worth of bread is not sufficient for them, that every one of them may receive a little."

⁸ One of his disciples, Andrew, Simon Peter's brother, said to him, ⁹ "There is a boy here who has five barley loaves and two fish, but what are these among so many?"

¹⁰ Jesus said, "Have the people sit down." Now there was much grass in that place. So the men sat down, in number about five thousand. ¹¹ Jesus took the loaves; and having given thanks, he distributed to the disciples, and the disciples to those who were sitting down; likewise also of the fish as much as they desired. ¹² When they were filled, he said to his disciples, "Gather up the broken pieces which are left over, that nothing be lost." ¹³ So they gathered them up, and filled twelve baskets with broken pieces from the five barley loaves, which were left over by those who had eaten. ¹⁴ When therefore the people saw the sign which Jesus did, they said, "This is truly the prophet who comes into the world." ¹⁵ Jesus therefore,

perceiving that they were about to come and take him by force
to make him king, withdrew again to the mountain by himself.

Chapter 6 opens with one of the few miracles that is
common to all the gospels: the feeding of the five
thousand. This miracle took place at the time of the
second Passover mentioned in the gospel (6:4). Later
in the chapter Jesus linked the miracle with the
communion by teaching about His body and His blood
(6:53). By this means the Old Testament feast and the
New Testament ordinance were firmly linked, and the
communion replaces and reinterprets the Passover.

The feeding of the five thousand was a simple
parable of the kingdom of God. Right at the centre of
that kingdom is the cross, which was declared when
Jesus took up the bread and broke it (Matthew 14:19).
This was the declaration that if the people of God are to
have any spiritual food, then the Son of God had to be
crucified to provide that food. There is no human
substitute for this food. Money cannot provide it, and
nor can any human effort. With the brokenness comes
the flow of life, and through brokenness alone. The
miracle itself was astounding. The account does not
indicate at what point the loaves and the fish were
multiplied, whether they saw the bread grow, or
whether they just kept breaking pieces off and yet it did
not diminish. The miraculous supply was so great that
all could eat and be filled and there was no limit to the
provision. This was abundance indeed, and with no
strain. The chapter went on to unfold the interpretation
that Jesus feeds the world with His body and blood not
with bread and fish.

The brokenness of Jesus on the cross is the
foundation of God's ways. God leads His disciples to be
broken bread in the same way. Brokenness for disciples
is not to give an atoning sacrifice, but rather to allow
the life of God to flow in their lives. When sinners
repent, they break their hearts open before God, and
the process begins. Humbling oneself before God in
self-emptying is the first step. Then this leads to a

pattern of life by which believers are quick to confess their faults, and are able to prefer one another in love. Life is always presenting opportunities to humble ourselves, and this means that if we embrace this way of life in the kingdom, then we will see abundance of blessing, and if we don't, we will find our hearts growing cold and hard.

What then is this brokenness? When a thing is broken it normally means that it has ceased to function. But in spiritual life it means it has begun to work. A broken will is one that has learned to give up its rights. When a broken person is overlooked, they do not notice, and if they do, they quickly repent of their wrong reaction. An unbroken disciple will be offended and hold grudges, and constantly manipulate circumstances in order that they be noticed and given their full recognition. A broken attitude of heart is most often revealed in our relationships, but it is also revealed in our response to pain and suffering, and to other things in our lives that either irritate or hinder us. The broken disciple will praise God in all things (not for all things). This does not mean that he or she will passively accept sickness, but it does mean that they will not grow bitter and resentful, but keep a thankful praising heart in the midst of suffering and sorrow.

All of these lessons are contained in the symbol of broken bread, and the lesson is later reinforced by the communion, when believers are taught once more to think of the character of Jesus as revealed in the cross, and to embrace it in their attitude to God and to each other. Brokenness is the foundation of our communion, because first of all God was broken on Calvary, and we are to be broken in our response.

However, the events in chapter 6 took a very different turn when the multitude began to hail Jesus as their King (6:15). This was exactly the kind of king or president that everyone could vote for: someone who provides free meals. It must have grieved Jesus that no-one had asked the true meaning of the miracle and he immediately withdrew up the mountain to pray. His kingdom will never come by the popular vote. If it did, then it could just as easily be destroyed by the will of the people. But the crowds did not give in easily and continued searching for this miracle worker. The disciples and the multitude crossed the lake by boat, but Jesus crossed the lake walking on the water.

Walking on water, the 8 signs and the 8 "I ams" of John's gospel

[16] *When evening came, his disciples went down to the sea.* [17] *They entered into the boat, and were going over the sea to Capernaum. It was now dark, and Jesus had not come to them.* [18] *The sea was tossed by a great wind blowing.* [19] *When therefore they had rowed about twenty-five or thirty stadia, they saw Jesus walking on the sea, and drawing near to the boat; and they were afraid.* [20] *But he said to them, "It is I. Don't be afraid."* [21] *They were willing therefore to receive him into the boat. Immediately the boat was at the land where they were going.*

It is in this chapter that two of the eight miracles of John's gospel occur: the feeding of the five thousand and walking on the water. It is necessary to pause at this point to reflect on the eight "signs" in John's gospel. It is notoriously difficult to get Bible scholars to agree on numerology. Someone once quipped that if you ask four Bible students for their views on a passage, you will always get at least 5 answers. If the question is asked "How many miracles or signs are there in John's gospel?" there is no definitive answer. John does not number the signs (though he does for the first and the second: see John 2:11 and 4:54), nor does he indicate whether all the "signs" are miracles. For example, Campbell Morgan interprets the cleansing of the temple as one of 8 signs.[3]

At this point it is worth asking why numerology is important? The numbers indicate the supernatural

---

[3] The Gospel of John, G. Campbell Morgan p. 7.

design of the Bible and underline the spiritual significance related to each number.

In addition to 8 signs there are also 8 times in John's gospel that Jesus expressed that He was the "I am". In chapter 6 the first of these "I ams" is introduced. Once more not all will agree whether these are seven or eight in number. Many have said there are seven, while once again Campbell Morgan finds eight.[4] It is probable that John did not consciously list eight signs and eight "I ams", but it certainly does not strain the text to point them out.

There are eight miraculous events in John's gospel[5]:

1. The water to wine (John 2:1-11).
2. The healing of the nobleman's son (John 4:46-54).
3. The lame man at the Pool of Bethesda (Jn 5:1-14).
4. The feeding of the five thousand (John 6:1-14).
5. Walking on water (John 6:15-21).
6. The healing of the Blind Man (John 9:1-7).
7. The resurrection of Lazarus (John 11:38-44).
8. The death and resurrection of Jesus (John 20:1-18).

These eight miracles are signs, carefully chosen by John to point to some characteristic of Jesus and to indicate some aspect of His ministry. Is there a symbolic meaning to this number? The name of Jesus has a numeric value in the Hebrew language of 888.[6] This is remarkable and once again points to the extraordinary nature of the Bible. The number eight occurs in several key points including the flood of Noah (Genesis 7:13, 1 Peter 3:20). It is also remarkable that the resurrection took place on the first day of the week, which can be seen as the eighth day. It was on the fiftieth day that

---

[4] The Gospel of John, G. Campbell Morgan p. 7.

[5] My list is different to that of G. Campbell Morgan.

[6] See Bullinger, Number in Scripture.

the Holy Spirit was poured out, and this is the first day of the eighth week. From all these references it can be inferred that the number eight is a symbol of the resurrection and of a new creation. Given this background to the eight miracles of John's gospel, they all point to the power of God in His creative and redemptive act on the cross.

All the eight signs listed above fit into this interpretation. These eight signs are linked and indicate a unified message.

1. The water to wine was the miracle of the new covenant in His blood.
2. The healing of the nobleman's son pointed to the poignant role of the Father in watching over the sufferings of His Son and His return to life.
3. The lame man was raised to health by the Giver of Life.
4. The multitudes were fed by the broken bread - the crucified Lamb of God.
5. Jesus walked on water to demonstrate that resurrection life lifts the believer to another plane of spiritual life and victory.
6. The blind man received washing for his eyes. This symbolised the washing of the Spirit through the cross.
7. Lazarus was raised to life, symbolising the power of death and resurrection in the believer.
8. Jesus died and rose again, opening the door for God's great redemptive act through the cross.

The Holy Spirit edited this material, perhaps unconsciously to John, in order to communicate a message in clarity and power.

In the same manner and for the same purpose there are eight "I Ams:"

1. I am the bread of life (John 6:35).
2. I am the light of the world (John 8:12).
3. Before Abraham was, I am (John 8:58).
4. I am the door (John 10:9).
5. I am the good shepherd (John 10:11).
6. I am the resurrection and the life (John 11:25).
7. I am the way the truth and the life (John 14:6).
8. I am the vine (John 15:1).

Some will argue that there are seven "I ams." Others will point out that in the Greek language Jesus says "I am" on several other occasions, such as John 6:20 where it is translated: "It is I". But let it be accepted for the moment that there are eight key declarations that link Jesus with the matchless name of Jahwe (Exodus 3:14). Once again, the number eight indicates the unifying principle of the power of God's redemptive act in the new creation through His death and resurrection.

The "I ams" stand in juxtaposition with the eight signs, and indicate the method of God in new creation. God does not do something for us, rather He IS something TO us. The central method of God is in His essential being, and in the power of His life applied to us and in us. This is a critical distinction between doing and being. It indicates first of all that God applies Himself to the human condition. On Calvary, the power that neutralised and destroyed evil in all its forms, was the presence of God Himself. This indicates that God Himself was and is personally and intimately involved in the redemption of the human race.

God's power is Himself. Moreover, there was something about the nature of sin that God removed by pouring Himself on it. Sin is the atmosphere that prevails apart from God's presence. Was there another method that God could have used? Could He have spoken to sin and removed it by His word of command? The answer must be "no", since it is inconceivable that God would have made His Son endure the cross unless there was no other way it could be done. Sin is the most powerful force in fallen humanity, a force that cannot be removed without the direct presence of God. The "I ams" also teach us that it is the continued presence of God that seals our salvation. This will be emphasised when Jesus later teaches the vital truth of abiding in the vine.

"I am the bread of life." (John 6:35)

[22] *On the next day, the multitude that stood on the other side of the sea saw that there was no other boat there, except the one in which his disciples had embarked, and that Jesus hadn't entered with his disciples into the boat, but his disciples had gone away alone.* [23] *However boats from Tiberias came near to the place where they ate the bread after the Lord had given thanks.* [24] *When the multitude therefore saw that Jesus wasn't there, nor his disciples, they themselves got into the boats, and came to Capernaum, seeking Jesus.* [25] *When they found him on the other side of the sea, they asked him, "Rabbi, when did you come here?"*

[26] *Jesus answered them, "Most certainly I tell you, you seek me, not because you saw signs, but because you ate of the loaves, and were filled.* [27] *Don't work for the food which perishes, but for the food which remains to eternal life, which the Son of Man will give to you. For God the Father has sealed him."*

[28] *They said therefore to him, "What must we do, that we may work the works of God?"*

[29] *Jesus answered them, "This is the work of God, that you believe in him whom he has sent."*

[30] *They said therefore to him, "What then do you do for a sign, that we may see and believe you? What work do you do?* [31] *Our fathers ate the manna in the wilderness. As it is written, 'He gave them bread out of heaven to eat.'"; ;*

[32] *Jesus therefore said to them, "Most certainly, I tell you, it wasn't Moses who gave you the bread out of heaven, but my Father gives you the true bread out of heaven.* [33] *For the bread*

of God is that which comes down out of heaven, and gives life to the world."

[34] They said therefore to him, "Lord, always give us this bread."

[35] Jesus said to them, "I am the bread of life. Whoever comes to me will not be hungry, and whoever believes in me will never be thirsty. [36] But I told you that you have seen me, and yet you don't believe. [37] All those whom the Father gives me will come to me. He who comes to me I will in no way throw out. [38] For I have come down from heaven, not to do my own will, but the will of him who sent me. [39] This is the will of my Father who sent me, that of all he has given to me I should lose nothing, but should raise him up at the last day. [40] This is the will of the one who sent me, that everyone who sees the Son, and believes in him, should have eternal life; and I will raise him up at the last day."

[41] The Jews therefore murmured concerning him, because he said, "I am the bread which came down out of heaven." [42] They said, "Isn't this Jesus, the son of Joseph, whose father and mother we know? How then does he say, 'I have come down out of heaven?'"

The first of the eight "I ams" is found here in chapter 6. The statement was provoked by the crowds who had crossed the lake seeking Jesus. They were bewildered because they were aware that He did not cross the lake by boat (6:25). Jesus answered their question in a manner which indicated that He was aware of their motive, and the scene was set for conflict. He told them that they were seeking Him for the lowest motive possible: free food. They were apparently not even seeking Him for miracles. The crowds stubbornly brought the discussion back to food, reminding Him of the great miracle of the manna in the time of Moses (6:31). Jesus turned the subject to food for the spirit, the inner man, and inferred that He was that food (6:33).

Then He made the plain statement that He is the bread of life. Jesus presented the crowds with Himself as the true answer to the need of every person. This is the only motive for seeking God that will lead us to true spiritual satisfaction: seeking God for Himself and not for what we can get out of Him. This takes spiritual truth onto a wholly different level. No man is ever nourished spiritually by any of the blessings that he may receive, or by any of the miracles that God may do for them.

True spiritual challenge begins when we have no needs, when we have no pain or sickness, no physical hunger or thirst. What will believers do when they have got beyond all need and are faced with the person of Jesus Christ? Then begins the true eternal ministry to a person's inner man, when they look at Jesus and see in Him something so beautiful and desirable that they forget all else in order to have Him. Moreover, the true power of salvation cannot be "owned". Christ's power is not in a teaching, a doctrinal emphasis, a second blessing or in spiritual exercise such as prayer or biblical knowledge. The power of Christ is Christ Himself and cannot be experienced without Him, His lordship and His presence.

Eating and drinking Jesus

52 The Jews therefore contended with one another, saying, "How can this man give us his flesh to eat?"
53 Jesus therefore said to them, "Most certainly I tell you, unless you eat the flesh of the Son of Man and drink his blood, you don't have life in yourselves. 54 He who eats my flesh and drinks my blood has eternal life, and I will raise him up at the last day. 55 For my flesh is food indeed, and my blood is drink indeed. 56 He who eats my flesh and drinks my blood lives in me, and I in him. 57 As the living Father sent me, and I live because of the Father; so he who feeds on me, he will also live because of me. 58 This is the bread which came down out of heaven—not as our fathers ate the manna, and died. He who eats this bread will live forever." 59 He said these things in the synagogue, as he taught in Capernaum.

⁶⁰ Therefore many of his disciples, when they heard this, said, "This is a hard saying! Who can listen to it?"

⁶¹ But Jesus knowing in himself that his disciples murmured at this, said to them, "Does this cause you to stumble? ⁶² Then what if you would see the Son of Man ascending to where he was before? ⁶³ It is the spirit who gives life. The flesh profits nothing. The words that I speak to you are spirit, and are life. ⁶⁴ But there are some of you who don't believe." For Jesus knew from the beginning who they were who didn't believe, and who it was who would betray him. ⁶⁵ He said, "For this cause I have said to you that no-one can come to me, unless it is given to him by my Father."

All of this was leading up to one of the most startling statements of Christ - that all who would have spiritual life must eat His flesh and drink His blood (6:53). Believers will automatically think of the communion table. That there is a connection between this chapter and the communion is obvious, but Jesus was not talking about the Lord's supper. He was talking about what the Lord's supper symbolises. A person may take the communion ten times a day for a thousand years and never receive any benefit. The physical emblems themselves have no power to impart blessing or sickness. Paul says:

> *"Therefore, whoever eats this bread or drinks this cup of the Lord in an unworthy manner will be guilty of the body and blood of the Lord. But let a man examine himself, and so let him eat of the bread and drink of the cup. For he who eats and drinks in an unworthy manner eats and drinks judgment to himself, not discerning the Lord's body. For this reason many are weak and sick among you, and many sleep."* (1 Corinthians 11:27-30 NKJV)

The danger in the partaking of the emblems lies in the hypocrisy of the heart, just as the benefit lies in having the eye of faith on Christ Himself and not on the symbol. The symbols of Christ can no more satisfy our hearts than a picture of a sumptuous feast can ever fill the stomach of a starving man.

So what does Jesus mean by eating His flesh and drinking His blood? Obviously, no-one ever has, or ever will drink His physical blood. No-one ever bit into His flesh, and on Calvary, no-one held a cup to catch the drops of blood. His physical death and agony were vital but they were not intended to feed us physically. The body and blood of Christ are to be spiritually received.

These two symbols indicate the very essence of the Godhead. A person has different aspects to their life and being. So one person may give money to a good cause, while another will give of their time. But if they give their life, they have given all that they are. The story is told of a young Vietnamese boy during the war whose sister had been badly injured. The doctor came to him and solemnly informed him that his sister needed a transfusion, and asked the boy if he would be prepared to give his blood. The boy went pale, but quickly nodded his consent. The doctor inserted a needle and drew out a measure of the boy's blood. When he had finished, the boy looked up in surprise. "Is that all?" he whispered. He had thought that the doctor wanted all of his blood and that he must die to save his sister.

The body and blood of Jesus Christ are His irreducible essence. On the cross when Jesus died, God was reduced to the raw, nuclear core of His being, and that is holy love. At its simplest, most basic level, the body and blood of Jesus are His direct, undiluted presence. We are to partake of the essence of God revealed at Calvary. We are to drink of His presence, His love, His holiness and His moral power, in liquid form by the Holy Spirit. The result is that we become an integral part of

His being, as joined to Him as a hand is joined to an arm, sustained by one life, one blood and controlled by one head. We do not become God, but we do become one with God.

Jesus teaches further the means by which we eat and drink. In John 6:35 He parallels "coming to Him" with eating, and "believing in Him" with drinking. We must simply come to Him and believe in Him, and this is so disarmingly simple. But then Jesus adds a word of clarification which is potentially discouraging. He says that no man can come to Him unless the Father draws him (6:44). He reinforces this by quoting Isaiah 54:13 (see also Jeremiah 31:34), indicating that only those who are taught by God can come to Him (6:45). He emphasised this truth yet again, teaching that it is by permission of the Father alone that anyone can ever come to Him (6:65). Jesus is by this means establishing the truth that there is no parallel in human life that can help us to eat His body and drink His blood. Doing this is unlike anything we have ever done before. It would be a mistake to rob it of its mystery and reduce it to some activity with which we are familiar. Far from being a normal everyday human activity, partaking of the communion is something new and wonderful.

Imagine for a moment a game of hide and seek. I take a pot of gold and hide it somewhere outside. The eager participants in the game will charge out of the house and into the garden, overturning every bucket and flower pot in their zeal to find the gold. When they are exhausted, and return begging for clues, I drop the news that the gold is somewhere between London and Edinburgh. This information is greeted with cries of "impossible!" and groans of disappointment. This illustration would be even more accurate if all those participating were blindfolded and their hands and feet tied together. Jesus was teaching that the things of His kingdom are not just hidden from the wise and the prudent, they are barred, locked and sealed behind impossible barriers.

So why tell us to come if we cannot come? The answer lies in the way we are to come. Taking the illustration a step further, I would then inform them, that if they would allow me to help, I will lead them by the hand right to the spot, and they will find it more quickly and surely than the most able-bodied man could ever hope to. The key is in becoming meek and teachable and allowing the Father to teach us the mystery of receiving this pure, undiluted, uncreated, life transforming presence of Jesus.

This beautiful truth, that Christ gave Himself on the cross as the bread of life, is taught in picture form in the showbread in the tabernacle. There are two Hebrew words for the showbread. The first is a phrase made up of two words in Exodus 25:30 meaning "the bread of the presence."[7] The second is translated "cake"[8] and is a word indicating that the bread has been pierced or punctured. Putting these two together, the result is "the pierced bread of the presence". Believers can feed on the direct pure presence of God in their hearts because Christ was pierced for us on the cross.

The test of true discipleship

[66] At this, many of his disciples went back, and walked no more with him. [67] Jesus said therefore to the twelve, "You don't also want to go away, do you?"

---

[7] Hebrew: "Lechem panyim" – literally "the bread of the presence".

[8] Hebrew "Challah" – literally "pierced".

68 Simon Peter answered him, "Lord, to whom would we go? You have the words of eternal life. 69 We have come to believe and know that you are the Christ, the Son of the living God."

70 Jesus answered them, "Didn't I choose you, the twelve, and one of you is a devil?" 71 Now he spoke of Judas, the son of Simon Iscariot, for it was he who would betray him, being one of the twelve.

At the end of John 6, many of His disciples abandoned Him because of this teaching. Why was it so offensive? The concept of drinking blood and eating flesh was offensive especially to the Jews. There was, moreover, an Old Testament ban on drinking blood (Leviticus 7:27). Of all the teachings of the New Testament this is the most startling departure from former ideas. Christ was teaching that we must partake of the very life-blood of God.

But the teaching has other offensive implications: most of all, that there is no appeal to the power of human ability to be a great disciple. The key to the Christian life is not the development of a great religious soul, but the receiving of the life of God to become our life. Even the act of receiving this life leaves no honour to the disciple, since he or she is incapable of receiving without divine help. Christ will never allow any room for our efforts to be glorified.

The final test of discipleship was the sifting of their motives. Were they seeking Him for Himself with unconditional surrender? Or were they partnering with Him as equals? We cannot negotiate the terms of our surrender to Him. There must be entire capitulation to Him, to His claims and all His ways. The twelve may have been bewildered, confused and even a little afraid of the things Jesus was now teaching. But they were persuaded that He was the Messiah, and there was no option but to submit themselves entirely to Him.

JOHN 7

RIVERS OF LIVING WATER

John 7 *After these things, Jesus was walking in Galilee, for he wouldn't walk in Judea, because the Jews sought to kill him. ² Now the feast of the Jews, the Feast of Booths, was at hand. ³ His brothers therefore said to him, "Depart from here and go into Judea, that your disciples also may see your works which you do. ⁴ For no-one does anything in secret while he seeks to be known openly. If you do these things, reveal yourself to the world." ⁵ For even his brothers didn't believe in him.*

⁶ Jesus therefore said to them, "My time has not yet come, but your time is always ready. ⁷ The world can't hate you, but it hates me, because I testify about it, that its works are evil. ⁸ You go up to the feast. I am not yet going up to this feast, because my time is not yet fulfilled."

Chapter 7 is the beginning of a group of chapters that cover the visit of Jesus to Jerusalem at the Feast of Tabernacles. This was in the early autumn, some 5 months before the Passover at which He was crucified. Chapter 7 covers the feast itself, while chapters 8, 9 and 10:1-21 cover the day after the feast ended. John's gospel describes a few days out of the life of Christ and there is no attempt to compose a full biography. Nearly all the material is from events which took place in Jerusalem. This is in stark contrast to the other gospels, which concentrate on events in Galilee.

At the opening of chapter 7, Jesus was in Galilee and crowds were setting out to go up to Jerusalem for the feast. His brothers goaded Him to go up to Jerusalem, possibly with a hint of sarcasm, suggesting that He should satisfy the multitudes who were wondering who He was. Amazingly, His brothers did not yet believe He was the Messiah.

The answer of Jesus was a further example of His eagle's perspective. Jesus was not acting according to any outward pressure - He was not reacting to the crowds, nor to His brothers - He was listening to His Father's voice. He referred to His time (7:6), which was the hour of the cross (17:1). While it is useless to speculate on when and how much He knew of the coming events, it is nevertheless clear that He walked to the drum beat of the Father's will.

[9] Having said these things to them, he stayed in Galilee. [10] But when his brothers had gone up to the feast, then he also went up, not publicly, but as it were in secret. [11] The Jews therefore sought him at the feast, and said, "Where is he?" [12] There was much murmuring among the multitudes concerning him. Some said, "He is a good man." Others said, "Not so, but he leads the multitude astray." [13] Yet no-one spoke openly of him for fear of the Jews. [14] But when it was now the middle of the feast, Jesus went up into the temple and taught. [15] The Jews therefore marvelled, saying, "How does this man know letters, having never been educated?"
[16] Jesus therefore answered them, "My teaching is not mine, but his who sent me. [17] If anyone desires to do his will, he will know about the teaching, whether it is from God, or if I am speaking from myself. [18] He who speaks from himself seeks his own glory, but he who seeks the glory of him who sent him is true, and no unrighteousness is in him. [19] Didn't Moses give you the law, and yet none of you keeps the law? Why do you seek to kill me?"
[20] The multitude answered, "You have a demon! Who seeks to kill you?"
[21] Jesus answered them, "I did one work and you all marvel because of it. [22] Moses has given you circumcision (not that it is of Moses, but of the fathers), and on the Sabbath you circumcise a boy. [23] If a boy receives circumcision on the Sabbath, that the law of Moses may not be broken, are you

angry with me, because I made a man completely healthy on the Sabbath? ²⁴ Don't judge according to appearance, but judge righteous judgment."

²⁵ Therefore some of them of Jerusalem said, "Isn't this he whom they seek to kill? ²⁶ Behold, he speaks openly, and they say nothing to him. Can it be that the rulers indeed know that this is truly the Christ? ²⁷ However we know where this man comes from, but when the Christ comes, no-one will know where he comes from."

He arrived at the feast discreetly, and fully aware of the danger (7:1, 10). Then at the middle of the feast He began to teach in the temple area. The eagle perspective is seen in the source of His teaching which so amazed the Jews (7:16-17). They were astounded that He had such wisdom and understanding without a formal education. Jesus explained that He had His understanding from the Father.

Then the controversies of previous chapters surfaced again, and there was conflict between the rulers and Jesus about healing and the Sabbath day. In the background there was confusion regarding His identity. The speculation was rife that this was the Christ (7:27).

²⁸ Jesus therefore cried out in the temple, teaching and saying, "You both know me, and know where I am from. I have not come of myself, but he who sent me is true, whom you don't know. ²⁹ I know him, because I am from him, and he sent me."
³⁰ They sought therefore to take him; but no-one laid a hand on him, because his hour had not yet come. ³¹ But of the multitude, many believed in him. They said, "When the Christ comes, he won't do more signs than those which this man has done, will he?" ³² The Pharisees heard the multitude murmuring these things concerning him, and the chief priests and the Pharisees sent officers to arrest him.
³³ Then Jesus said, "I will be with you a little while longer, then I go to him who sent me. ³⁴ You will seek me, and won't find me. You can't come where I am."
³⁵ The Jews therefore said among themselves, "Where will this man go that we won't find him? Will he go to the Dispersion among the Greeks, and teach the Greeks? ³⁶ What is this word that he said, 'You will seek me, and won't find me;' and 'Where I am, you can't come'?"

Then Jesus stood in the temple and lifted His voice to make the first of two great declarations. He cried out for all to hear that all knew who He was and where He was from (7:28). This was a startling claim and goes to the heart of the whole work of evangelism. Jesus declared that everyone recognised Him and His divine origin. There are two sides to this claim which baffle the mind. Firstly, He claimed that human beings know things that no-one has taught them. Secondly, He claimed to be the key that makes sense of every human being's life. It is an arresting thought that human beings have an instinct that tells them who Jesus is. It is alluded to in Jeremiah 8:7, where the Lord is appalled by the neglect of this instinctive knowledge.

> *"Even the stork in the heavens*
> *Knows her appointed times;*
> *And the turtledove, the swift, and the swallow*
> *Observe the time of their coming.*
> *But My people do not know the judgment of the LORD."*

It should not be surprising that the Creator's imprint is on all His creation, including the human race. But this has profound implications for the spiritual responsibility of the individual. It affirms the same truth that the apostle Paul taught in Romans 1:18-19

> *"For the wrath of God is revealed from heaven against all ungodliness and unrighteousness of men, who suppress the truth in unrighteousness, because what may be known of God is manifest in them, for God has shown it to them."*

When confronted with the person of Christ, humanity is faced with an awakening of a deep awareness about the true God.

The implication is that Christ is the key to each individual's life. This is in itself the only explanation behind the powerful and sudden conversions that occurred in the New Testament and since. Human lives are so damaged that it is no longer obvious what their ultimate purpose is. This can be illustrated from the world of antiques, where occasionally an object whose use is long forgotten, will be unearthed from an attic. No-one can remember and there are no instruction manuals to explain. So the object is then discarded or put to some other inappropriate use. The human heart can be likened to a bell that is half buried in earth, and encrusted with rust. It may be turned upside down and used as a cooking pot. In the same way, individuals seek to find the purpose to their life, and seek to find it in pleasure, fame, money or success. The result is emptiness and meaninglessness, or even worse: despair. The suicide rate is highest among rich, educated nations. Lonely people seek despairingly for some meaning to their lives, and drink deeply from the wells of physical or mental pleasure, but find no meaning there. To return to the image of the bell, Jesus is the only one who can strike it and make it resonate with meaning and purpose. As soon as we meet Jesus there is a deep sense of the meaning of life. Our destiny is friendship with God, as fundamentally as the glove was made for a hand. Jesus is not merely a religious alternative to other pleasures. He is the reason we were created. As soon as He is presented to the inner conscience, the bell resonates, the rust falls off, and the life becomes alive with a sense of the wonderful plan and destiny God has for each human being. He is wonderful and He is to be allowed to have that role in our lives that not only heals our woes, but also makes us come alive to the ultimate purpose of our existence. This is the explanation behind the conversion of Saul of Tarsus, who had sought fulfilment in religion and found only emptiness until he met Christ on the Damascus road. It also explains the reactions of the guards sent to arrest Jesus in this chapter: they were so struck by His teaching that they were unable to act.

This chapter also shows the unwillingness of Jesus to engage in arguments about His identity. The argument developed about the birthplace of Christ. Many were convinced that He was the Christ (7:40) but it was well known that He had come from Galilee, and that Messiah must come from Bethlehem (7:41-2). This was a technical error on the part of the rulers and the crowds, and it would have taken but a moment for Jesus to correct it. But He remained silent on the subject, begging the question "Why?" The answer lies in the fact that our faith cannot rely on superficial proofs. When Yuri Gagarin purportedly said that he "saw no God" on his orbit of earth[9], many might celebrate this as a proof that there is no God. But such trivial comments will never satisfy the seeking heart. Jesus did not correct the assumption that He had been born in Galilee, knowing that earnest, seeking souls would find out the truth for themselves, and not be put off by such superficial objections. If He had affirmed that He was from Bethlehem, He knew that this would not lead the sceptics to faith, since doubt is based as much on choices made, more than on evidence presented.

[37] Now on the last and greatest day of the feast, Jesus stood and cried out, "If anyone is thirsty, let him come to me and drink! [38] He who believes in me, as the Scripture has said, from within him will flow rivers of living water." [39] But he said this about the Spirit, which those believing in him were to receive. For the Holy Spirit was not yet given, because Jesus wasn't yet glorified.

At the height of the feast Jesus uttered His second great cry, inviting all to come to Him to receive rivers of living water, referring to the Holy Spirit. On the last day of the feast, the priests had a tradition of drawing water from the pool of Siloam and pouring it into an opening in the side of the altar, causing the water to come out of the front. This great cry of Jesus would have been interpreted as a commentary on that action. Jesus identified Himself as the sacrifice on the altar, from whom the living water proceeds. He was inviting the crowds to come to Him and receive the great gift He had earlier spoken of to the Samaritan woman.

---

[9] Quoted in *"To Rise from Earth"* by Wayne Lee, 1996.

This great cry of Jesus is important for its implications for our understanding of how the Holy Spirit works. Here Jesus locates the source of the Spirit in Himself. John's commentary on the verse indicates that the Holy Spirit is given through Calvary, following the glorification of Jesus in heaven. This is a vital emphasis; in that it is only as Jesus and His cross are proclaimed that the Holy Spirit works. This is paralleled by an event in Exodus 17:1-7, when Moses gave the nation water to drink by smiting the rock. This was such a powerful and simple prophecy of Calvary: Christ the rock was smitten and from Him the Spirit flowed. Then in Numbers 20:1-13, the same event was re-enacted, but this time there was no need for Moses to smite the rock, he only needed to speak to it for it to give forth its water. By this, God gave the understanding that Christ would be crucified once, for the outpouring of the Holy Spirit on all people in all generations. No further sacrifice of prayer and fasting, no human intensity or concentration can now "pay" for an outpouring of the Holy Spirit. Calvary was a finished, perfect work, and all can now receive by simple believing prayer. This whole picture is completed in John 19:34 when the Roman soldier pierced the side of Jesus and water and blood gushed out. The lesson was simple: the water of the Holy Spirit is obtainable only in and through the person and the sacrifice of Jesus Christ.

This great statement on the Spirit in John 7:37-9 also enlarges on the effect of the gift in those who receive. The Holy Spirit is not merely flowing through God's people as water through a channel. The Holy Spirit is located in the believer like a fountain, a source of life. The plural "rivers" indicates that the Holy Spirit will flow in great diversity, in rivers of faith, prayer, power, love and so on.

Jesus also established thirst as the great condition for receiving the Holy Spirit. At first sight this was a very commonplace condition for receiving the Spirit, since every human being experiences some degree of thirst every few hours. But the thirst that Jesus is speaking of, is the raging thirst of a person lost in the dry barren desert, with a blackened tongue and a parched throat. This is the thirst of the sinner who is in the despairing darkness of separation from God. There is an inner emptiness that makes the soul cry out to God. Jesus is declaring that it is this thirst that will direct a soul to the discovery of the Holy Spirit. It is not intellectual curiosity, nor religious intensity, and certainly not long prayer in itself that will bring a person to drink of the Spirit. This thirst is a longing for a life that is close to God, it is a consciousness that life cannot continue without a deeper discovery of the eternal God, in His love and power. This thirst will lead people to lay aside religious correctness, and pray from the heart.

Jesus then identified two actions that lead us to receive the Holy Spirit, namely "coming" and "believing". The action of coming to Jesus has an element of mystery. Coming to Jesus is not to be equated with going forward for prayer at a meeting, nor is it a matter of saying the right words. Jesus is to be reached by faith and by pressing through the veil of dullness that clothes our souls. We are to turn to Him whom we cannot see, and consciously bring our lives before Him. There we must believe in Him. The believer that receives the Holy Spirit is not merely believing He exists. He has gone a stage further in trusting in Christ, and entrusting His life to Him. There is a foundation of surrender in the faith that receives the Holy Spirit.

It is at this point that Jesus might be expected to explain the way this gift will be manifested. There are so many who direct the hearts of believers to outward signs, but here Jesus pointed us to the effect of the gift. The gift of tongues is to be ardently sought after (1 Corinthians 14: 1 and 5), but it was not this gift that Jesus underlined. He described the abundance of rivers as the effect of the Spirit's coming in fullness.

Jesus Himself is our example here, and wherever He went rivers flowed out from Him, touching lives with forgiveness, healing and love. But most of all, His life flowed with rivers of communion with His Father, of peace in the midst of adversity, and of worship that carried Him heavenwards on eagle's wings. Those who came into contact with Jesus would have been conscious of the Holy Spirit. They would have felt the Spirit like waves flowing on the shores of their lives. Some would have felt so engulfed with wonder and awe at God's love revealed, as the Spirit touched them. This must have been the effect on that day in Jerusalem at the Feast of Tabernacles, as they listened and became convinced that they were in the presence of God's Messiah (7:40).

Could this be the Messiah?

40 Many of the multitude therefore, when they heard these words, said, "This is truly the prophet." 41 Others said, "This is the Christ." But some said, "What, does the Christ come out of Galilee? 42 Hasn't the Scripture said that the Christ comes of the offspring of David, and from Bethlehem, the village where David was?" 43 So a division arose in the multitude because of him. 44 Some of them would have arrested him, but no-one laid hands on him.

The crowds were stunned by this cry of Jesus in the temple precincts. As the debate raged around Him, several focused on the fact that Jesus was from Galilee (He probably had a Galilean accent). It would have been easy for Jesus to engage with this error and defend Himself by stating the amazing fact that He had been born in Bethlehem and that He was of the house of David. So why did He not correct this misconception? The answer lies in the simple truth that objections to the person of Jesus Christ fall into two categories. First, there are the sincere questions asked by seeking hearts. Secondly, there are the objections that are excuses for rejecting Him. In this case Jesus must have known that the ones making the objection were not seeking to remove doubts about Him, but were endeavouring to justify their rejection of Him.

The darkness of religious pride

45 The officers therefore came to the chief priests and Pharisees, and they said to them, "Why didn't you bring him?"

[46] *The officers answered, "No man ever spoke like this man!"*

[47] *The Pharisees therefore answered them, "You aren't also led astray, are you?* [48] *Have any of the rulers believed in him, or of the Pharisees?* [49] *But this multitude that doesn't know the law is cursed."*

[50] *Nicodemus (he who came to him by night, being one of them) said to them,* [51] *"Does our law judge a man, unless it first hears from him personally and knows what he does?"*

[52] *They answered him, "Are you also from Galilee? Search, and see that no prophet has arisen out of Galilee.*

The chapter concludes with the scene in the Sanhedrin. The officers had been sent to arrest Jesus, but had been paralysed by the sheer wonder of His word and presence. The Pharisees pouted with religious indignation, scorning the ignorance of the common people who believed in Christ (7:49). Nicodemus was forced to timidly raise His voice in dissent, only to be roundly dismissed as a Galilean (7:52). The awful truth is here revealed that religious authorities, coupled with theological and intellectual superiority, have a terrifying power to be the very centre of opposition to the living Christ. The Scripture is filled with dire warnings about the deadly power of religious pride to blind the human heart.

JOHN 8

THE FOURTH WATERPOT:
THE WOMAN TAKEN IN ADULTERY

7 *53 Everyone went to his own house,*

8 *1 but Jesus went to the Mount of Olives. 2 Now very early in the morning, he came again into the temple, and all the people came to him. He sat down and taught them. 3 The scribes and the Pharisees brought a woman taken in adultery. Having set her in the middle, 4 they told him, "Teacher, we found this woman in adultery, in the very act. 5 Now in our law, Moses commanded us to stone such women.; What then do you say about her?" 6 They said this testing him, that they might have something to accuse him of.*

But Jesus stooped down and wrote on the ground with his finger. 7 But when they continued asking him, he looked up and said to them, "He who is without sin among you, let him throw the first stone at her." 8 Again he stooped down and wrote on the ground with his finger.

9 They, when they heard it, being convicted by their conscience, went out one by one, beginning from the oldest, even to the last. Jesus was left alone with the woman where she was, in the middle. 10 Jesus, standing up, saw her and said, "Woman, where are your accusers? Did no-one condemn you?"

11 She said, "No-one, Lord."

Jesus said, "Neither do I condemn you. Go your way. From now on, sin no more."

12 Again, therefore, Jesus spoke to them, saying, "I am the light of the world. He who follows me will not walk in the darkness, but will have the light of life."

The last verse of chapter 7 gives the detail that everyone went home, but Jesus went to the Mount of Olives, from where He went to the temple in the morning. This is a poignant detail in that the implication is that Jesus went to His home, spending all night in prayer to the Father. Whether He prayed all night or part of it is of secondary importance. The significant detail is the location: the Mount of Olives, probably Gethsemane. This was the place where olives were cultivated in quiet gardens and then crushed to obtain oil - Gethsemane means "olive press". Jesus was communing with His Father and was soaking in the fragrant anointing of His loving presence. This was the key to Jesus' ministry, that He was constantly filled with this matchless oil of grace and healing power. The tabernacle and the priests were all anointed with oil mixed with spices, and as a result there would have been a beautiful, unique fragrance wherever and whenever they were engaged in the ministry. When Jesus came to the temple in the morning the crowds were drawn to the anointing that flowed from His life as He taught them.

The scene was suddenly disturbed by the arrival of the scribes and Pharisees bringing a woman whom they had caught in the very act of adultery. Their attitude completely lacked the oil of grace, and there was no fragrance in their accusing words. They had not been communing with God. Their intention was devious, in that they were seeking to trap Jesus into either condoning adultery by His love and forgiveness, or approving the execution of the woman by stoning. Jesus' response was to write on the ground. It is useless to speculate what He may have written, but there are only two occasions when the finger of God writing is mentioned in Scripture: Exodus 31:18 and Daniel 5:5. The connection was thus made between Jehovah (who wrote the law on tables of stone and gave it to Moses) and Jesus who now interpreted that same law to sinners. Jesus and Jehovah are one. King Belshazzar had also seen the finger of God write words on the palace wall, words that spelt his impending doom. If the act of Jesus had brought the references in Moses and Daniel to the mind of the scribes, it would have reinforced the terrible convicting power of God's holy presence.

The Pharisees persisted in placing before Him what they believed to be a trap from which there was no escape. But then Jesus reversed the trap, and caught them in their own sin. He answered that only a sinless person had the right to condemn another, and then returned to His writing on the ground. The Pharisees were convicted by their own conscience (8:9) and one by one they walked away.

Jesus then addressed the woman, offering her the three things that every human being needs:

1. forgiveness of sins (8:11)
2. power to liberate her from the slavery of sinful lusts (8:11).
3. the friendship of Jesus to sustain her through life (8:12).

The first need of the human race is for forgiveness. The guilt of the human heart is a bottomless pit of pain and torment. It may be covered up through excuses such as "everyone does it!" or "I am not doing any one any harm!" But the truth is that our sins cut us off from the source and centre of joy, which is having a good conscience before God and man. Anyone exposed in the way this woman was, would have been overwhelmed with embarrassment and shame. The Pharisees were the first in a long line of accusers, including her own husband and children if she were married, and the wife and children of the man she had slept with.

Sin and madness are sometimes not easy to distinguish. Many will ask "was she bad or mad?" The answer is that human behaviour is illogical. People are driven to words and actions that are appallingly harmful and self-destructive, to others and to themselves.

Beyond this, if the woman had any spiritual desire for God, it would have died in the face of such personal failure. She would have been convinced that her hope of heaven was gone, and she could only expect condemnation from the courts of men and God. This is why Jesus is the master healer of the human condition. He made us, He understands us, and goes right to the centre of our need. His word comes always with power to fulfil what He says. He spoke words of forgiveness and broke the terrible burden of guilt in her heart.

The second need of the human heart is for power to break the endless cycle of sinful habits. Sins are like weeds; they multiply and grow faster than our cherished ideals. Sin is a power that mocks the brightest minds, and enslaves the strongest wills. Bill Clinton was an Oxford graduate, who attained the position of the most powerful man in American politics, yet he was powerless to resist his baser instincts and was humiliated in his affair with Monica Lewinsky.

Jesus's words *"Go and sin no more"* would have come with almighty power to break the reign of lust in her heart. The word of Jesus cast out devils, healed lepers and raised the dead. His word enters the darkest caverns of human need and brings authority, light and salvation.

The third need of the human heart is to walk with Jesus in the light and so have constant strength for all of life's situations. The woman would have to return to her husband, who might have refused to receive her back. She might have been barred from the synagogue. The fact that we are forgiven and empowered does not mean that all our problems will disappear. God does not leave us after saving us, but invites us to follow Him and receive the light of His love. Daily walking with Jesus brings the wisdom that enables us to persevere through suffering and pain as we learn to walk in paths of righteousness.

The identity of Jesus – the eternal Son who came down from heaven

[13] The Pharisees therefore said to him, "You testify about yourself. Your testimony is not valid."

[14] Jesus answered them, "Even if I testify about myself, my testimony is true, for I know where I came from, and where I am going; but you don't know where I came from, or where I am going. [15] You judge according to the flesh. I judge no-one. [16] Even if I do judge, my judgment is true, for I am not alone, but I am with the Father who sent me. [17] It's also written in your law that the testimony of two people is valid.; [18] I am one who testifies about myself, and the Father who sent me testifies about me."

[19] They said therefore to him, "Where is your Father?"

Jesus answered, "You know neither me nor my Father. If you knew me, you would know my Father also." [20] Jesus spoke these words in the treasury, as he taught in the temple. Yet no-one arrested him, because his hour had not yet come. [21] Jesus said therefore again to them, "I am going away, and you will seek me, and you will die in your sins. Where I go, you can't come."

[22] The Jews therefore said, "Will he kill himself, because he says, 'Where I am going, you can't come'?"

[23] He said to them, "You are from beneath. I am from above. You are of this world. I am not of this world. [24] I said therefore to you that you will die in your sins; for unless you believe that I am he, you will die in your sins."

[25] They said therefore to him, "Who are you?"

Jesus said to them, "Just what I have been saying to you from the beginning. [26] I have many things to speak and to judge concerning you. However, he who sent me is true; and the things which I heard from him, these I say to the world."

[27] They didn't understand that he spoke to them about the Father. [28] Jesus therefore said to them, "When you have lifted up the Son of Man, then you will know that I am he, and I do nothing of myself, but as my Father taught me, I say these things. [29] He who sent me is with me. The Father hasn't left me alone, for I always do the things that are pleasing to him."

The huge problem in the hearts and minds of the Jewish leaders was the identity of Jesus. This is the issue that every human being must come to terms with. When Peter confessed that Jesus is the Messiah (Matthew 16:16), he was giving voice to the dawning realization in the hearts of all the disciples that Jesus was not merely another prophet. Later on, it was Thomas who first confessed that Jesus was God (John 20:28). For subsequent generations it has been commonplace to accept His divinity without fully grasping the enormity of this claim. In this section five significant claims were made by Jesus:

1. Jesus claimed that God the Father was at work to produce faith in His Son Jesus (8:17-18). Once more, as He had stated in John 5:37, He asserted that the Father and He were witnessing to His identity. This is the claim that the Father works in the hearts of human beings to make His Son known. Jesus had said the same thing in Matthew 11:27, when He stated that no-one can know the Son except by the grace of the Father. In Matthew 16:17, Jesus attributed Peter's recognition of Jesus as Messiah to the hidden activity of the Father.

2. Jesus knew where He was from and where He was going (8:21). Throughout His life, Jesus demonstrated a knowledge that He was pre-existent with the Father (see also John 16:28 and 17:24). He also knew that He was going back to the Father and that He must return home by way of the cross.

3. Jesus was the "I am" coming from above (8:24). Jesus claimed to be "from above," that He had come down from heaven (John 3:13). John 8:24 can be translated *"Unless you believe that "I am", you will die in your sins."* The teaching of John is, that it is of eternal importance to recognise that Jesus is the Messiah, and that this realization will lead to transformation and empowerment (Matthew 16:16-19). The refusal to recognise the manifold witness about Jesus Christ would deny a person access to the only means of salvation. Of all people, those living in Israel in the days of Jesus had no excuse in rejecting Him.

4. Jesus knew He would soon be crucified and that then His identity would be confirmed. The literal translation of John 8:28 is *"When you lift up the son of man, you will know that "I am"."* He later said that it is through this lifting up that He would draw all humanity to Himself. Jesus knew throughout His time on earth that He would do something on the cross that would result in an explosion of revelation about Him. That explosion was the day of Pentecost. Jesus later said it was expedient for Him to go away, for otherwise the Holy Spirit would not be poured out (John 16:7).

5. Jesus was one with the Father (John 8:19 and 29). Jesus stated that He was in perfect harmony with the person of the Father and that this bond was absolute and unshakable. The serenity of Christ was based on His deep intimacy with the Father. He was secure in the Father's love.

The true nature of si

30 As he spoke these things, many believed in him. 31 Jesus therefore said to those Jews who had believed him, "If you remain in my word, then you are truly my disciples. 32 You will know the truth, and the truth will make you free."

33 They answered him, "We are Abraham's offspring, and have never been in bondage to anyone. How do you say, 'You will be made free'?"

34 Jesus answered them, "Most certainly I tell you, everyone who commits sin is the bondservant of sin. 35 A bondservant doesn't live in the house forever. A son remains forever. 36 If therefore the Son makes you free, you will be free indeed. 37 I know that you are Abraham's offspring, yet you seek to kill me, because my word finds no place in you. 38 I say the things which I have seen with my Father; and you also do the things which you have seen with your father."

39 They answered him, "Our father is Abraham."

Jesus said to them, "If you were Abraham's children, you would do the works of Abraham. 40 But now you seek to kill me, a man who has told you the truth which I heard from God. Abraham didn't do this. [41] You do the works of your father."

They said to him, "We were not born of sexual immorality. We have one Father, God."

[42] Therefore Jesus said to them, "If God were your father, you would love me, for I came out and have come from God. For I haven't come of myself, but he sent me. [43] Why don't you understand my speech? Because you can't hear my word. [44] You are of your father, the devil, and you want to do the desires of your father. He was a murderer from the beginning, and doesn't stand in the truth, because there is no truth in him. When he speaks a lie, he speaks on his own; for he is a liar, and the father of lies. [45] But because I tell the truth, you don't believe me. [46] Which of you convicts me of sin? If I tell the truth, why do you not believe me? [47] He who is of God hears the words of God. For this cause you don't hear, because you are not of God."

[48] Then the Jews answered him, "Don't we say well that you are a Samaritan, and have a demon?"

[49] Jesus answered, "I don't have a demon, but I honour my Father and you dishonour me. [50] But I don't seek my own glory. There is one who seeks and judges. [51] Most certainly, I tell you, if a person keeps my word, he will never see death."

[52] Then the Jews said to him, "Now we know that you have a demon. Abraham died, as did the prophets; and you say, 'If a man keeps my word, he will never taste of death.' [53] Are you greater than our father, Abraham, who died? The prophets died. Who do you make yourself out to be?"

[54] Jesus answered, "If I glorify myself, my glory is nothing. It is my Father who glorifies me, of whom you say that he is our God. [55] You have not known him, but I know him. If I said, 'I don't know him,' I would be like you, a liar. But I know him and keep his word. [56] Your father Abraham rejoiced to see my day. He saw it, and was glad."

[57] The Jews therefore said to him, "You are not yet fifty years old! Have you seen Abraham?"

[58] Jesus said to them, "Most certainly, I tell you, before Abraham came into existence, I AM."

[59] Therefore they took up stones to throw at him, but Jesus was hidden, and went out of the temple, having gone through the middle of them, and so passed by.

This chapter exposed the huge error in the way the Pharisees thought about the nature of sin. The Pharisees believed that the woman taken in adultery was a sinner because she had committed such a blatant transgression, and this was correct. Their mistake was in believing that they were not sinners, because they had not committed this sin. When Jesus said that only a sinless man could judge another, He was not accusing them of adultery. Nor is it to be assumed that they all left because of sexual immorality. These were men of moral stature, with a deep commitment to ethical behaviour. Their problem did not lie in blatant unrighteousness, but in barefaced self-righteousness of the worst kind, because it was cloaked in religion.

The world is made up of the unrighteous and the self-righteous. The path of true righteousness is only attainable through repentance and faith. Most people believe that if they have not committed a criminal offence then they are good people. Some religious people believe they are morally superior to the rest of the human race. But Jesus here taught that the only standard of righteousness that is acceptable to God is absolute moral perfection, both in the conscious and the unconscious life. It is this that Jesus taught the Pharisees and the crowd who were watching. The result of the searching word and presence of Jesus, was to convict all of sin. This is the first step for all who would be saved.

The Pharisees evidently soon returned to engage him in arguments about His claims. The conflict soon came back to the question of what sin really is. The clash reached its climax when Jesus declared to those who were beginning to believe in Him, that knowing the truth would set them free from sin (8:32). This provoked the most absurd response, that they had never been in bondage to anyone (8:33). This may have been a political statement, and if it was, it was patently untrue. In the long history of Israel, political freedom had lasted but a few hundred years at most. The previous six hundred years had been years of occupation by foreign powers: the Babylonians, the Persians, the Greeks and then the Romans. If it was a statement of spiritual freedom, then it was spectacularly complacent. The ark of the covenant had been lost for centuries. The priesthood had grown corrupt and obsessed with making profit in the temple precincts, through money-changing and the sale of animals for sacrifice. The nation of Israel had a long history of slavery to foreign powers and bondage to idolatry and sin.

Jesus then left no room for misunderstanding, by stating plainly that whoever commits sin is a slave to it. He then gave the promise that He was able to set those who follow Him free from sin, and really free. This is a most searching statement about sin, that it is a bondage to another will and power that is greater than us.

Jesus then pointed out to the Jews the distinction between being natural sons of Abraham and spiritual sons. He acknowledged their physical descent from Abraham (8:37) but questioned their spiritual affinity with him. He explained that any true son of Abraham would not reject Him (8:39-40). The exchange became even more heated as the Jews implied that He was an illegitimate child (8:41). They then made the claim that they were children of God (8:41). Jesus then made His most devastating statement about sin, that it is essentially a spiritual kinship and affinity with the devil (8:44).

Jesus made the obvious statement that the devil is a liar and a murderer. He then went one step further to point out that the same murderous thoughts were passing through their hearts, as they reacted with scorn to His claims. Jesus exposed the shocking possibility that there is a murderer and liar in each of us. The Jews rejected this possibility by mocking such a claim and accusing Him of being a Samaritan and demon possessed (8:48, 50). But then at the end of the exchange they took up stones to kill Him, paradoxically attempting to kill the only sinless one amongst them (8:7; 59).

The assertion that sin makes us children of the devil is shocking to every reader of these words, just as it was shocking to the Pharisees. The shock is based on the fact that the devil is the very epitome of evil. The truth is that as human beings pass through life, they will be faced with the choice of two ways: that of God revealed through His son Jesus, and that of the devil. When we are at first presented with such an option, most people will refuse to make a choice. The demands of Jesus are so radical that most pause before surrendering to His person and His demands. The idea that some would choose the path of the devil is monstrous to most readers and will be rejected. But the words of Jesus point to the inevitable consequences of our choices. If we humble ourselves and receive Jesus Christ as Lord then we will become children of God. If we follow the way of self and pride, then we will find ourselves in company with the prince of darkness.

When Jesus was on trial, Pilate sought to align himself with Jesus and actively steered the proceedings to have him released (John 19:12). He must have realised that crucifying Jesus was a grave act of injustice. Pilate then forced the issue by presenting the chief priests and the people with a choice: Jesus or Barabbas. Barabbas was a murderer (Mark 15:7). There can be no doubt that no-one wanted Barabbas to be released onto their streets. But given the choice between Jesus and Barabbas, they were forced to follow their irrational hatred of Jesus and allow a murderer to be let loose. Pilate sat on the fence refusing to make a decision. But his inaction was a choice. To refuse to choose is to choose. None are exempt from this colossal battle raging for the souls of human beings.

This passage also contains two of the great "I am" statements. Jesus said He was the light of the world (8:12). In the context he was claiming to be sinless and the source of spiritual light for a dark world. His claim to be free from sin was repeated in this chapter when He challenged them to find any grounds on which to accuse Him (8:46).

The second "I am" statement was the claim to have been alive before Abraham: *"Before Abraham was, I am,"* (8:58). By this He was claiming to be the pre-existent Son of God before His birth. It was the claim to be eternal and divine.

The clash of this chapter is breath-taking. It is the unavoidable truth that every human being will have to face the fact of Jesus at some point or other and come to terms with His awesome being and authority. The clash is between darkness and light, Satan and God, sin and Jesus. Human beings often decline such a choice, and prefer to sit on the fence. But the choice cannot be avoided. Only if Jesus were not who He claims to be could a human being ever hope to escape Jesus as Judge. Once the possibility is entertained that Jesus is the eternal, sinless Son of God, there is no more room for any to be indifferent to His teaching and His claims. The Jews in this chapter stood before the light of the world and rejected Him. They retreated at this point into the self-righteous protection of their religion. But such protection is vain, and can only postpone the awful day of judgment, when He will assert His claims in full, as God in human form.

The conflict between love and righteousness

This encounter opened up the great questions regarding God's dealing with humanity. The trap that the Pharisees set for Jesus exposed the underlying conflict between forgiveness and righteousness. Would He condemn the adulteress or forgive her? Would Jesus preach love or righteousness? Surely it is impossible to preach both. Jesus would either sacrifice love on the altar of righteousness or righteousness on the altar of love. Which would it be?

This passage actually does not answer this riddle, but leaves it till later events have unfolded. But this question lies at the heart of the gospel and it is important to see how God resolved it. Put simply, the riddle is this: how can a God of love simply forgive unrighteousness? Does this not in the end condone it and allow it? Should not a holy God punish the wicked? This riddle is answered at the cross, where love and holiness met. The following story indicates in some small measure the love of God that was revealed on Calvary.

James and Henry were close friends. They grew up together in a small village in Cornwall. James and Henry were inseparable and spent hours together wandering the fields and lanes around the village. They went fishing together and went on long bike rides exploring the beautiful countryside. They were inseparable and most people thought they were brothers.

When they left school Henry went to university and studied law. It was not long before he had risen through the ranks and was appointed a high court judge. But James had flair and an uncanny ability to sell any product that was going. James bought and sold and made a lot of money and occasionally a lot of losses. The two friends drifted apart and soon all communication ceased.

James discovered that he could make a lot more money by cutting corners, occasionally telling a lie. Without noticing, the small lies led to bigger ones and little by little he sold out his conscience to the god of money. James was clever and made sure he was never caught by the law.

It was when he turned forty years old that he had an opportunity he couldn't resist. He found a piece of land for sale that he planned to develop into holiday cottages. He calculated that he could make a huge five-fold profit of his investment, meaning that if he invested £500,000 he would make a profit of £2.5 million. The more he could invest, the more profit he could make. So he advertised his scheme and received great interest. He went to visit dozens of retirees who were seeking to invest their life savings. Thanks to his silver tongue, within a few months he had accumulated £5 million to invest in his scheme.

But James wasted a lot of the money enjoying life in the fast lane. He was so sure that he would make a massive profit that he went on expensive holidays and bought expensive fast cars. He lavished money on local government officials, especially those in the planning department, whose approval he needed to build his holiday paradise. He did buy a huge plot of land and building materials for the proposed holiday village, but the money was running out. James couldn't help himself and hid his financial problems by producing expensive glossy brochures and persuading more and more people to invest their life savings in his company. On 1 October 1929 James used the last of the money he had raised to clear the site ready for construction to begin, deluding himself that he would be able to raise more money to finish the project. It was only a few weeks later on 28th October that the stock market crashed in New York unleashing a world-wide wave of bankruptcies and unemployment. The land James had bought was now worth nothing, because no-one was buying. James went bankrupt and the police began to take notice of his activities.

The investors lost everything and were badly shaken - one even committed suicide. The fraud department was called in to investigate James' business practice and the case went to the High Court. The presiding judge was James' boyhood friend Henry.

When Henry saw his old friend's name on the upcoming case list, his heart sank. Although the two had grown apart over the years, Henry had followed James' career at first with interest and then with dismay as he observed the marks of foul play.

The case was prepared over several months and then heard over a period of 2 weeks. Henry listened impassively to all the evidence against his friend. Henry himself had served many years as a judge and was now a very wealthy man. He had invested his money wisely and had lost nothing in the great depression that followed the stock market crash *of 1929. Henry listened to the case with deep sorrow and foreboding. At the end of the trial the jury returned the only possible verdict that James was guilty of maliciously and callously manipulating people to invest in his hare-brained scheme. The foreman read the verdict "Guilty as charged."*

Sentencing was set for the following week. Henry was hardly seen in his chambers and to everyone's surprise he no longer drove in his Bentley to the courthouse. He was even seen taking the bus, something he hadn't done for years.

On the day of sentencing, James stood before his boyhood friend, now a forbidding judge. Henry's expression was severe as he recounted the years of fraud that had culminated in the latest scheme. He concluded by sentencing James to 10 years of hard labour. There were gasps in the courtroom at the severity of the sentence. The blood drained from James' face and he had to steady himself for fear he would collapse. He was tempted to be resentful that his friend could do this to him, but the judge was still speaking. "However," said Henry, "this sentence will be waived if the accused reimburses the whole amount borrowed of £5 million, together with interest to each investor of 5%." James hung his head in shame and despair. He had lost all his money.

To James' amazement, Henry then laid aside his wig and gown and came down to stand beside his friend. He presented him with a cheque for the whole amount. Henry had spent the past few weeks selling his car, his home and scraping together every last penny he could, to pay his friend's debt in full.

James went pale with shock. He had been steeling himself for a prison sentence. But he was totally unprepared for such an act of extravagant generosity. In fact, he was appalled when he realised what his friend had done. He protested strongly; his voice thick with tears. Above all he felt unworthy of such kindness and mercy. But Henry would not be moved and at last James fell sobbing into his friend's arms. The two friends were now both penniless, but embraced each other and left the court with their bond of brotherly love deeper than ever.

Amazingly, Jesus never spelt out the enormous cost of forgiveness when He freely dispensed it to guilty human beings. He often seemed to make light of His imminent sufferings, receiving His reward in the joy and gladness that His forgiveness brought to fallen sinners. In the story, Henry sold everything to release his friend from his dire need. On the cross, Jesus paid for our sin by suffering the righteous punishment that was due to us. Jesus proved Himself to be our friend by taking our place. Yet He also judged sin with all the wrath of God vented on Jesus on the cross. There, God broke sin's power by His righteous and loving act of redemption. The answer to the question posed by the Pharisees was in the loving heart of Jesus. It would be as if He took the stoning that the woman's sin deserved, in order that she might be forgiven.

JOHN 9

THE FIFTH WATERPOT:
THE BLIND MAN

9 *As he passed by, he saw a man blind from birth.* **²** *His disciples asked him, "Rabbi, who sinned, this man or his parents, that he was born blind?"*

³ *Jesus answered, "This man didn't sin, nor did his parents; but, that the works of God might be revealed in him.* **⁴** *I must work the works of him who sent me while it is day. The night is coming, when no-one can work.* **⁵** *While I am in the world, I am the light of the world."* **⁶** *When he had said this, he spat on the ground, made mud with the saliva, anointed the blind man's eyes with the mud,* **⁷** *and said to him, "Go, wash in the pool of Siloam" (which means "Sent"). So he went away, washed, and came back seeing.* **⁸** *The neighbours therefore, and those who saw that he was blind before, said, "Isn't this he who sat and begged?"* **⁹** *Others were saying, "It is he." Still others were saying, "He looks like him."*

He said, "I am he." **¹⁰** *They therefore were asking him, "How were your eyes opened?"*

¹¹ *He answered, "A man called Jesus made mud, anointed my eyes, and said to me, 'Go to the pool of Siloam and wash.' So I went away and washed, and I received sight."*

¹² *Then they asked him, "Where is he?"*

He said, "I don't know."

The ninth chapter opens with Jesus and His disciples escaping from the mob that was about to stone Him (8:59). Jesus was untroubled and calm despite the threat to His life. As He passed by, Jesus noticed the blind man, and the disciples posed the question about the origin of his sickness. They wanted to know whether the blindness was caused by a sin his parents had committed, or even some sin of his own. The second part of their question was odd in that they evidently believed that the man might have sinned in the womb before he was born, so causing his blindness. They may have believed that the blindness was a punishment for a sin that he would commit after he was born.

Jesus again gave the eagle perspective, and explained that God would have the last word on this man's condition. All would in the end be for the glory of God. It is astonishing how little Jesus probed into the past life of those He counselled and helped. Some have speculated that each human life is made up of generations of curses, sins and traumatic events in the distant past, that have produced the complex problems that are present in so many people. While such speculation is fascinating, there is no evidence that such probing is either necessary or useful. Jesus cut right across the past as He handled lives, and drew attention, not to the source of problems, but to their solution: Himself. In the case of the blind man, He did not look at the causes but at the ultimate purpose of the man's condition.

Jesus did not ask the man for permission to heal him, but spat on the ground to make clay, and anointed the man's eyes. Jesus was giving a visual aid regarding His ministry to sinners. The man was a simple picture of the condition of every human being. The eye symbolises the human heart, with its extreme sensitivity. The clay symbolises the uncleanness of the heart, causing spiritual blindness and irritating the soul, as clay or sand would irritate the eye. Human beings are protective of their inner life, and keep people at arm's length. This is not wrong and it is perfectly normal just as we would not let anyone touch our physical eyes. In the same way, there is almost no-one to whom we would dare reveal the tender secrets of our inner life. There may be some rare, skilful counsellors who have proved a loving aptitude and an ability to be discreet, but the only one who can touch us at the deepest level and heal us, is Jesus Christ.

The picture was so very simple. Jesus commanded the man to go to the pool of Siloam and wash. It is important to remember that this was the day after the Feast of Tabernacles, when the priests had drawn water from the pool of Siloam and poured it into the altar, from where it had flowed out. That last day of the feast, Jesus had cried out that if any were thirsty, they should come to Him and drink. Jesus sent the blind man to wash in the waters of the pool of Siloam, which was moreover the lowest point in Jerusalem. It is a simple and obvious fact that water always flows in the lowest part of the valley, and the Holy Spirit can only be known by those who will humble themselves to the point when they can receive the divine whispers of grace through the gentle, meek, dove-like Spirit of God.

The blind man did not object, and there must have been a sense of anticipation in his heart, for he simply obeyed. As difficult as it must have been, he made his way the half mile from the temple, through the streets of Jerusalem, to the appointed place. There, as he splashed the water on his face, and rinsed the mud from his eyes, the miracle took place: his eyes were cleansed, and recreated. The story does not tell of his reaction, but he must have shouted with wonder at the things he saw for the first time in his life. He could see colour, from the blueness of the sky to the green of the trees. He would have observed the exquisite design of a baby's eye, and the artistic beauty of flowers. He probably commented on everything, brimming over with joy and amazement. The transformation was so complete that some of his former friends were unsure whether he was the same man (9:9).

The events of this chapter explain the purpose of God in giving the Holy Spirit to His people. The Holy Spirit cleanses the heart, and creates it anew, producing the ability to see God with the inner eye of faith. Later Jesus told His disciples that they alone would be able to see Him (16:16). Jesus had told Nicodemus that only through the inner renewing of the Holy Spirit can anyone see the kingdom of God (3:3). The action of God is then twofold: cleansing - the removal of impurity - and the creation of spiritual ability that was formerly not there. The heart of every person yearns for purity and the ability to sense and have fellowship with God. This yearning is fulfilled in the gift of the Holy Spirit.

The conflict with the Pharisees

¹³ They brought him who had been blind to the Pharisees. ¹⁴ It was a Sabbath when Jesus made the mud and opened his eyes. ¹⁵ Again therefore the Pharisees also asked him how he received his sight. He said to them, "He put mud on my eyes, I washed, and I see."

¹⁶ Some therefore of the Pharisees said, "This man is not from God, because he doesn't keep the Sabbath." Others said, "How can a man who is a sinner do such signs?" So there was division among them. ¹⁷ Therefore they asked the blind man again, "What do you say about him, because he opened your eyes?"

He said, "He is a prophet."

¹⁸ The Jews therefore didn't believe concerning him, that he had been blind, and had received his sight, until they called the parents of him who had received his sight, ¹⁹ and asked them, "Is this your son, whom you say was born blind? How then does he now see?"

²⁰ His parents answered them, "We know that this is our son, and that he was born blind; ²¹ but how he now sees, we don't know; or who opened his eyes, we don't know. He is of age. Ask him. He will speak for himself." ²² His parents said these things because they feared the Jews; for the Jews had already agreed that if any man would confess him as Christ, he would be put out of the synagogue. ²³ Therefore his parents said, "He is of age. Ask him."

²⁴ So they called the man who was blind a second time, and said to him, "Give glory to God. We know that this man is a sinner."

²⁵ He therefore answered, "I don't know if he is a sinner. One thing I do know: that though I was blind, now I see."

²⁶ They said to him again, "What did he do to you? How did he open your eyes?"

[27]He answered them, "I told you already, and you didn't listen. Why do you want to hear it again? You don't also want to become his disciples, do you?"
[28]They insulted him and said, "You are his disciple, but we are disciples of Moses. [29]We know that God has spoken to Moses. But as for this man, we don't know where he comes from."
[30]The man answered them, "How amazing! You don't know where he comes from, yet he opened my eyes. [31]We know that God doesn't listen to sinners, but if anyone is a worshiper of God, and does his will, he listens to him.; ; [32]Since the world began it has never been heard of that anyone opened the eyes of someone born blind. [33]If this man were not from God, he could do nothing."
[34]They answered him, "You were altogether born in sins, and do you teach us?" Then they threw him out.

The man was taken to the Pharisees who immediately seized on the fact that Jesus had healed him on the Sabbath day. Yet again, the chief enemy of the work of God was their religious prejudice. The Sabbath day observance, along with circumcision, had become the central tenets of Judaism. Jesus performed seven miracles on the Sabbath day[10]evidently choosing to challenge the shallow hypocrisy of their Sabbath day observance. He did this by exposing their evident lack of compassion for those suffering and their absence of faith to be of any real help to those in need.

In Luke 13 Jesus was angry with the Pharisees for their lack of compassion for the sick woman:

> *"The Lord then answered him and said, "Hypocrite! Does not each one of you on the Sabbath loose his ox or donkey from the stall, and lead it*

---

[10] Jesus deliberately performed these seven miracles on the Sabbath day: (1) Lame man at Bethesda John 5 (2) Woman bowed down Luke 13:10 ff. (3) Blind man John 9 (4) Dropsy Luke 14:1-6 (5) Withered hand Matt 12:9-14 (6) Unclean spirit Mark 1:21-26 (7) Burning up with a fever Mark 1:29-31

away to water it? "So ought not this woman, being a daughter of Abraham, whom Satan has bound, - think of it - for eighteen years, be loosed from this bond on the Sabbath?"" (Luke 13:15-16 NKJV)

At the healing of the blind man, the Pharisees concluded that Jesus was not from God, because of His attitude to the Sabbath (9:16). The conflict intensified as the man himself challenged the Pharisees to explain how a sinner could heal the sick (9:32-33). The Pharisees changed tack and attempted to prove that no miracle had taken place and that the man had not been born blind. They then received abundant proof that the healing was genuine by interviewing his parents (9:20-21).

The man was given a final interview in which he was obviously expected to denounce Jesus. Instead of this, he gave the common-sense reply of a man in the face of a miracle: *"One thing I know: that though I was blind, now I see."* (9:25).   He proceeded to draw the conclusion that the Pharisees might wish to become His disciples.   This provoked a firm rejection of Jesus and an affirmation of their faith in Moses (9:28-9). The blind man marvelled at their spiritual ignorance, and he was excommunicated (9:34).   This meant that he could no longer trade or be an active member of Jewish society. He was to be considered as if he were dead to his relatives and the religious community. Jesus heard of this harsh judgment, and sought out the man and revealed Himself to him as the Son of God (9:36-37). The man believed and worshipped Jesus as God. Jesus received this worship, which would indeed have been outrageous, unless He was truly God in human form.

These exchanges are tinged with humour and sadness.   The humour is in the simple wisdom of the healed man, who appeared to enjoy confronting the Pharisees with the miracle and its implications.   The sadness was in the wilful blindness of the Pharisees. They obtained the proof that a miracle had indeed taken place, and then proceeded to demonstrate that proof of

109

a miracle does not lead automatically to faith. Faith comes to the heart that is willing to surrender to the authority and person of Jesus: faith involves moral choice. Their unbelief was not from confusion, but from a refusal to believe the overwhelming evidence of their conscience and established facts. Their pursuit of proof was thus shown to be a search for excuses to reject Jesus, not for grounds to receive Him.

The sadness was further compounded in their misuse of authority when they excommunicated the healed man (9:34). The punishment was severe but the healed man was brave and steadfast in the face of their persecution and made his choice to be a follower of the despised Messiah.

The light of the world

> [35] Jesus heard that they had thrown him out, and finding him, he said, "Do you believe in the Son of God?"
> [36] He answered, "Who is he, Lord, that I may believe in him?"
> [37] Jesus said to him, "You have both seen him, and it is he who speaks with you."
> [38] He said, "Lord, I believe!" and he worshiped him.
> [39] Jesus said, "I came into this world for judgment, that those who don't see may see; and that those who see may become blind."
> [40] Those of the Pharisees who were with him heard these things, and said to him, "Are we also blind?"
> [41] Jesus said to them, "If you were blind, you would have no sin; but now you say, 'We see.' Therefore your sin remains.

When Jesus revealed Himself to the man as the Son of God, he responded with worship. This doesn't mean that He took out his song book and sang a few choruses. His worship would have been the stilled awe that comes over a soul in the presence of the king. Few were able to put in words what they slowly became aware of, but he gave to Jesus the worship that is reserved for God alone. The man was giving to Jesus not merely the respect due to a prophet, but the reverence that belongs exclusively to God. The man did not say it, but he believed that Jesus was God. Jesus affirmed to the man that this is why He came into the world, to open men's eyes to see who He is. He also came to expose false shepherds, who claimed to have spiritual depth and authority but could not recognise the Messiah standing before them.

The Pharisees overheard the conversation and challenged him to explicitly apply these comments to them: *"Are we blind also?"* Jesus gave the astonishing reply that ignorance equals innocence, and that it is a wrong response to light that makes a person guilty before God. So, at the end of the chapter, the blind man received his sight because of his consciousness of need, while the Pharisees, with their sharp minds and clear sight, were blinded by their pride and their refusal to admit their need of Jesus.

JOHN 10

THE GOOD SHEPHERD

10 "Most certainly, I tell you, one who doesn't enter by the door into the sheep fold, but climbs up some other way, is a thief and a robber. **²** But one who enters in by the door is the shepherd of the sheep. **³** The gatekeeper opens the gate for him, and the sheep listen to his voice. He calls his own sheep by name, and leads them out. **⁴** Whenever he brings out his own sheep, he goes before them, and the sheep follow him, for they know his voice. **⁵** They will by no means follow a stranger, but will flee from him; for they don't know the voice of strangers." **⁶** Jesus spoke this parable to them, but they didn't understand what he was telling them.

⁷ Jesus therefore said to them again, "Most certainly, I tell you, I am the sheep's door. **⁸** All who came before me are thieves and robbers, but the sheep didn't listen to them. **⁹** I am the door. If anyone enters in by me, he will be saved, and will go in and go out, and will find pasture. **¹⁰** The thief only comes to steal, kill, and destroy. I came that they may have life, and may have it abundantly. **¹¹** I am the good shepherd.; , , The good shepherd lays down his life for the sheep. **¹²** He who is a hired hand, and not a shepherd, who doesn't own the sheep, sees the wolf coming, leaves the sheep, and flees. The wolf snatches the sheep, and scatters them. **¹³** The hired hand flees because he is a hired hand, and doesn't care for the sheep. **¹⁴** I am the good shepherd. I know my own, and I'm known by my own; **¹⁵** even as the Father knows me, and I know the Father. I lay down my life for the sheep. **¹⁶** I have other sheep, which are not of this fold. I must bring them also, and they will hear my voice. They will become one flock with one shepherd. **¹⁷** Therefore the Father loves me, because I lay down *my life, that I may take it again. [18] No-one takes it away from me, but I lay it down by myself. I have power to lay it down, and I have power to take it again. I received this commandment from my Father."*

[19] Therefore a division arose again among the Jews because of these words. [20] Many of them said, "He has a demon, and is insane! Why do you listen to him?" [21] Others said, "These are not the sayings of one possessed by a demon. It isn't possible for a demon to open the eyes of the blind, is it?"

This chapter division is misleading in that chapter 10 is a continuation of the dialogue of chapter 9, following the healing of the blind man. Chapter 9 closed with the paradox that it was the Pharisees who were wilfully blind because they would not accept the two-fold evidence that was presented to them. The first proof that Jesus was the Messiah, was the indisputable miracle of the healing of the blind man. The second was the awakening of their conscience through the presence and the words of Jesus. Their guilt was underlined by the words of Jesus, that if they were truly blind, they would not be morally reprehensible at all (9:41). It is an astonishing fact that the deepest guilt comes not from what we have done, but from the moral cowardice to face up to truth of which we are conscious, when God speaks to us.

This challenge to the Pharisees underlies all that Jesus now taught in this tenth chapter. He addressed the fact that His sheep were hearing his voice (10:3), just as the blind man had heard Jesus and obeyed Him without being able to see Him. The chapter opens with a parable about the sheep fold. This parable has two applications, the first being that the sheep fold is Israel, and the second that the sheep fold is the human heart.

Taking the sheepfold to signify Israel, then the doorkeeper (10:3) was John the Baptist who was sent of God to open the door of the nation to Him. Christ the good shepherd presented Himself to the nation without deviousness, in an open, direct manner. The sheep were free to decide without tricks or pressure of any kind, and they flocked to Him for they recognised the voice of God. Other false shepherds acted in a different manner, using

113

underhand methods to deceive the sheep, and such were thieves and robbers. These false shepherds were the supposed spiritual guardians of the nation: the scribes, the Pharisees and the Sadducees. Their role was to recognise and point to the Messiah, but instead they had enslaved the nation to religious superstition. Moreover, they had established their own authority and were lording over the sheep, usurping the authority of God in the lives of the believers. But they had gone further using underhand methods for financial gain. They had made money from the temple sacrifices. On His last visit to Jerusalem Jesus called them "a den of robbers." (Mark 11:17).

Taking the sheepfold to signify the human heart, then it means that human beings may for a while be taken in by religious fraudsters. But deep down there is a consciousness of the authentic voice of God, who comes to the front door of the human life. God does not trick His way into human lives, but addresses the will directly and openly. Jesus Christ was disarmingly frank, challenging each person to make up their mind about Him. Jesus had confidence in His sheep to distinguish between His true voice and that of the false shepherds. Jesus is the true shepherd who will not flee when danger approaches, whereas the hireling flees. Those whose hearts are not full of love will walk away from conflict and danger, and abandon the church with indifferent hearts.

Jesus is the true shepherd of Israel and of the human race. He fulfilled this, not by academic qualifications, nor by occupying some office in a religious institution, but by laying down His life on the cross. The cross was not an accident, nor was it the plan of man or devil. It was the plan of God and Jesus laid His life down of His own free will. He said in 10:18 that no-one was able to take His life from Him, and that He had the absolute right and power to both lay it down and take it up again. There is a sublime purity in the words of Jesus, and by them many came to faith, though His words also provoked intense controversy (10:19-21).

The image of the good shepherd would have been familiar to the hearers in the first century. The role of a shepherd was to live with His flock, spending time with them on the hillsides, seeking out fresh pastures during drought and protecting the flock from predators. The sheep would have known his voice and would come to his call. At night the shepherd would make an enclosure and lie down in the entrance as a living door. Enemies would not be able to enter, and wayward sheep would not be able to wander out of the fold. When Jesus said *"I am the door,"* it was all a part of the truth contained in *"I am the good shepherd"*. Moreover, the word "good" is the Greek word "kalos" that can also be translated "beautiful". Jesus is the good shepherd and is also full of that splendour that shines forth from the brightness of God's being:

> *"Out of Zion, the perfection of beauty, God will shine forth." (Psalm 50:2 NKJV)*

Jesus is the perfection of moral and spiritual beauty that are the perfect love of God. Jesus is filled with compassion and courage, two qualities that constrained Him to lay down His life for the sheep.

Jesus uttered two of the great "I am" statements in this chapter: *"I am the door"* (verse 9) and *"I am the good shepherd"* (verse 14). When He said He was the door, He meant a door of salvation. This corresponds to the door smeared with blood on the first Passover in Egypt (Exodus 12:7). Jesus is the door to fellowship with the Father (John 14:6) because He shed His blood to make the way open. He is also the door to closer fellowship with God:

> *"Therefore, brethren, having boldness to enter the Holiest by the blood of Jesus, by a new and living way which He consecrated for us, through the veil, that is, His flesh" (Hebrews 10:19-20 NKJV)*

When sinners come to Jesus they pass from death to

life. As they continue with Him, they will find Him to be a door to be clothed with power from on high and a door for closest communion with the Father. Jesus said that all a person had to do was knock and the door would be opened (Luke 9-13).

Jesus declared that He is the good shepherd and it is as we stay close to Him that we know His watchful care over our lives. We often think it is our responsibility to take ourselves deeper. But Jesus is revealing that our one need is to stay close to the shepherd. If we do this, He will lead us to fresh pastures and to still waters and our soul will be restored (Psalm 23 – the Shepherd's psalm).

The Feast of Dedication

22 It was the Feast of the Dedication at Jerusalem. 23 It was winter, and Jesus was walking in the temple, in Solomon's porch. 24 The Jews therefore came around him and said to him, "How long will you hold us in suspense? If you are the Christ, tell us plainly."

25 Jesus answered them, "I told you, and you don't believe. The works that I do in my Father's name, these testify about me. 26 But you don't believe, because you are not of my sheep, as I told you. 27 My sheep hear my voice, and I know them, and they follow me. 28 I give eternal life to them. They will never perish, and no-one will snatch them out of my hand. 29 My Father who has given them to me is greater than all. No-one is able to snatch them out of my Father's hand. 30 I and the Father are one."

31 Therefore the Jews took up stones again to stone him. 32 Jesus answered them, "I have shown you many good works from my Father. For which of those works do you stone me?"

33 The Jews answered him, "We don't stone you for a good work, but for blasphemy: because you, being a man, make yourself God."

34 Jesus answered them, "Isn't it written in your law, 'I said, you are gods?' 35 If he called them gods, to whom the word of God came (and the Scripture can't be broken), 36 do you say of him whom the Father sanctified and sent into the world, 'You blaspheme,' because I said, 'I am the Son of God?' 37 If I don't do the works of my Father, don't believe me. 38 But if I do them,

though you don't believe me, believe the works, that you may know and believe that the Father is in me, and I in the Father."
    [39] They sought again to seize him, and he went out of their hand. [40] He went away again beyond the Jordan into the place where John was baptizing at first, and he stayed there. [41] Many came to him. They said, "John indeed did no sign, but everything that John said about this man is true." [42] Many believed in him there.

The scene now changed from the Feast of Tabernacles and the events following it, to the Feast of Dedication, known today as Hanukah. This feast takes place towards the end of December, some 3 months after the Feast of Tabernacles. The Feast of Dedication was not instituted by God in any of the writings of Moses or the Old Testament. It was kept as a celebration of the courageous act of Judas Maccabaeus in cleansing the temple in 174 BC. This was to reverse the outrageous defilement of the temple in 176 BC by Antiochus Epiphanes. The Seleucid rulers had governed Palestine from Antioch in Syria following the death of Alexander the Great. Through successive governments, there had been a gradual erosion of Jewish values and culture. But when Antiochus came to the throne, he banned circumcision and Sabbath-day observance, and imposed heavy taxes on Israel. The culmination of his desecration of the Jewish faith came when he ordered pigs to be offered to the Greek god Zeus on the altar of the temple in Jerusalem. The family of a certain priest named Matthias Maccabeus led the rebellion against this abomination of desolation. They successfully halted this blasphemous desecration of the Jewish faith, though they did not end the Seleucid rule.

Jesus was in Jerusalem at this feast commemorating the Maccabean revolt. By His presence He gave His divine approval to the feast and what it represented. This is not of itself remarkable since Daniel had prophesied the events described above (Daniel 11:31-32). There the Maccabean brothers and others are described as follows: *"But the people who know their God shall be strong, and carry out great exploits."* *(Daniel 11:32).* Jesus honoured their memory, their faith and their heroic deeds. Astonishingly, in the midst of this feast, the Jewish leaders committed an act of blasphemous desecration, that exceeded the abominable deed of Antiochus Epiphanes. Their rejection of Jesus boiled over and they took up stones to kill Him (verse 31). On this occasion they failed, but three months later at the next Passover feast, they succeeded in rejecting and crucifying the Messiah.

The Jewish leaders confronted Jesus, demanding that He state openly whether He was the Messiah. Jesus reminded them of what He had done and said three months earlier (10:26). He was referring to the miraculous healing of the blind man. He added the simple truth that no-one was able to snatch His sheep from His hand (10:28) and reinforced this by including His Father in this promise, and stating that no-one can snatch a believer from His Father's hand.

Jesus was expressing the great truth of our eternal security. In weighing up these words it is essential to place Scripture alongside other Scriptures, otherwise wrong conclusions will be drawn. Jesus said that no-one can take a believer away from God. That truth stands as the foundation of our security when there are three forces involved: first, God who holds us; second, we who trust Him; third, an enemy who tries to snatch us from God. Jesus taught that we should never fear the devil or any foe; they cannot snatch us from God's hand.

However, in other places the focus is on our relationship with God, with no third party to threaten us. Later in John's gospel, Jesus gave clear warnings that we must abide in Him if we are to continue to enjoy that security. In chapter 15, Jesus taught that unfruitful branches will be cut off (15:6). This does not mean that our salvation is fragile. God does not quickly cut branches out of the vine that He has carefully grafted in through the death of His Son. But the Bible teaches the fear of the Lord, and gives many warnings to cultivate this fear. Paul wrote:

"But I keep under my body, and bring it into subjection: lest that by any means, when I have preached to others, I myself should be a castaway." (1 Corinthians 9:27 KJV)

The word "castaway" is the Greek word "adokimos" and is used to refer to reprobates in 2 Corinthians 13:5-6. The same word refers to that which is rejected by God in Hebrews 6:8. Focusing exclusively on the security of the believer might weaken the fear of the Lord. The Bible exhorts believers to holy, loving conduct and warns of consequences for those who wander from that path:

"For if, after they have escaped the pollutions of the world through the knowledge of the Lord and Saviour Jesus Christ, they are again entangled in them and overcome, the latter end is worse for them than the beginning. For it would have been better for them not to have known the way of righteousness, than having known it, to turn from the holy commandment delivered to them." 2 Peter 2:20-21 NKJV *(see also Revelation 3:16).*

Our salvation is strong and is strengthened by these sober warnings to maintain a walk with God in holiness.

The exchange of words between Jesus and the Jewish leaders provoked the unbelieving Jews to take up stones to kill Jesus (10:31). This clash was ignited by the claim of Jesus to be God's Son and to be one with Him (10:30). Jesus then reminded them of the enigmatic Scripture in which the Psalmist prophetically declares *"You are gods!"* (Psalm 82:6). At first this Scripture is arresting and even shocking. By quoting this verse, Jesus reminded the Pharisees that His claim to be God should not have been surprising since it was God's intention to make all human beings God-like!

The tragedy is that human beings have partaken of such a base form of life that our expectation is to be eternally imperfect and morally weak. Yet in the beginning God created man in His own image, after His likeness (Genesis 1:26-27). This is only shocking if we interpret it to mean that we should be all-knowing, omnipresent and almighty. God made man to be a loving, thinking, moral being. These qualities are God-like, and human beings were made to be one with God and to be absorbed into His being, from which they would live and have eternal life. Human beings cannot become God, and that is because human beings have one huge difference (among many others) that sets them apart from the divine: their complete dependence on God. God is not dependent on anyone, but human beings are totally dependent on God.

These statements may seem disconnected to the casual reader, but they are themes to which John returns again and again in his gospel. Believers are to be partakers of the very essence of God (His body and blood). Believers are to become one with God, and be indwelt and filled with His love and life. This will be the theme of later chapters and the subject of His great prayer in chapter 17.

JOHN 11

THE SIXTH WATERPOT: LAZARUS

The raising of Lazarus was the greatest miracle that Jesus performed, and it is full of spiritual meaning. The story can be divided into three movements:
1. The crisis of Lazarus' sickness and death.
2. The arrival of Jesus in Bethany.
3. The miracle at the tomb.

1. The crisis of Lazarus' sickness and death

11 *Now a certain man was sick, Lazarus from Bethany, of the village of Mary and her sister, Martha.* ²*It was that Mary who had anointed the Lord with ointment and wiped his feet with her hair, whose brother, Lazarus, was sick.* ³*The sisters therefore sent to him, saying, "Lord, behold, he for whom you have great affection is sick."* ⁴*But when Jesus heard it, he said, "This sickness is not to death, but for the glory of God, that God's Son may be glorified by it."* ⁵*Now Jesus loved Martha, and her sister, and Lazarus.* ⁶*When therefore he heard that he was sick, he stayed two days in the place where he was.* ⁷*Then after this he said to the disciples, "Let's go into Judea again."*

⁸*The disciples asked him, "Rabbi, the Jews were just trying to stone you. Are you going there again?"*

⁹*Jesus answered, "Aren't there twelve hours of daylight? If a man walks in the day, he doesn't stumble, because he sees the light of this world.* ¹⁰*But if a man walks in the night, he*

stumbles, because the light isn't in him." [11] *He said these things, and after that, he said to them, "Our friend, Lazarus, has fallen asleep, but I am going so that I may awake him out of sleep."*

[12] *The disciples therefore said, "Lord, if he has fallen asleep, he will recover."*

[13] *Now Jesus had spoken of his death, but they thought that he spoke of taking rest in sleep.* [14] *So Jesus said to them plainly then, "Lazarus is dead.* [15] *I am glad for your sakes that I was not there, so that you may believe. Nevertheless, let's go to him."*

[16] *Thomas therefore, who is called Didymus, said to his fellow disciples, "Let's go also, that we may die with him."*

The chapter opens with a description of Jesus' relationship with Mary, Martha and Lazarus. The simple fact was stated that He loved them (11:5). There are three further Scriptures that describe His relationship with them.

1. John mentions (11:2) that Mary, the sister of Lazarus, was the woman who washed Jesus' feet and wiped them with her hair. The implication is that this was the same woman mentioned in Luke 7:36-50 when Jesus dined in the house of Simon a Pharisee. This beautiful act of worship was repeated in John 12:1. The information is insufficient to be dogmatic, but it is indisputable to conclude that Mary was one of several women whose lives had been deeply touched and changed by the love and forgiveness of Jesus. The result was extravagant worship.

2. In Luke 10:38-42 we read that Martha invited Jesus into their home. Martha was preoccupied with serving, and Mary was apparently helping her at first. Then Mary was drawn away from the kitchen by a desire to sit at His feet and not to miss any of the words falling from His lips. Jesus commended Mary's action and described it as the essential element of true discipleship. Jesus was not condemning Martha's practical gifts, but was identifying His order of priorities. Jesus said that *"one thing was needful"* and that was the

positioning of the disciple's soul to hear Jesus speak. Lazarus was probably present at these visits, but no mention was made of him.

3. Mark 11:1 and 11 reveal the truth that Bethany became Jesus' home whenever He visited Jerusalem.

When Lazarus fell sick, Mary and Martha sent a brief message to Jesus, informing Him that *"he whom You love is sick."* Their expectation was clear: we are your close friends, and You have the power to heal, so come quickly and heal him. Jesus was some 30 miles away on the other side of the Jordan, a walk of two days. As they nursed their brother, they would have kept anxious watch for the return of the messenger, and for the imminent arrival of Jesus. As Lazarus' condition worsened, they may have pleaded with their brother to cling to life a little longer, since they were certain that Jesus could heal and that therefore He would heal.

Then came the disappointment: the messenger returned without Jesus, and without any assurance of His intervention. There was no sign of Jesus. Then came the nightmare: Lazarus stopped breathing. It is probable that Lazarus himself was at peace as he died, and was more distressed by his sisters' grief than his own impending death. This can be deduced from Jesus' comment in 11:25-26. When Jesus said: *"He who believes in Me, though he may die, yet shall he live"*, He may well have been commenting specifically on the faith of Lazarus.

Back across the Jordan, Jesus had the eagle perspective. He knew in Himself that Lazarus had died, and it was at this point that the narrative has the most arresting comment: *"Lazarus is dead. And I am glad for your sakes that I was not there, that you may believe,"* (11:14-15). This comment should not surprise us entirely, since Jesus had waited for Lazarus to die. What is most startling is that Jesus wanted things to get worse before they got better. Often, we pray for a swift patch up of the situation, but God wants to effect a deeper miracle than we ever imagined.

It is at this point that we need to remember the six waterpots, and to keep in view that what is being described is the ministry of the Holy Spirit. Review for a moment the meaning of the infilling of the Holy Spirit: with Nicodemus it was new birth; with the woman of Samaria, it was the healing of a failed moral and spiritual life; with the man by the pool of Bethesda it was the healing of his paralyzed limbs; with the woman taken in adultery it was the restoration to moral purity and power; with the blind man it was the recovery of sight. Finally, we have the sixth waterpot, and for Lazarus the gift of living water was life from the dead. The gift of the Holy Spirit is the radical regeneration of our lives, but this regeneration is not possible without death.

Note at this point the four meanings of the word "death" in the Bible:
- Sin, or separation from God, Genesis 2:17.
- The second death: eternal separation from God, Revelation 20:14.
- Physical death which is consistently referred to as sleep (Psalm 13:3, Daniel 12:2, 1 Thessalonians 4:14).
- The death of Jesus, Romans 6:3.

The first meaning of the word death is separation from God, indicating a state of heart that cannot sense God in any clear way. This state is not permanent and can be reversed, but the second death is also separation from God. But this death is eternal and irreversible. The third biblical use of the word indicates that physical death is to be likened to going to bed at the end of a hard day's work. The labouring man or woman falls gladly into their bed to rest, and so it should be at the end of our earthly life. But the fourth and final meaning of the word death is triumphant. The death of Jesus was voluntary and by faith. It was not the inevitable result of sin, rather it was an act of God to destroy both sin and death. When Jesus died, death died. When He rose from the dead, the reversal of the fall took place, and by that death, humanity is restored to everlasting fellowship with God. This is the full meaning that the eagle had in view when He said *"Lazarus is dead. And I am glad."* When Jesus died there was tragedy and triumph, but the triumphant joy of resurrection swallowed up the anguish of the cross, as Jesus said it would. He said that the cross would be like labour pains, and that once the victory was won, the sorrow would be swallowed up by incredible joy (John 16:19-22).

2. The arrival of Jesus in Bethany

[17] So when Jesus came, he found that he had been in the tomb four days already. [18] Now Bethany was near Jerusalem, about fifteen stadia away. [19] Many of the Jews had joined the women around Martha and Mary, to console them concerning their brother. [20] Then when Martha heard that Jesus was coming, she went and met him, but Mary stayed in the house. [21] Therefore Martha said to Jesus, "Lord, if you would have been here, my brother wouldn't have died. [22] Even now I know that whatever you ask of God, God will give you." [23] Jesus said to her, "Your brother will rise again."

[24] Martha said to him, "I know that he will rise again in the resurrection at the last day."

[25] Jesus said to her, "I am the resurrection and the life. He who believes in me will still live, even if he dies. [26] Whoever lives and believes in me will never die. Do you believe this?"

[27] She said to him, "Yes, Lord. I have come to believe that you are the Christ, God's Son, he who comes into the world."

[28] When she had said this, she went away and called Mary, her sister, secretly, saying, "The Teacher is here and is calling you."

[29] When she heard this, she arose quickly and went to him. [30] Now Jesus had not yet come into the village, but was in the place where Martha met him. [31] Then the Jews who were with her in the house and were consoling her, when they saw Mary, that she rose up quickly and went out, followed her, saying, "She is going to the tomb to weep there." [32] Therefore when Mary came to where Jesus was and saw him, she fell down at his feet, saying to him, "Lord, if you would have been here, my brother wouldn't have died."

[33] When Jesus therefore saw her weeping, and the Jews weeping who came with her, he groaned in the spirit, and was troubled,

The reaction of Martha was typically practical, but Mary collapsed into despair. On hearing that Jesus had come, Martha wasted no time and set out to meet Him. Martha's faith was both practical and triumphant. She had sorrow that Jesus had not come in time to heal her brother. But she expressed her confidence that "even now" at this lowest point, Jesus was still able to obtain any blessing if He chose to pray for it. Martha was expressing that her faith was not sufficient of itself to pray for a miracle, but her faith in Christ was undiminished. This is a vital distinction since so often the believer is faced with baffling circumstances which are beyond his or her faith. It is at such moments that believers must commit themselves in faith to Jesus, trusting that He is able to work in great power beyond what they can ask or believe (Ephesians 3:20). This is true at many moments in our lives, but especially when we receive the power of the Spirit to raise us from spiritual death. Thank God that He works in us according to His power, far beyond what we are able to ask or think.

Jesus declared that her brother Lazarus would rise from the dead. Martha reacted with the kind of faith that pushed God's power into the distant future. Yes, we believe that God can raise the dead, but not today, not in our circumstances. Martha's faith made the power of God recede into the dim and distant "last day" (11:24). Jesus brings His miraculous resurrection power into the here and now: *"I am the resurrection and the life. He who believes in Me, though he may die, he shall live. And whoever lives and believes in Me shall never die. Do you believe this?"* (John 11:25-26).

Jesus made the arresting claim that whoever lives and believes in Him will never die. This could not mean that believers will never die physically. It meant that they will never be separated from God – spiritual death, but will enjoy an unbroken relationship with God for all eternity. Martha's response was to affirm her belief that Jesus was the Messiah, and thus became the first woman to clearly confess this, just as Peter was the first man.

Martha called Mary, and Jesus waited for Mary to come where He was. He wanted her to rise from her shock and disappointment and to come to Him. So often we wait for God to come to us, but we must raise our eyes to look where He is. Often our perspective is so clouded by grief and tragedy, that we fail to see that God is not grieving in the same manner. Jesus had already declared to His disciples that Lazarus was not dead, but only asleep. This meant that Lazarus was in the safe hands of God, and enjoying the bliss of the direct Presence of God. Perhaps he was in the bosom of Abraham like his namesake in Luke 16:23.

Mary fell sobbing and broken at the feet of Jesus, and repeated the same words that Martha had spoken, but this time with a greater depth of disappointment and anguish. Martha was grieving but she was not sobbing inconsolably. Mary had entered into a dark place in her grief. It is easy for believers to speak negative things to their own soul. Perhaps Mary was wondering whether God heard her prayers, whether He still loved her. Perhaps she thought that God was punishing her. Mary had entered into a tomb of her own.

Jesus Himself began to be shaken with great sobs of grief. This was not the sorrow of bereavement, since He had already declared His knowledge that Lazarus was not dead (separated from God) but only asleep (his body had been laid aside while his spirit was in paradise). Moreover, He knew that Lazarus was but moments away from coming back to life. What moved Jesus to tears was the heartache of Mary (11:33) and the pain of the human race, struggling to cope with the awfulness of death, equipped with such a narrow perspective and weak faith. The Jews who were comforting Mary commented on the depth of Jesus' love when they saw Him weeping. This is a manifestation of the incalculable love of God expressed both individually at our personal sorrows and universally for the whole world.

3. The miracle at the tomb

34 Jesus said, "Where have you laid him?"
They told him, "Lord, come and see."
35 Jesus wept.
36 The Jews therefore said, "See how much affection he had for him!" 37 Some of them said, "Couldn't this man, who opened the eyes of him who was blind, have also kept this man from dying?"
38 Jesus therefore, again groaning in himself, came to the tomb. Now it was a cave, and a stone lay against it. 39 Jesus said, "Take away the stone."
Martha, the sister of him who was dead, said to him, "Lord, by this time there is a stench, for he has been dead four days."
40 Jesus said to her, "Didn't I tell you that if you believed, you would see God's glory?"
41 So they took away the stone from the place where the dead man was lying. Jesus lifted up his eyes, and said, "Father, I thank you that you listened to me. 42 I know that you always listen to me, but because of the multitude standing around I said this, that they may believe that you sent me." 43 When he had said this, he cried with a loud voice, "Lazarus, come out!"
44 He who was dead came out, bound hand and foot with wrappings, and his face was wrapped around with a cloth.
Jesus said to them, "Free him, and let him go."
45 Therefore many of the Jews who came to Mary and saw what Jesus did believed in him.

Jesus approached the tomb in this atmosphere of grief and despondency. No-one expected a miracle at this point. Jesus repeated what Martha had already expressed, that He knew that His prayers would be answered (11:42). This is the ultimate place of security: that we are saved by the prayers and faith of Jesus. There is deep peace and joy in knowing that our salvation does not depend on our ability to hold on and believe, but on His ability to hold on to us.

Then Jesus cried out with a loud voice and called out the name of Lazarus. The voice that could awaken a whole graveyard singled out one alone, and so it had to be or the whole burial ground would have erupted. The voice of Jesus reached beyond the physical realm into the Spirit. Whatever Lazarus was conscious of at that moment was not included in the accounts of John. Perhaps he was resting in the bliss of fellowship with Abraham, as the Lazarus of Luke 16:22. Speculation is futile, but the fact remains that the voice of Jesus called him back to his mortal body, and Lazarus awoke in the tomb. The voice of Jesus had sent His presence into that tomb and filled it with life.

Lazarus got up and walked out of the cave where he was buried. His body was wrapped in graveclothes, so that he could walk and breathe, but he was still hindered by the symbols of his death and burial. Jesus commanded the bystanders to remove the graveclothes. So it is that after the miracle of new birth, many believers still bear the marks and influence of their former lives. The followers of Jesus are to minister the love and encouragement that enables believers to lay aside the garments and habits of an earthly carnal life and to put on the garments of resurrection.

The miracle was sublime, and the reaction of Mary and Martha is not described and must be imagined. In calling forth Lazarus, Jesus also had called Mary out of her tomb of despairing grief. Mary and Martha must have passed in seconds from sorrow to shock to joyful amazement at the sight of their brother alive after four days in the tomb. The resurrection changes everything forever. There can be no more room for pessimism, nor unbelief. Once Christ has demonstrated His total authority over death, there is no further enemy to fear.

Lazarus himself must have been radically transformed in his thinking and approach to life. Many grow wiser with the approach of death, as they focus on what is truly important in the light of eternity. Once we have died and are enjoying eternal life in heaven, it may be assumed that we will be overwhelmed with the sense of relief and amazement at an unseen world, that surpasses everything seen or known in this place of shadows. But what wisdom then, does a person have, who is then allowed to return from that world of bliss and to speak again to this world?

This is the whole point of the resurrection, that life does not cease with death, nor will it merely continue without a body. At the return of Christ, believers shall be given a new body. The whole point of resurrection is that it is a transformation as from a caterpillar to a butterfly, from a seed that resembles a speck of dust or dirt to a breath-taking orchid. Resurrection is not merely life after death, it is life that is raised to another plane, to another dimension, which no human mind can truly grasp before we get there.

It must be assumed that if the horrors of eternity without God and the bliss of eternity with Him were fully grasped, then no-one would reject the offer of Christ. Nevertheless, the offer of Christ is to die now, in spirit to the power of sin and flesh, and to rise in newness of life through the gift of the Holy Spirit. The great need is for radiant believers whose lives demonstrate the reality of resurrection now.

This miracle is a declaration that there is no-one too corrupted by immorality, unbelief or religious pride, that cannot be totally transformed by the power of the resurrection of Jesus. The point that can be easily overlooked is that in order to experience His power we must first become like Him in His death. Jesus teaches us how to die. To do this, we surrender in faith into His loving arms, trusting Him to raise us into life abundant.

The reaction of the rulers

46 But some of them went away to the Pharisees and told them the things which Jesus had done. 47 The chief priests therefore and the Pharisees gathered a council, and said, "What are we doing? For this man does many signs. 48 If we leave him alone like this, everyone will believe in him, and the Romans will come and take away both our place and our nation."

49 But a certain one of them, Caiaphas, being high priest that year, said to them, "You know nothing at all, 50 nor do you consider that it is advantageous for us that one man should die

for the people, and that the whole nation not perish." [51] *Now he didn't say this of himself, but being high priest that year, he prophesied that Jesus would die for the nation,* [52] *and not for the nation only, but that he might also gather together into one the children of God who are scattered abroad.* [53] *So from that day forward they took counsel that they might put him to death.* [54] *Jesus therefore walked no more openly among the Jews, but departed from there into the country near the wilderness, to a city called Ephraim. He stayed there with his disciples.*
[55] *Now the Passover of the Jews was at hand. Many went up from the country to Jerusalem before the Passover, to purify themselves.* [56] *Then they sought for Jesus and spoke with one another as they stood in the temple, "What do you think—that he isn't coming to the feast at all?"* [57] *Now the chief priests and the Pharisees had commanded that if anyone knew where he was, he should report it, that they might seize him.*

As incredible as it may seem, the Jewish leaders were not drawn to open their hearts to Jesus by this miracle, but were threatened by it. It was this miracle that provoked the plot to kill Him (11:53). They also planned to kill Lazarus (12:10-11). The paradox of killing a man who raises the dead or who had been raised from the dead never seems to have occurred to them. But such is the insanity of sinful humanity, and never is it more strongly and horribly expressed than in the guise of religion.

The Pharisees felt they were losing their power and control over the people. They were reproved by a word of prophecy from Caiaphas the High Priest. John pointed out that Caiaphas did not speak this from himself, indicating that the Spirit of God rested on the office that he held, even though he was unworthy of that office. This is a warning to all who are in positions of authority and influence in the church. God may honour His word and use us, but that does not mean that our lives are right with God.

Caiaphas spoke the word without understanding it himself. He obviously believed that the death of Jesus was necessary to protect Israel from Roman cruelty. He believed that God was sanctioning his rejection and hatred of Jesus. Caiaphas saw that the death of Jesus would be for the blessing of Israel and beyond, though he had no idea how this would be worked out. He saw the expediency of removing Jesus, but failed to see that the cross would be the basis of reconciling sinners with a holy God. Caiaphas was a mouthpiece for truth that he himself could not grasp. Events were moving swiftly to their climax in the final confrontation between the Jewish leaders and the Messiah.

JOHN 12

THE CALM BEFORE THE STORM

12 Then six days before the Passover, Jesus came to Bethany, where Lazarus was, who had been dead, whom he raised from the dead. ² So they made him a supper there. Martha served, but Lazarus was one of those who sat at the table with him. ³ Therefore Mary took a pound of ointment of pure nard, very precious, and anointed Jesus's feet and wiped his feet with her hair. The house was filled with the fragrance of the ointment. ⁴ Then Judas Iscariot, Simon's son, one of his disciples, who would betray him, said, ⁵ "Why wasn't this ointment sold for three hundred denarii, and given to the poor?" ⁶ Now he said this, not because he cared for the poor, but because he was a thief, and having the money box, used to steal what was put into it. ⁷ But Jesus said, "Leave her alone. She has kept this for the day of my burial. ⁸ For you always have the poor with you, but you don't always have me."

⁹ A large crowd therefore of the Jews learned that he was there, and they came, not for Jesus' sake only, but that they might see Lazarus also, whom he had raised from the dead. ¹⁰ But the chief priests conspired to put Lazarus to death also, ¹¹ because on account of him many of the Jews went away and believed in Jesus.

Chapter 12 opens with a prophetic picture of the church. There were five elements to this scene:

1. Martha served (12:2). In the exultant joy of the resurrection of Lazarus, it might be thought that all practical concerns would be swept away. But

this is not the case. The truth of resurrection does not negate the practical dimensions of life, it enhances them. Martha and all practical individuals should draw great comfort and inspiration from the simple fact that Martha is here described serving Christ and her risen brother. What did she cook? Martha would have prepared the best feast possible, ministering to her beloved master with radiant joy.

2. Lazarus ate and drank with Jesus in the wonder of resurrection from the dead. Believers have died and are risen with Christ. They are to sit at the table of the king and eat and drink the very presence of Almighty God. The gathering of God's people is to have a touch of heaven about it, since the exultant life and victory of the cross is imparted to His people now. Believers have the unique privilege of dying before they die. They die spiritually to sin and death itself and are then free from all the worries and fears that assail those whose lives are dominated by this present evil age.

3. Mary broke her expensive bottle of perfume and poured it over His feet. The perfume of love rising in the worship of God's people refreshes the heart of God, and brings a washing to those engaged in it. This was a re-enactment of the extravagant love that she had expressed when she first met Him. Jesus here comments that she was preparing Him for burial (12:7). This is a most touching comment, because some days later the women came to the tomb of Jesus to anoint His dead body, only to find that the opportunity had passed (Luke 24:1). Mary may have had a revelation of His impending death, and there may have been something she sensed of the gathering storms and the inevitable clash between darkness and light. The lesson for us

is to take the opportunities to express our love to Him every time they are presented.

4. Judas Iscariot expressed his cynical view of Mary's extravagant love, and brought it down to the level of economic expediency, heavily mixed with hypocrisy and greed (12:5-6). This discordant note is so obviously out of place in such a sublime scene. The tragedy is that everywhere the church is formed, there, conflict and opposition will also be found. The betrayal of Christ was not only the heartbreak of the first band of disciples; it is a tragic element that is present throughout church history.

5. In the background, the members of the Sanhedrin were plotting to kill Jesus. The chief priests represent organised religion that looks on true believers with disdain. The group of disciples around Jesus were amateurish and untrained in matters of theology. The priests were calculating and envious, and most of all lacking any affection for Jesus Christ. Professionalism in the church can kill the trusting child in us that Jesus seeks to cultivate among His people.

The raising of Lazarus was the ultimate sign of John's gospel, and the pinnacle of Jesus' ministry to the needs of the human race. The next step was the cross, when Jesus would enter the dark tomb of the human race and raise humanity out of sin and death.

The triumphal entry into Jerusalem

12 On the next day a great multitude had come to the feast. When they heard that Jesus was coming to Jerusalem, 13 they took the branches of the palm trees and went out to meet him, and cried out, "Hosanna! Blessed is he who comes in the name of the Lord, the King of Israel!"
14 Jesus, having found a young donkey, sat on it. As it is written, 15 "Don't be afraid, daughter of Zion. Behold, your King comes, sitting on a donkey's colt." 16 His disciples didn't

understand these things at first, but when Jesus was glorified, then they remembered that these things were written about him, and that they had done these things to him. 17 The multitude therefore that was with him when he called Lazarus out of the tomb and raised him from the dead was testifying about it. 18 For this cause also the multitude went and met him, because they heard that he had done this sign. 19 The Pharisees therefore said among themselves, "See how you accomplish nothing. Behold, the world has gone after him."

The crowd that greeted Jesus was made up of pilgrims who had come to the feast, and probably included a large number from Galilee. The crowd was filled with great anticipation, as Jesus was welcomed as Messiah and King. Jesus entered Jerusalem on a donkey, which was a symbolic declaration that He came for peace and not for war. The full quote from Zechariah indicates the contrast with the war horses that would be cut off by Messiah:

> *"Rejoice, O people of Zion! Shout in triumph, O people of Jerusalem! Look, your king is coming to you. He is righteous and victorious, yet he is humble, riding on a donkey-- riding on a donkey's colt. I will remove the battle chariots from Israel and the warhorses from Jerusalem. I will destroy all the weapons used in battle, and your king will bring peace to the nations. His realm will stretch from sea to sea and from the Euphrates River to the ends of the earth." (Zechariah 9:9-10 NLT)*

This entry into Jerusalem is also in contrast to the second coming of Christ at the height of the battle of Armageddon. Then He will come to exercise judgment – not to save. (Revelation 19:11-21).

The whole of Jerusalem was stirred at His arrival and was buzzing with the news of the most recent miracle in Bethany (12:17-18). There was near panic among the Pharisees as they realised that the whole world was going after Jesus (12:19): they were losing control.

The Greeks seek Jesus

²⁰ Now there were certain Greeks among those who went up to worship at the feast. ²¹ These, therefore, came to Philip, who was from Bethsaida of Galilee, and asked him, saying, "Sir, we want to see Jesus." ²² Philip came and told Andrew, and in turn, Andrew came with Philip, and they told Jesus. ²³ Jesus answered them, "The time has come for the Son of Man to be glorified. ²⁴ Most certainly I tell you, unless a grain of wheat falls into the earth and dies, it remains by itself alone. But if it dies, it bears much fruit. ²⁵ He who loves his life will lose it. He who hates his life in this world will keep it to eternal life. ²⁶ If anyone serves me, let him follow me. Where I am, there my servant will also be. If anyone serves me, the Father will honour him.

Now the scene turned to a moment of relative calm. A group of Greeks had heard of Jesus and had come to see Him. The Greeks represent the whole Gentile world, which had been largely excluded from the ministry of Jesus. They presented their request to Philip. Jesus was then approached to see if He would grant an audience to the Greeks. Jesus' answer was startling: no, He wouldn't see them. This meant that the hour for preaching and teaching had passed and the long-awaited hour of His death had now come. He described His death by comparing Himself to a seed that must fall into the ground and die or abide alone (12:24). He was describing the necessity of His death in order to be able to provide salvation for all the nations, and thus bear true fruit from His life's work. His mission was to be the sacrifice for sins that would reconcile both Jew and Greek to God.

He then applied this same image of the seed to all His followers. The only basis of effective ministry is to lose one's life. This little key opens a big door for all who can receive it. The key to preaching is to be dead to self, and this is the key to all activity in the kingdom. The man or woman who is motivated by desire for fame or wealth will betray the values of the kingdom and bear little or no fruit for eternity. Fruit can only come if there is a letting go of all, in order to die by faith with Christ. Christ's death was first and foremost a substitutionary death: He bore our punishment. But it was also in complete identification with us, in that by it we can also die. This makes the death of Jesus a door into a world of fruitful service. The life of a believer can easily be made fruitless by worldly desires or hurts and disappointments that weigh down and suffocate our spiritual life. Jesus here gives the way of escape: that we can become as dead as He to the allurements of the world, and to a self-centred way of life.

Dying to self and the world is the counterpart to becoming alive to God, to His voice, His presence and His love. The seed that refuses to fall into the ground will remain alone and unblessed. The seed that dies will spring up with abundant new life. It is a hard path at first, but with patient application, it leads to abundant fruit. To refuse the cross is to choose a much harder path, abiding in hardness and barrenness.

The voice of the Father

[27] *"Now my soul is troubled. What shall I say? 'Father, save me from this time?' But I came to this time for this cause.* [28] *Father, glorify your name!"*
Then a voice came out of the sky, saying, "I have both glorified it, and will glorify it again."
[29] *Therefore the multitude who stood by and heard it said that it had thundered. Others said, "An angel has spoken to him."*
[30] *Jesus answered, "This voice hasn't come for my sake, but for your sakes.* [31] *Now is the judgment of this world. Now the prince of this world will be cast out.* [32] *And I, if I am lifted up from the earth, will draw all people to myself."* [33] *But he said this, signifying by what kind of death he should die.* [34] *The multitude answered him, "We have heard out of the law that the Christ remains forever.; How do you say, 'The Son of Man must be lifted up?' Who is this Son of Man?"*

Jesus was troubled and a great cry escaped from His heart: *"Father, glorify your name!"* (12:28). The result was startling as a voice like thunder immediately responded. The Father had spoken from heaven at the baptism of Jesus, and on the mount of transfiguration. Each time He had pointed to His Son and declared His love for Him. This is an incredibly simple fact that lies at the foundation of God and His universe. He loves His Son. Anyone who rejects God's Son cannot feel at home in God's universe. This passion for and pride in His Son are what motivates the Father. He lives for and through His Son and Jesus lives for and through His Father.

The effect on the crowd was bewilderment, and few understood what had happened. This was not because God does not have clear diction! It was because the crowds were so out of tune with God's heart. Some heard merely a loud noise; others sensed the miraculous dimension and thought it was an angel. John recorded the words: *"I have both glorified it, and will glorify it again."* To those who love and serve Jesus, there is a joyous anticipation of what God will do to exalt and present His Son in every succeeding generation of the human race. In some measure, every prayer is to be for the glory of Jesus. Even our prayers for salvation are to bring glory to Him. The history of grace is the history of how God is glorifying His Son for His obedience unto death.

Jesus commented on the Father's words and made three observations. First, God was speaking to the world, not to Jesus. Second, the hour of God's triumph over evil had come. In the cross the devil was about to lose His last vestiges of power over human beings, who would turn to God in faith. Third, the lifting up of the Son of God on the cross would trigger the world-wide harvest of all nations. All tongues and tribes would come to Christ as the cross is preached, revealing the heart of God in all His matchless love and power.

The cross is the greatest revelation of God in all eternity. Something is revealed there that surpasses any other expression of God's being. Just as pressure brings out extraordinary qualities of character, so the pressure of the cross revealed the infinity of God's love.

Walk while you have the light

* 35 Jesus therefore said to them, "Yet a little while the light is with you. Walk while you have the light, that darkness doesn't overtake you. He who walks in the darkness doesn't know where he is going. 36 While you have the light, believe in the light, that you may become children of light." Jesus said these things, and he departed and hid himself from them. 37 But though he had done so many signs before them, yet they didn't believe in him, 38 that the word of Isaiah the prophet might be fulfilled, which he spoke, "Lord, who has believed our report? To whom has the arm of the Lord been revealed?" 39 For this cause, they couldn't believe, for Isaiah said again,*

40 "He has blinded their eyes and he hardened their heart,
lest they should see with their eyes,
and perceive with their heart,
and would turn,
and I would heal them."

41 Isaiah said these things when he saw his glory, and spoke of him. 42 Nevertheless even many of the rulers believed in him, but because of the Pharisees they didn't confess it, so that they wouldn't be put out of the synagogue, 43 for they loved men's praise more than God's praise.

44 Jesus cried out and said, "Whoever believes in me, believes not in me, but in him who sent me. 45 He who sees me sees him who sent me. 46 I have come as a light into the world, that whoever believes in me may not remain in the darkness. 47 If anyone listens to my sayings, and doesn't believe, I don't judge him. For I came not to judge the world, but to save the world. 48 He who rejects me, and doesn't receive my sayings, has one who judges him. The word that I spoke will judge him in the last day. 49 For I spoke not from myself, but the Father who sent me, he gave me a commandment, what I should say, and what I should speak. 50 I know that his commandment is eternal life. The things therefore which I speak, even as the Father has said to me, so I speak."

From verse 35 to the end of the chapter, Jesus explained the key principle of living and walking in the light of revelation given by God. Jesus said in 12:35-6 that we must walk while we have the light or darkness will overcome us. Moreover, it is walking in the light that will cause us to become sons of light. Rejecting Christ and His words will result in self-condemnation, in that Jesus did not come to condemn but to save the world (12:47). It is the receiving or rejecting of Him that will be the basis on which each person is judged.

Jesus here teaches that it is not our responsibility to turn the light on. Rather it is the responsibility of each individual to respond fully to the light, and by walking in the light, make that light to become an integral and inseparable part of our life. When a person acts upon revelation received, that revelation stays with them. On the other hand, when a person neglects to act upon what they have received, then the revelation is lost, and it will one day be brought back as a condemnation of that person.

This changes the whole approach to life; in that we realise that our sole responsibility before God is to treasure what He has sown into our lives. God's touch and God's word bring an awakening of the soul to God, which is to be treasured and prized above diamonds and rubies. It is beyond price, because His touch is not meant to be a distant memory, but rather a door to deeper revelations and friendship with God. 2 Corinthians 3:18 speaks of being transformed from glory to glory, and Romans 1:17 speaks of going from faith to faith. The light that Christ gives us, is the first step on a walk, that goes right into the centre of that light, in the holy of holies. The alternative is to go round and round the same spot and so never to discover the deeper things of God. The result is monotony. Whoever finds their Christian life dull and repetitive, has stopped walking in the Light. Whoever walks in the light has begun the adventure of faith.

Christianity is often reduced to a community experience. The result is that we attend meetings and services and relate to a church hierarchy and to Christian friends. The will of God is that our community life be the expression of a company of people who are all walking with God in their private lives. Such Christianity is full of light, joy and expectation.

John quoted Isaiah in this section from two crucial prophecies. The first is from Isaiah 53:1, when Isaiah saw the cross and grieved in anticipation that the Messiah would be misunderstood and rejected. Isaiah looked into the future and saw the events described in the gospels.

The second quote was from Isaiah 6:10, in which Isaiah was given a message of caution to the nation of Israel. The warning was that if the nation did not respond to the word of God and the moving of God's grace, then their ability to perceive truth would be taken away. Isaiah was explaining the spiritual principle that if people will not respond, then their ability to understand will be removed. God was warning every person in every generation, that free will and the ability to respond are gifts of grace and not to be taken for granted.

God never does this intending to reject people. Rather, God intends to awaken people who are sleep walking into eternity, with little regard for God or His grace. The inner paralysis should shock people to realise their dreadful neglect of the kindness and mercy of God. God was giving this warning to a generation that had received the greatest visitation in all history. The revival that took place in the three years of Jesus' ministry was astounding. There had never been such a period in all the history of Israel. God was walking in human form in the streets, preaching, teaching and doing signs and wonders. The response was equally astonishing. The scholars who pored over the prophecies, rejected and crucified their Messiah. John pointed out that Isaiah saw the glory of Jesus' day, and that glory was the core message of His prophecy (12:41).

JOHN 13

THE WASHING OF THE DISCIPLES' FEET

13 *Now before the feast of the Passover, Jesus, knowing that his time had come that he would depart from this world to the Father, having loved his own who were in the world, he loved them to the end. ² During supper, the devil having already put into the heart of Judas Iscariot, Simon's son, to betray him, ³ Jesus, knowing that the Father had given all things into his hands, and that he came from God, and was going to God, ⁴ arose from supper, and laid aside his outer garments. He took a towel and wrapped a towel around his waist.*

Chapter 13 opens with a description of the inward thoughts of Jesus. John observed what Jesus was thinking, but does not explain how he knew. John was not a mind-reader, but was looking at Jesus and identifying with Him. This is the attitude of one who loves Him, and is free from self. Most people attend meetings with a sense of deep inward need, conscious of their problems, and are sifting and evaluating everything that is said, to see how it relates to their agenda. John was free and able to look at Him and immerse Himself into Jesus.

What then did John see in the face of Jesus? He saw destiny, love, authority and humility. He could see the destiny of Jesus, knowing that His hour to leave the

world and return to the Father was come (13:1). He saw
authority because He saw that Jesus knew that all things
were now given into His hands by the Father (13:3). He
saw love because He could see that Jesus would fulfil
the demands of love, and go all the way in suffering for
the sin of the world (13:1). He saw humility because
Jesus laid aside His garments and despite the fact that
the rule of the whole universe was given to Him, He
clothed Himself with the garments of a slave. It is the
uniting of absolute authority with total humility that is
so breath-taking.

> *⁵ Then he poured water into the basin, and began to wash
> the disciples' feet and to wipe them with the towel that was
> wrapped around him. ⁶ Then he came to Simon Peter. He said
> to him, "Lord, do you wash my feet?"*
> *⁷ Jesus answered him, "You don't know what I am doing
> now, but you will understand later."*
> *⁸ Peter said to him, "You will never wash my feet!"*
> *Jesus answered him, "If I don't wash you, you have no part
> with me."*
> *⁹ Simon Peter said to him, "Lord, not my feet only, but also
> my hands and my head!"*
> *¹⁰ Jesus said to him, "Someone who has bathed only needs
> to have his feet washed, but is completely clean. You are clean,
> but not all of you." ¹¹ For he knew him who would betray him,
> therefore he said, "You are not all clean." ¹² So when he had
> washed their feet, put his outer garment back on, and sat down
> again, he said to them, "Do you know what I have done to
> you? ¹³ You call me, 'Teacher' and 'Lord.' You say so correctly,
> for so I am. ¹⁴ If I then, the Lord and the Teacher, have washed
> your feet, you also ought to wash one another's feet. ¹⁵ For I
> have given you an example, that you should also do as I have
> done to you. ¹⁶ Most certainly I tell you, a servant is not greater
> than his lord, neither is one who is sent greater than he who
> sent him. ¹⁷ If you know these things, blessed are you if you do
> them. ¹⁸ I don't speak concerning all of you. I know whom I
> have chosen. But that the Scripture may be fulfilled, 'He who
> eats bread with me has lifted up his heel against me.' ¹⁹ From
> now on, I tell you before it happens, that when it happens, you
> may believe that I am he. ²⁰ Most certainly I tell you, he who
> receives whomever I send, receives me; and he who receives
> me, receives him who sent me."*

The scene was the upper room, and Jesus was about
to eat the Passover and share the first communion with

His disciples. At the door there would have been a bowl and a towel, waiting for a servant to take up his duties and wash the feet of the esteemed guests. Today it would have been like a doorman, or a waiter taking the coats from customers in a restaurant. But here the bowl lay untouched, because none of the twelve saw it as their responsibility. How their cheeks must have burned with embarrassment, when the Master took on Himself the task and washed their feet one by one, from headstrong Peter all the way down to treacherous Judas. Peter was typically impetuous and swung from resisting Jesus, and refusing to let Him wash His feet, and then insisting that Jesus wash Him entirely (13:9).

When Jesus washed the disciples' feet, He was revealing the heart of God and the nature of God's kingdom and the church. It is sometimes reported that the queen of England might visit a family in some poor area of her kingdom. Such a great act of humility attracts reporters and TV cameras. But this is worlds away from the act of Jesus. If the queen rolled up her sleeves and took upon herself the cleaning of toilets in a homeless centre, the press would be on the scene. But if she did it every day, the press would soon lose interest. Jesus Christ did not do acts of humility to impress. He did them because they flowed from His character and nature. Jesus was most at home dressed as a slave, taking the lowest place and washing His disciples' feet. Their feet would also have been dusty and smelly. If it were announced that there would be a service with foot-washing, everyone who attended would make sure their feet were clean beforehand. But in this case, it was not merely a symbolic act - it was a necessary one and Jesus was completely at home doing it

By this act Jesus revealed the true foundation of godly leadership and set an example for all leaders and believers to follow. He also revealed the function of the church to be a place of washing. Every time believers meet, it is to be ministered to by Jesus. The medium of washing is the love of God, which reaches our souls through the water of the Holy Spirit and of the Spirit/word ministered (Ephesians 5:26). This cleansing power of the Spirit brings to us the love of God. Only as the meeting of God's people is in this same mind and power, can there be real transformation and refreshing of hearts to continue the journey of faith.

There are many facets to the truth of washing that Jesus expressed in the upper room. First, He said that unless we are washed, we have no part in Him (verse 8). He was emphasizing purity as the foundation of the kingdom of God. The believer must be clean and cannot present him or herself to God without the work of the Holy Spirit to cleanse the heart. This is one of the constant themes of John's gospel. Inner cleansing is the chief work of the Holy Spirit, from the moment of conversion to the great work of the baptism with the Spirit. The Psalmist asked the question:

"Who may ascend into the hill of the LORD? Or who may stand in His holy place? He who has clean hands and a pure heart." (Psalm 24:3-4 NKJV)

The writer to the Hebrews affirms that without holiness, none shall see the Lord (Hebrews 12:14). Jesus points every believer to the place of cleansing, as we surrender our lives to Him.

The second aspect of washing, is that it is not to be experienced once only, but continually. Jesus said that there is a foundational washing that clears up the deep polluting power of sin. Jesus affirmed that all the disciples, except Judas, had already experienced His power to make them clean. But then He continued to say that His disciples needed regular washing. He was referring to the contact of the believer with the world, through which believers can be defiled. Believers are to allow Jesus to minister washing daily, enabling them to walk free of bitterness and attitudes that mar our lives.

Believers are touched with the burdens, the weariness and troubles of the world. Jesus told the disciples that if He did not continually wash their feet, they would ultimately not belong to Him. He assured them that they had already been cleansed by receiving Him, but that they would need regularly washing through His love, His word and His presence. Believers must gather together, to cooperate with God in the fulfilling of this ministry, or the churches will ultimately deteriorate and be as dry and dusty as the world. Powerful cleansing had already begun through their fellowship with Jesus, but continual cleansing is a necessary part of the Christian's walk.

The hour of darkness

[21] When Jesus had said this, he was troubled in spirit, and testified, "Most certainly I tell you that one of you will betray me."

[22] The disciples looked at one another, perplexed about whom he spoke. [23] One of his disciples, whom Jesus loved, was at the table, leaning against Jesus' breast. [24] Simon Peter therefore beckoned to him, and said to him, "Tell us who it is of whom he speaks."

[25] He, leaning back, as he was, on Jesus' breast, asked him, "Lord, who is it?"

[26] Jesus therefore answered, "It is he to whom I will give this piece of bread when I have dipped it." So when he had dipped the piece of bread, he gave it to Judas, the son of Simon Iscariot. [27] After the piece of bread, then Satan entered into him.

Then Jesus said to him, "What you do, do quickly."

[28] Now nobody at the table knew why he said this to him. [29] For some thought, because Judas had the money box, that Jesus said to him, "Buy what things we need for the feast," or that he should give something to the poor. [30] Therefore having received that morsel, he went out immediately. It was night.

[31] When he had gone out, Jesus said, "Now the Son of Man has been glorified, and God has been glorified in him. [32] If God has been glorified in him, God will also glorify him in himself, and he will glorify him immediately. [33] Little children, I will be with you a little while longer. You will seek me, and as I said to the Jews, 'Where I am going, you can't come,' so now I tell you. [34] A new commandment I give to you, that you love one another. Just as I have loved you, you also love one another. [35] By this everyone will know that you are my disciples, if you have love for one another."

Jesus moved from the sublimity of this symbolic act to the reality of the disciples' state of heart. Jesus affirmed that one of the 12 would imminently betray Him (13:18-21). This provoked perplexity among the disciples, as they looked in themselves and wondered if they had the awful potential to betray and destroy the Son of God. The word of Jesus was searching, because He did not openly identify the betrayer, which left all the disciples looking inward. Matthew tells us that they all were exceeding sorrowful and began to say one after another "*Lord, is it I?*" (Matthew 26:22). They could only have asked this because they suspected that they were capable of it.

But John the beloved apostle was the exception. He was leaning his head on Jesus' shoulder and was enjoying the peace and love that he sensed in the person of Christ. Peter was not in this attitude, and whispered to John to ask who the traitor was. Astonishingly, Peter was unable to ask the Master. He was awkward and unable to receive the love of God as deeply as God intended him to. Peter feared that he might be the one who would destroy God's Messiah, and he was not far from the truth, given that he would soon deny knowing Him. John alone asked a different question, asking which of the others would betray Jesus. From the security of love, John knew he would be strengthened not to betray Him.

In answer to this question, Jesus still did not openly point to Judas. By means of a sign, He gave to John alone the understanding that Judas was the traitor. He told John that the traitor was the one to whom He would give a sop. Some have speculated that this action was one of singling out Judas to honour him. It is certainly true that by this act, Jesus was expressing love and affection to Judas. The remarkable fact is that when Judas received it, Satan entered into him. Something was triggered in Judas' heart by this act of love. Perhaps it was jealousy or shame or a combination of many dark thoughts. Judas was a lover of money and constantly stole from the common purse (John 12:6). It was this love of money that moved him finally to betray Jesus for personal gain. Jesus reaching out to him provoked a startling reaction that allowed Satan to fill his heart with even darker thoughts. When the word of God is preached and Christ is exalted in His love and purity, human beings react with a wide spectrum of responses. Some fall at His feet in surrender, while others are filled with scorn and anger.

The outcome was that Judas left the upper room and was not present at the communion and the exalted teaching that came in the following chapters. John records that *"He went out immediately. And it was night."* (13:30). Jesus had said that the night was coming (9:4), and once more in John's writings, the words are poignant with spiritual meaning.

The departure of Judas was the signal for the final act to begin. Jesus spoke of this as the time when He would be glorified (13:31). He passed over the horror of the suffering that would precede the glory of His resurrection and ascension. He began to unfold the teaching that would comfort the disciples and prepare them for the inauguration of the new covenant with the outpouring of the Holy Spirit. He comforted them with words that show that He knew in advance what was going to happen. Nothing that happened in the next 24 hours took Him by surprise.

He introduced this phase of His teaching by announcing a new commandment, which would be a foundation of a new covenant. The mark of His people would be love. One may rightly conclude from this that no-one can claim to be a disciple of Jesus Christ unless their chief aim in life is to love. God's intention has never changed, no more than God has ever stopped being love. Love is not an attribute of God, for God is love, and therefore all God's attributes are attributes of love. God does not cease to be love when He is angry or when He exercises judgment. Love must rule in power and strength. But love did not fill the hearts of the Old

149

Testament saints. They were changed by their contact with the God of love. But in the new covenant, God would fill His disciples with the Spirit of love, and love would prevail and rule supreme.

The pride of Peter

36 *Simon Peter said to him, "Lord, where are you going?"*
Jesus answered, "Where I am going, you can't follow now, but you will follow afterwards."
37 *Peter said to him, "Lord, why can't I follow you now? I will lay down my life for you."*
38 *Jesus answered him, "Will you lay down your life for me? Most certainly I tell you, the rooster won't crow until you have denied me three times.*

The final phase of chapter 13 is marked by the gentleness with which Jesus began to guide Peter through his deepest hour of trauma. Peter was grieved that he could not follow Jesus, slowly grasping that Jesus was about to leave them by dying a terrible death. Peter affirmed that he would follow Jesus even to death.

The words that Jesus addressed to Peter are sublime and full of promise. He gently explained to Peter that it was beyond Peter's capacity to follow Him into death. He said: *"You cannot follow Me now."* These are words that must be grasped by every disciple, who longs to follow Jesus in His fire of total devotion to the Father's will. Any person who gets close to Jesus Christ will begin to burn with that same ardent passion. Then Jesus gave Peter the great promise: *"But you shall follow Me afterward."* These words - *"You cannot"* *"but you shall"* = are the amazing promise of God to all His people. We face the impossible weakness and failure of our own devotion. We all fail to meet the standard of love, of prayer, of sacrifice. But through the ruins of our failure comes the sure and certain promise of God: you shall love, you shall be a man or woman of prayer, you shall surrender all to God.

Between these two statements there was a depth of brokenness and a baptism of power. Judas, Caiaphas and Pilate all had the same spiritual weakness as Peter, but they would not follow, break, yield, surrender and believe. If only we will follow on through all the impossibilities of our spiritual bankruptcy, we shall discover that what we cannot do, the Holy Spirit will magnificently empower us to do.

Peter did not know himself, and was heading for failure, but this failure was foreknown by Jesus. He knows the failure of every human being before they fall. Jesus does not judge any man by his last failure. No human being need be defined by their moments of spiritual collapse, whether their wilderness lasts a day, a year or a decade. Peter was restored a few days later; King David languished in sin for over a year; Manasseh spurned God for most of his adult life. But God was waiting for them all when they finally turned to Him. God knows our weaknesses and asks only one thing of us: that we will turn to Him and be healed, changed and empowered by His matchless grace.

JOHN 14

THE WATER EXPLAINED

The Holy Spirit reveals the trinity

14 "Don't let your heart be troubled. Believe in God. Believe also in me. *2* In my Father's house are many homes. If it weren't so, I would have told you. I am going to prepare a place for you. *3* If I go and prepare a place for you, I will come again, and will receive you to myself; that where I am, you may be there also. *4* You know where I go, and you know the way."

5 Thomas said to him, "Lord, we don't know where you are going. How can we know the way?"

6 Jesus said to him, "I am the way, the truth, and the life. No-one comes to the Father, except through me. *7* If you had known me, you would have known my Father also. From now on, you know him, and have seen him."

8 Philip said to him, "Lord, show us the Father, and that will be enough for us."

9 Jesus said to him, "Have I been with you such a long time, and do you not know me, Philip? He who has seen me has seen the Father. How do you say, 'Show us the Father?' *10* Don't you believe that I am in the Father, and the Father in me? The words that I tell you, I speak not from myself; but the Father who lives in me does his works. *11* Believe me that I am in the Father, and the Father in me; or else believe me for the very works' sake.

After Jesus had washed their feet, He began to teach explicitly about the Holy Spirit. He no longer used parables and symbols such as water. This section contains the most important teaching about the person and work of the Holy Spirit in the whole Bible. Jesus was here giving instruction about patterns of life that are only possible through a deep work of God to renew our nature, leading to consciousness of the indwelling of the Holy Spirit.

The section opens with the familiar phrase: *"Let not your heart be troubled."* These words should be read without a break from the last words of chapter 13, in which Jesus had foretold Peter's denial. The words of Jesus must have had a devastating effect on Peter, but also on all the disciples. Jesus was teaching us that whenever we are tempted to sink into despair, there will be a moment of choice. We must not **let** anxiety and fear fill our hearts. Jesus told them that the antidote to a troubled heart is to believe in God, who is present and within reach. Jesus said *"You believe in God, believe also in Me."* We are prone to believe in a distant God, whose help might not always be available. Here, Jesus focused their attention on Him, present and available. Jesus is God with us, God at hand, God incarnate, who has come to bring God's presence and salvation within the reach of every human being.

Jesus then turned to the theme of the Father's house. This is a theme that He had already addressed in the preceding days, when He had cleansed the temple and declared that God's house is to be a house of prayer (Mark 11:17). Jesus said that there are *"many abiding places"* in this great house. The word "mansion" (the King James translation of this verse) is unfortunate, since it has connotations of the luxurious houses of wealthy people. The Greek word refers to the action of abiding and the root word occurs 14 times in this passage (from John 14:1 to 15:17). It occurs in 14:10, when Jesus says it is the Father "dwelling in Him" who does the works. It refers to the fact of God abiding or dwelling in us, and that we are to abide in Him. With this understanding, it is immediately clear that Jesus is not referring to heaven, but to a spiritual house. Christ saw His physical body as His Father's house (John 2:19-21). The New Testament later teaches that the church is the Father's house (Ephesians 2:19-22). This little word "abide" is the key word in chapter 15:1-17, where it occurs no fewer than 10 times and refers to the consciousness of the indwelling Christ, and the complementary activity of the believer to guard that consciousness.

So, the "place prepared" is a home in Christ now, not only after the second coming. We enter into the place prepared for us when the Holy Spirit comes and Jesus receives us to Himself. This is repeated in 14:18 when He assured them, that He would not leave them orphans, but would come to them. He affirmed this again in 14:28 when He said He was going away and would come back to them. These promises are the great confidence of the believer, who has a home while in this world with all its wars, conflicts and uncertainties. Every believer has a path prepared and a secure future, because he has a home in Christ, who has promised to be always with and in Him.

Jesus assured them that they knew where He was going and also knew the way. It is surprising that Thomas flatly contradicted the Lord. The freedom with which Thomas did this reveals the degree of acceptance and ease they felt with Him. He did not belittle them or chastise them when they displayed ignorance of spiritual things. He took their questions seriously and affirmed the truth that He was going to the Father and that He was the way to the Father (14:6).

Jesus spoke the seventh "I am", stating that He was the way, the truth and life. This verse demonstrates the great passion of Jesus – to introduce His followers to His father. It also is a new way that He is speaking of. Jesus made a new and living way for the believer to enter the Holy of Holies:

> Therefore, brethren, having boldness to enter the Holiest by the blood of Jesus, by a new and living way which He consecrated for us, through the veil, that is, His flesh (Hebrews 10:19-20 NKJV).

154

Jesus is Himself the way. This means that it is as we surrender to Him that we find ourselves able to come to the Father. It also means that Jesus is the only way to know God. He is the only mediator between God and any man or woman.

Jesus then asserted that to know Him was to also know the Father. When Philip claimed that it would be sufficient if they could be shown the Father, Jesus was amazed that they did not know the secret of His life, despite the fact they have been together for so long. It would be like being a life-long friend of David Beckham and yet not know that he is a footballer! The Father was the passion of Jesus, the centre of His life and the explanation of all that He was and had achieved.

It is at this point that it should dawn upon us that the coming of the Holy Spirit is not just our introduction to the third person of the trinity, but rather our introduction to the trinity as a whole. The Bible is not the unfolding of God in three stages: stage one - the Old Testament revealing the Father; stage two - the gospels revealing the Son and stage three - the Acts of the apostles revealing the Holy Spirit. As has often been said: "The new is in the old concealed, the old is by the new revealed." The fact is that in the Old Testament neither Father, Son or Holy Spirit were openly revealed. The emphasis there was on the revelation of God the creator, the God of Abraham, Isaac and Jacob, the God of Israel. Moreover, no Old Testament saints addressed God as Father. Neither Abraham, Moses nor the writers of the Psalms prayed to Him saying "our father". The trinity was revealed in types and figures in the Old Testament. But the direct revelation comes in the New Testament. When Jesus taught His disciples, there were flashes of revelation that He was the Son of God (Matthew 16:16). But the clear steady stream of revelation came with the indwelling Spirit. By the Spirit abiding in them, believers know the Father, the Son and the Holy Spirit.

The Holy Spirit creates close union in prayer

[12] Most certainly I tell you, he who believes in me, the works that I do, he will do also; and he will do greater works than these, because I am going to my Father. [13] Whatever you will ask in my name, I will do it, that the Father may be glorified in the Son. [14] If you will ask anything in my name, I will do it.

Of all the promises connected with the coming of the Holy Spirit, this one is the most arresting. Jesus said that His followers would have a relationship with God in prayer identical to His. He said that whatever we ask in His name will be given to us. Such a promise is comforting and challenging. All of these promises point to the potential resources of the believer. Most believers will pass through a phase of testing this promise by asking the Father for many minor things. Some will wonder if the promise is real when their prayers are not answered as they imagined. The Bible confirms in many places that God will answer the prayers of those whose lives are in step with the heart and mind of God. These verses should not cause us to think that we can have whatever we ask. They should cause us to seek to fellowship with God, to absorb His purity, His love and His will. If we do this, we will discover that our prayers are in line with the will of God. Jesus summed up the will of God in the phrase: *"that the Father may be glorified in the Son".* All prayers that are prayed from such a motive will be answered.

Even more striking is that Jesus stated that those who receive His Spirit will do greater works than He did. We will all protest that no-one has ever done greater works of power than Jesus, though there may be many examples of miracles that equal His. (For example, John Welch, the Scottish covenanter raised a young nobleman from the dead[11]). But few have had such a range and abundance of miracles to come anywhere near the wonders performed by the Son of God.

---

[11] Howie, *Biographica Scotiana*

The explanation of this promise lies in the power of the Holy Spirit to cleanse hearts from sin and to create a community of selfless love. This was a miracle that was never performed by Jesus during His ministry on earth. It was, however, the central focus of the apostles. It is astonishing that Peter and Paul in their writings did not advocate signs and wonders and did not even recount all the many miracles they performed. They rather consistently and persistently emphasised unity, purity and love.

Loving Jesus: the key to receiving the Holy Spirit

[15] If you love me, keep my commandments. [16] I will pray to the Father, and he will give you another Counsellor, that he may be with you forever: [17] the Spirit of truth, whom the world can't receive; for it doesn't see him and doesn't know him. You know him, for he lives with you, and will be in you. [18] I will not leave you orphans. I will come to you.

In the upper room Jesus was teaching about the work of the Holy Spirit: the water that would fill the six waterpots. Here He gave the great key to receiving the baptism with the Holy Spirit: *"If you love Me"*. The Holy Spirit loves Jesus and whoever receives the Holy Spirit must have the same passion. It is clear from these verses that salvation generally precedes the baptism with the Holy Spirit.

Later in this gospel, Mary Magdalene is seen searching for the dead body of Jesus, motivated by her deep love for Him. Her focus was not on an experience of the Spirit but on the person of Christ. So often the Holy Spirit is presented as a means to obtain power or vivid spiritual experiences. But such an emphasis can exalt selfish desires and lead believers away from the fullness. The key to the whole work and ministry of the Holy Spirit is to love and exalt Jesus Christ.

No-one can love Jesus unless the Holy Spirit has begun to reveal Him to us. Jesus explained here that only believers can receive the Holy Spirit in fullness.

They know the Spirit's power with them, and through the baptism with the Holy Spirit they will know the power of His indwelling in them.

Some will insist that these phrases "with you" and "in you" indicate two stages of the indwelling of the Holy Spirit, first in salvation and then in full salvation. There are different ways in which this may be understood and explained. However, we can only know the full wonder of dwelling in Christ and Christ in us through the baptism with the Holy Spirit. This also explains why the baptism with the Spirit is what makes us members of His church (1 Corinthians 12:13). These phrases indicate a step from knowing Christ's salvation, to letting Him be our life. The great focus of the gospel of John is the place in which believers know Him as our life.

The work of the Holy Spirit: to make Jesus known to His own

¹⁹ *Yet a little while, and the world will see me no more; but you will see me. Because I live, you will live also.* ²⁰ *In that day you will know that I am in my Father, and you in me, and I in you.* ²¹ *One who has my commandments and keeps them, that person is one who loves me. One who loves me will be loved by my Father, and I will love him, and will reveal myself to him."*

²² *Judas (not Iscariot) said to him, "Lord, what has happened that you are about to reveal yourself to us, and not to the world?"*

²³ *Jesus answered him, "If a man loves me, he will keep my word. My Father will love him, and we will come to him, and make our home with him.* ²⁴ *He who doesn't love me doesn't keep my words. The word which you hear isn't mine, but the Father's who sent me.* ²⁵ *I have said these things to you while still living with you.* ²⁶ *But the Counsellor, the Holy Spirit, whom the Father will send in my name, will teach you all things, and will remind you of all that I said to you.* ²⁷ *Peace I leave with you. My peace I give to you; not as the world gives, I give to you. Don't let your heart be troubled, neither let it be fearful.*

Jesus then introduced the characteristic of the church age, that Jesus would continue to be seen and known, but only to the church and not openly to the world (verse 19). The Holy Spirit makes it possible for believers to walk with God in the quietness of their heart as they see or perceive Him through the Holy Spirit.

Jesus said that it is by this that we will have life (verse 19), but not physical life, rather the life that is in Jesus. When the Bible speaks of life and death it is easy to think that it is referring to bodily life. In Eden God warned Adam that if he ate of the tree of the knowledge of good and evil, he would surely die. When he swallowed the forbidden fruit, he died to God and became alive to sin and darkness. In this sense Jesus was the "deadest" man who ever lived because he was dead to sin. He was also the most alive human being who ever lived, because of His perfect consciousness of God. This is the consciousness of being in the Father and in the Son (verse 20). This explains why humanity is dead in trespasses and sins (Ephesians 2:1).

That believers have eternal life is one of the most amazing claims of the Bible. Archaeologists have found seeds in the tombs of the Pharaohs. They lie in the dust as inconspicuous as grains of sand. Yet they have the spark of life in them. When the mere whiff of humidity touches them, they reveal the life hidden in their dry shell, and green shoots appear. The question of what constitutes even basic plant life baffles scientists. It has proved impossible to produce any form of life in the laboratory. The Bible tells us that human beings had life in the beginning but lost it through sin. Humanity has existence but not life. Life is through the presence of God in the heart of a human being. Once we receive the divine touch through the Holy Spirit, it is like waking up from a long dreamless sleep. It is to rise from the dead.

Judas (not Iscariot) then asked how Jesus could be known to His own and hidden to the world. His question reveals the paradox that believers have rock-like certainty about God, while the world is unable to grasp the simplest facts about Him. Jesus further explained that the key to this is the indwelling of Father, Son and

Holy Spirit. The Father makes His home in the believer (verse 23) and the Holy Spirit begins His work of instructing believers from the inside.

Being taught by the Spirit is another foundation stone of the new covenant. Jeremiah had prophesied that all would know God from the least to the greatest (Jeremiah 31:34). John later affirmed that the believer does not need to be taught by men (1 John 2:27) but that believers know all things through this inner anointing. John is not teaching that believers know all there is to know. The Holy Spirit will not teach us mathematics, Greek, Hebrew or how to play the piano. John is referring to the things that *only* the Holy Spirit can teach. There are things that only man can teach, and other more important matters that can only be taught through the Holy Spirit. God uses people through the gifts of the Spirit, but only the Spirit can reveal the Father and His matchless love.

The result of the awareness of God indwelling us will be peace (verse 27) and such peace as is not known except by believers. The mark of any Christian who is making real spiritual progress will be a steadily increasing depth of supernatural peace.

The centrality of the Father

> *28 You heard how I told you, 'I go away, and I come to you.' If you loved me, you would have rejoiced, because I said 'I am going to my Father;' for the Father is greater than I. 29 Now I have told you before it happens so that when it happens, you may believe. 30 I will no more speak much with you, for the prince of the world comes, and he has nothing in me. 31 But that the world may know that I love the Father, and as the Father commanded me, even so I do. Arise, let's go from here.*

Jesus once more emphasised that He was not going to death, but to the Father. The cross was a point on His journey, but His destination was the Father. Here Jesus gave two great revelations about His relationship with the Father: first that His Father was greater than

He, and second that He went to the cross to demonstrate His love for the Father.

Jesus said His Father was greater than He, and so revealed the order in the trinity. The Father was the centre of Jesus' life and the centre of the Godhead. Jesus worshipped His Father (John 4:22-23). He honoured and obeyed Him (John 8:29; Luke 22:42). The prayer of Jesus in John 17 demonstrates the deep reverence and awe with which Jesus related to His Father. God is infinite, eternal, omnipresent and omniscient, but He is also beautiful in depths of fathomless, shimmering magnificence. Jesus is immeasurable in His love and holiness, and it is astonishing that He Himself is filled with awe at the greater glory and wonder of the person of His Father.

Jesus said that He was going to the cross to demonstrate to the world that He loved the Father. This is one of the greatest things He ever taught: that His love for His Father led Him to offer His life on the cross. Jesus was conscious that there is a purpose, filled with love and grace, that lies at the bedrock of the universe and is in the heart of the Father in heaven.

JOHN 15

THE WATER TURNED TO WINE

The place of abiding.

15 *"I am the true vine, and my Father is the farmer. ² Every branch in me that doesn't bear fruit, he takes away. Every branch that bears fruit, he prunes, that it may bear more fruit. ³ You are already pruned clean because of the word which I have spoken to you. ⁴ Remain in me, and I in you. As the branch can't bear fruit by itself unless it remains in the vine, so neither can you, unless you remain in me. ⁵ I am the vine. You are the branches. He who remains in me and I in him bears much fruit, for apart from me you can do nothing. ⁶ If a man doesn't remain in me, he is thrown out as a branch and is withered; and they gather them, throw them into the fire, and they are burned. ⁷ If you remain in me, and my words remain in you, you will ask whatever you desire, and it will be done for you.*

⁸ "In this my Father is glorified, that you bear much fruit; and so you will be my disciples. ⁹ Even as the Father has loved me, I also have loved you. Remain in my love. ¹⁰ If you keep my commandments, you will remain in my love; even as I have kept my Father's commandments, and remain in his love. ¹¹ I have spoken these things to you, that my joy may remain in you, and that your joy may be made full.

Jesus used the parable of the vine to explain the Christian life. He returned to the earlier theme of turning water to wine, since that is precisely what a vine does. It sucks up water through its roots and as it passes through the branches, it produces grapes. Moreover, the vine is a perfect image of this process, since the vine is a weak tree, quite unlike the mighty cedar of Lebanon or the English oak. The vine is weak and must be supported by a piece of wood. We are immediately transported in our mind's eye to the cross, where Christ the vine was nailed to a piece of wood. In a moment of total weakness, Jesus produced the fruit of eternal salvation. The tree of life is not described in Genesis 2, but the inner logic of the Bible compels one to believe it was a vine. Jesus Himself is the true vine, the true tree of life.

It is amazing that we are made one with Him to the extent that we are branches of this tree. We have no life unless we abide in the vine. By this simple image we are introduced to the vitally important teaching, that we are not only to receive the Holy Spirit, but abide, live and walk in the Spirit.

Abiding in the vine is achieved as the believer discovers the conscious presence of God in a new dimension. This is new and was unknown to the believers of the Old Testament. It is what Hebrews describes as *"a new and living way"* into the Holy of Holies through the blood of Jesus. This is also why this teaching was only given on the night before He died, because it would only be possible to abide in the vine through the coming of the Holy Spirit. The dimension of life revealed in the upper room, is the inner life of Christ, imparted to His followers through the Spirit. This is life that enables us to soar on eagles' wings.

Jesus further described this whole realm as abiding in the love of God (verse 9). Believers have access to a place, where holiness and love are the very air they breathe. The discipline of abiding has been intellectualised and reduced to abiding in the doctrine of Christ. The result is spiritual dryness. It is only as we consciously abide in His loving presence, that life flows through the branches.

Abiding is achieved through entering into the Holy of Holies by faith. It is important to recognise that Jesus Christ is not in the Holy of Holies, rather He is that place. There can be no holiness without Him and it is vain to think of attaining any moral or spiritual stature, without a growing and living relationship with Him.

Abiding is also maintained through obedience to the Spirit as He touches our hearts with understanding of His will and His word.

> "He that says he abides in Him ought also to walk as He walked." I John 2:6.

The Holy Spirit searches the heart and sheds light on our walk, revealing not merely activities that must stop, but motives that must be cleansed. Carnal activity is fundamentally selfish. The Holy Spirit relentlessly challenges us to bring our inner life to the cross to be cleansed and purged. If we disregard the Holy Spirit's convicting touch, we will find the inner light of Christ growing dim and our fellowship growing theoretical and unreal. The power of the church is ultimately in direction proportion to the reality of the inner lives of her members.

The aim and consequence of abiding is fruit. Often this is interpreted as souls won through our witness. But that is a secondary result of abiding. The primary result is fruit in our character. The fruit that God seeks is Christ-like motives, resulting in Christ-like behaviour, in short: love.

Love is the highest goal of the Christian, and is described in 1 Corinthians 13 in terms of motives and inner desires. Love then is a fruit. God cannot create love, since it would be as false as plastic flowers or artificial fruits. Neither can human beings produce love on their own. God is love. He is love without effort and every instinct and movement of His being is from love. Human beings are made in His image, and there is a deep marriage between God and humanity. Humanity was made in the image of love with the capacity to develop a loving disposition by allowing God to reign in their hearts. Christ becoming a human being indicates the degree to which God has invested Himself in the human race. It also reveals that it is Christ in us that makes us truly human. If God is not in our life, we are like a sophisticated computer with no power cable. There may be limitless potential, but it is only achieved through God in our lives.

The marvellous result of abiding in Christ is the appearance of qualities of character that are a combination of God and man blending in oneness. It is awesome to be loved by God, but it is equally breath-taking when love is formed in our soul. The essence of love is to be carried away by the power of the Spirit, away from selfish living, to look at God and worship Him. Love can never flourish without this foundation. Love appears and grows as we discover His life-giving presence, and it grows and spreads to colour every part of our personality, as we pour ourselves out to Him. Love for others is inevitable if we continue to abide, because the Holy Spirit will fashion us to do exactly what God would do. He shapes us to notice others and to live for them. Thus, love is the beautiful fragrance of Christ, manifest through us. It is also the freedom from selfishness that so long hindered the will of God being fulfilled in us.

Jesus taught that God seeks fruit (verse 4), more fruit (verse 2) and much fruit (verses 5 and 8). Abiding in Christ is the only way to achieve this goal. There is no other. If we neglect this inner life of the Spirit, we will grow dry and fruitless. We will wither, our love for God will grow dry and our hearts will be a desolate wasteland. There is a warning here that such branches will be cut out of the vine and burnt. How sobering, that a branch may be in Him and yet not abide in Him! This explains the wide variety of conduct among Christians and contains a warning that salvation must be obtained and then made strong through continued cooperation with the Holy Spirit. There is often fierce debate about whether a Christian may lose his or her salvation. This passage contains a warning, that there are deep consequences of living a carnal, selfish life.

Jesus added a significant detail to this teaching in verse 7, when He said that we are to abide in Him and in His word. The word of God to which He refers is the Spirit-breathed word of the Scriptures. There is a prophetic quality to every page of the Bible. When taken up by the Spirit, the Bible becomes life-changing. Jesus said that the result of this abiding will be a closeness to God in prayer. All we need to do is attend to Him and His inward promptings and we shall discover the delight of an effective prayer life. This in itself will provide still more fruit that glorifies God.

From this verse we can learn the art of praying the Bible. Prayer is never to be merely mechanical, for that would make it purely impersonal. But if we take the Bible in hand and use it as a springboard to talk to God and let Him talk to us, then we will find that it will be an open door that inspires us to reach out to God in faith, with a clear object in view. Abiding in His word is the art of meditation:

"Reading without meditation is unfruitful; meditation without reading is hurtful; to meditate and to read without prayer upon both is without blessing." William Bridge, (a Puritan writer).

The teaching of John 15 is to open the spiritual life to the delight of a walk with God that is effective, life changing and impacts the world we live in.

The final result of this way of life is joy. When we delight ourselves in God, there is an unconscious light in our whole being which contrasts with the emptiness and tarnished ways of sin. There is no greater beacon of light than a believer in a loving, close walk with God through His Son Jesus Christ. Joy is a wall of defence around the heart and a strong tower of protection against the attacks of Satan. God always intended that following Him would bring abundant joy to His children.

The New Commandment

12 "This is my commandment, that you love one another, even as I have loved you. 13 Greater love has no-one than this, that someone lay down his life for his friends. 14 You are my friends, if you do whatever I command you. 15 No longer do I call you servants, for the servant doesn't know what his lord does. But I have called you friends, for everything that I heard from my Father, I have made known to you. 16 You didn't choose me, but I chose you and appointed you, that you should go and bear fruit, and that your fruit should remain; that whatever you will ask of the Father in my name, he may give it to you.
17 "I command these things to you, that you may love one another.

The teaching in the upper room was the introduction to the new covenant, which was to be inaugurated following His death, resurrection and ascension. The outpouring of the Holy Spirit was to so change those who believed in Him that they would be able to follow His new commandments. Christ was introducing *"a new and living way"* of life (Hebrews 10:20).

"But now we have been delivered from the law, having died to what we were held by, so that we should serve in the newness of the Spirit and not in the oldness of the letter." (Romans 7:6 NKJV)

Jesus had said in chapter 13:34, that it was His new commandment that His followers should love one another as He had loved them. He defines this love as being one of sacrifice for one another. The world tramples over others, but the love of God lays itself down in sacrifice. This love is impossible without the coming of the Spirit and our abiding in Christ through the Spirit.

The outcome of fruit bearing, of growing a life of love for God and man, is friendship with Jesus. Those who embrace a life of love, will be welcomed into the exalted state of being His friends. This is greater than the title of apostle, bishop, prophet, pastor, elder, president or king. When Jesus calls us His friends, it is because we have understood what makes Him tick. We share the same life, the same goals and we are partaking of the same instinct to lay our lives down, giving up all our comforts, rights and preferences in order to reveal God as He really is. Such a life is entirely supernatural and can only be cultivated through an attitude of loving friendship with God - enjoying His company, seeking His presence and yielding to His will and His ways.

As we follow this path, we will become increasingly aware that it is God who chose us and not we who chose Him. Every true believer must be motivated by love and will be increasingly aware of the beauty and wonder of God's being. But this did not begin with us. God loved us before we ever loved Him. He thinks we are wonderful and is Himself deeply in love with the human race. He counts each one as unique and possessing a potential for beauty and perfection. God loved us and chose us before the foundation of the world to be perfected in love. He thinks we are wonderful and nothing can deter Him from pursuing His divine plan of love.

The resulting persecution

[18] *If the world hates you, you know that it has hated me before it hated you.* [19] *If you were of the world, the world would love its own. But because you are not of the world, since I chose you out of the world, therefore the world hates you.* [20] *Remember the word that I said to you: 'A servant is not greater than his lord.' If they persecuted me, they will also persecute you. If they kept my word, they will also keep yours.* [21] *But they will do all these things to you for my name's sake, because they don't know him who sent me.* [22] *If I had not come and spoken to them, they would not have had sin; but now they have no excuse for their sin.* [23] *He who hates me, hates my Father also.* [24] *If I hadn't done among them the works which no-one else did, they wouldn't have had sin. But now they have seen and also hated both me and my Father.* [25] *But this happened so that the word may be fulfilled which was written in their law, 'They hated me without a cause.'*

26 "When the Counsellor has come, whom I will send to you from the Father, the Spirit of truth, who proceeds from the Father, he will testify about me. 27 You will also testify, because you have been with me from the beginning.

Jesus explained His exalted goal for His followers and then turned to the inevitable reaction of the world to those who walk closely with Him. As Paul later said:

"Yes, and all who desire to live godly in Christ Jesus will suffer persecution." (2 Timothy 3:12)

Jesus described this inevitable persecution as irrational. It is hatred for God *"without a cause"* (verse 25). The more the believer walks with the world, the less they will provoke it or reveal its sins. The more a believer walks in the ways of holiness and love, which are rooted in the presence of God, the more the world will feel exposed. Jesus provoked most hatred from the religious members of society. When the Pharisees heard Him speak and saw the miracles He did, they became conscious of the deep emptiness of their religious practices. Jesus here made the startling assertion that this persecution is hatred of God. When provoked, it is passionate and blind. It was revealed in all its raw intensity when the Sanhedrin saw Stephen in radiant union with God, and then gnashed at him with their teeth and with seething anger stoned him to death. Jesus here prophesied such events, and asserted that it is all motivated by hatred of the Father and hatred of all that the Father does.

Jesus again mentioned the imminent arrival of the Helper, the Paraclete, the Comforter, who is the Holy Spirit. He explained that the main role of the comforter was to testify of Jesus, to reveal Him, to make Him known. In the same way, believers who receive the Holy Spirit will be witnesses to what they know of Jesus by the revelation of the Holy Spirit. The Holy Spirit is the revealer of God's heart. There can be no greater witness of God than the activity of the Holy Spirit in the hearts of human beings. To reject the Holy Spirit is to reject the loving touch of God, and such rejection has serious consequences. It would be like rejecting the light of the sun in favour of the feeble torch light of the human mind.

JOHN 16

THE END OF PARABLES

The coming persecution

16 *"I have said these things to you so that you wouldn't be caused to stumble.* ***²*** *They will put you out of the synagogues. Yes, the time comes that whoever kills you will think that he offers service to God.* ***³*** *They will do these things because they have not known the Father, nor me.* ***⁴*** *But I have told you these things, so that when the time comes, you may remember that I told you about them. I didn't tell you these things from the beginning, because I was with you.*

Jesus emphasised that all kinds of trouble would inevitably accompany the coming of the Holy Spirit and the inauguration of the new covenant. He asserted this strongly in order to prevent believers from being stumbled by the coming waves of persecution. It is easy for new Christians to expect that all who hear the gospel will immediately believe, and that the resulting community will be a foretaste of heaven on earth, with untroubled peace and joy. The history of the church has been one of fierce opposition from both political and religious institutions. Thousands of believers died at the hands of Roman emperors and medieval popes.

Jesus never taught that the church age would be perfect. In the parable of the wheat and the tares (Matthew 13:24-30 and 36-43), Jesus taught that the kingdom age would not be a pure field of wheat, but that there would be other elements that disturb and trouble the kingdom. In the parable of the sower, (Matthew 13:3-8), Jesus taught that believers would struggle with issues in their own lives. He explained that not all who receive the gospel would inevitably proceed to a fully fruitful life. In the earliest years of the church, the chief persecutors were the Jewish authorities that had rejected Jesus. But Jesus was looking far into the future, to the time when the church would be established with earthly institutions that would also persecute believers. Moreover, He was referring to living assemblies where carnal men would rise to positions of power and influence and persecute believers. John refers to such a situation in his third epistle:

> "*I wrote to the church, but Diotrephes, who loves to have the pre-eminence among them, does not receive us. Therefore, if I come, I will call to mind his deeds which he does, prating against us with malicious words. And not content with that, he himself does not receive the brethren, and forbids those who wish to, putting them out of the church.*"
> (3 John 1:9-10)

The long history of the church is a story of divisions on a grand and a local scale. The first martyr to die at the hands of the church was Priscillian, bishop of Avila in Spain. He and five other believers were condemned by a church council and executed in Trieste in 385 AD. This marked the beginning of many long, sad chapters of the church, when it was wedded with powers of government and especially the power to torture and execute. As the church departed from spiritual life, so there were two churches, the church visible and the church invisible.

The coming of the Holy Spirit

⁵ But now I am going to him who sent me, and none of you asks me, 'Where are you going?' ⁶ But because I have told you these things, sorrow has filled your heart. [7] Nevertheless I tell you the truth: It is to your advantage that I go away, for if I don't go away, the Counsellor won't come to you. But if I go, I will send him to you.

Jesus taught His disciples that His departure was necessary in order for the Holy Spirit to indwell them in a new dimension, previously unknown. Why was it necessary? Simply because the sacrifice of the cross was needful to prepare human hearts to be indwelt of the holy presence of God. It is often the case that believers will set aside time to seek God for the gift of the Holy Spirit. This may lead to the belief that the Holy Spirit can only be poured out if believers make exceptional efforts. However, this Scripture affirms that the price has been fully paid at the cross for the outpouring of the Holy Spirit. Believers must lay their lives on the altar, not to pay for an outpouring, but to position their souls to receive what Christ has already purchased in full.

The work of the Holy Spirit

[8] When he has come, he will convict the world about sin, about righteousness, and about judgment; [9] about sin, because they don't believe in me; [10] about righteousness, because I am going to my Father, and you won't see me any more; [11] about judgment, because the prince of this world has been judged.

In these verses Jesus outlined further effects that will follow the outpouring of the Holy Spirit. He will convict the world of unseen truths, that cannot be understood any other way than by His direct influence. The Holy Spirit will impress three truths on the conscience: the fact of sin, the fact of righteousness and the fact of judgment.

1. The fact of sin. It is often readily assumed that we need revelation to know and understand God. The truth is that human beings cannot understand any of the foundational truths about God or themselves, without the Holy Spirit. Sin is not merely moral failure; it is a spiritual

173

disease that is destroying the inner life of every human being. Like most physical diseases, it has a dormant stage, when a person may believe they are in good health. But when it breaks out in all its force, it destroys everything in its path. The first thing that it destroys is our ability to sense God, but it goes on to rob us of peace and inner strength. The outworking of sin leads to the devastation of personality, marriages, relationships, and ultimately sanity itself. We may think all is well until we are convicted of sin. Then we cry out with an inner despair, that unless God intervenes, we are hopelessly lost. Conviction of sin will be present in meetings where the Holy Spirit is given free rein. It is also an unconscious side-effect of being in the presence of a person in close fellowship with God and full of the Holy Spirit. If we believe God and receive this blessing, people around us will be affected.

2. The fact of righteousness. True righteousness must also be revealed, since it is not based on good works but on a right relationship with God. It is vital that the heart be in tune with God and the result is not merely moral uprightness, but a fragrance that lights up the whole life with purity.

3. The fact of judgment. The dark clouds of impending judgment hang over all that is taking place on earth in the affairs of humankind. The crimes of humanity cry out for justice, from the war crimes of the Nazis to the malicious abuse of children. There must be a judgment or evil will have triumphed unscathed. Satan, the prince of darkness, was judged at the cross and defeated. The defeat of Satan is made evident through the preaching of the gospel and the activity of the Holy Spirit in all who believe the gospel.

The teacher

[12] "I still have many things to tell you, but you can't bear them now. [13] However when he, the Spirit of truth, has come, he will guide you into all truth, for he will not speak from himself; but whatever he hears, he will speak. He will declare to you things that are coming. [14] He will glorify me, for he will take from what is mine, and will declare it to you. [15] All things that the Father has are mine; therefore I said that he takes of mine and will declare it to you.

Jesus taught them that the Holy Spirit would reveal to them things that they were unable to understand or even bear at this point. Jesus revealed that in the relationship of the three persons of the trinity, the Holy Spirit is the servant, listening to the Father with rapt attention and communicating what He hears to believers. He reveals all truth, which means intellectual understanding of the great facts of our salvation. But it also refers to truth pertaining to behaviour. He is the ultimate teacher of what to say and how to say it. He grants wisdom and grace to live a supernatural life of love. If the Holy Spirit is a listener, how much more should believers attend to Him with an attentive ear. Our chief inner faculty is the ability to listen to the whisper of the witness of the Holy Spirit, who grants an inner assurance that enables believers to live for God with joy and confidence.

As soon as we sense the Holy Spirit is grieved, or that our hearts have become dull and unaware of Him, then we must stop and seek refreshment of our inner faculties that enable us to be taught by the Holy Spirit. The Holy Spirit teaches us "all things", but this does not mean He teaches us history, geography, Hebrew and Greek. There are things that the Spirit cannot teach us, and things that we cannot learn any other way than by listening to the voice of God in our hearts. Through the Spirit we have assurance of sins forgiven an inner knowledge that we are His children - and no book can teach us these things. The Holy Spirit teaches us all things that refer to the wonder of an inner life with God.

The result of developing a listening servant attitude to God through the Spirit, will be that God will be glorified. This is the aim of the Spirit - to glorify God. It is to become the aim of every believer to allow the Holy Spirit to shape in us the same mind of the Spirit, in other words to live for the glory of God. What does the Holy Spirit hear? He is the one who communicates the deep things of God:

> *"But God has revealed them to us through His Spirit. For the Spirit searches all things, yes, the deep things of God."* (1 Corinthians 2:10)

The deepest things of God are all revealed in the love of God that motivated and planned Calvary. The Holy Spirit moves when Christ is glorified and His cross is preached, for these are the two themes revealing the hidden riches of the Godhead. God is wonderful, amazing, breath-taking and those who receive the Spirit and His revealing activity, are brought into ever-deeper love for God.

Seeing the invisible

[16] *A little while, and you will not see me. Again a little while, and you will see me."*

[17] *Some of his disciples therefore said to one another, "What is this that he says to us, 'A little while, and you won't see me, and again a little while, and you will see me;' and, 'Because I go to the Father'?"* [18] *They said therefore, "What is this that he says, 'A little while'? We don't know what he is saying."*

[19] *Therefore Jesus perceived that they wanted to ask him, and he said to them, "Do you inquire among yourselves concerning this, that I said, 'A little while, and you won't see me, and again a little while, and you will see me?'* [20] *Most certainly I tell you that you will weep and lament, but the world will rejoice. You will be sorrowful, but your sorrow will be turned into joy.* [21] *A woman, when she gives birth, has sorrow because her time has come. But when she has delivered the child, she doesn't remember the anguish any more, for the joy that a human being is born into the world.* [22] *Therefore you now have sorrow, but I will see you again, and your heart will rejoice, and no-one will take your joy away from you.*

At the simplest level, Jesus was prophesying His resurrection, when He said that they would not see Him for a short while. The three days that He was in the tomb were days of unspeakable grief for the disciples, and Jesus assured them that they would end with joy. This joy would be comparable to that of the birth of a baby after the trauma of child birth. But these words also have relevance to all believers who receive the baptism with the Holy Spirit. One of the greatest works of the Holy Spirit is to make Jesus Christ intimately and feelingly known to His followers. Believers "see the invisible One." Believers who have not yet known this deeper work of the Holy Spirit are missing out on the deeper joys of the new covenant. Christ is known by experience. In these chapters Jesus speaks of hearing and seeing Him, but He is referring most importantly to the inner faculties by which He lived. He only did what He saw the Father do:

> "Most assuredly, I say to you, the Son can do nothing of Himself, but what He sees the Father do." (John 5:19)

Jesus did not see the Father in a physical form, nor did He constantly hear the Father speak in an audible voice. Jesus was teaching that the Holy Spirit will grant to the believer the same inner life that He has, having the same intimate fellowship with the Father.

Close relationship with God in prayer

23 "In that day you will ask me no questions. Most certainly I tell you, whatever you may ask of the Father in my name, he will give it to you. 24 Until now, you have asked nothing in my name. Ask, and you will receive, that your joy may be made full. 25 I have spoken these things to you in figures of speech. But the time is coming when I will no more speak to you in figures of speech, but will tell you plainly about the Father. 26 In that day you will ask in my name; and I don't say to you that I will pray to the Father for you, 27 for the Father himself loves you, because you have loved me, and have believed that I came from God. 28 I came from the Father, and have come into the world. Again, I leave the world, and go to the Father."

Jesus taught that He was the mediator by which we can come to the Father. Here He taught that after He has brought us there, His mediation will cease. This does not mean that our need of His redeeming blood ceases, or that we do not need the mediator to constantly renew our relationship with the Father. Rather, it means that we are brought into full and free open relationship with God the Father, and Christ steps back to allow us to enjoy that amazing depth of love.

Jesus taught that the fruit of the coming of the Holy Spirit will be a closer walk with God in prayer. Many of us long for this, but the Bible teaches us that it is already ours by right. We must become what we are. We must begin to let our minds catch up with what God has already done in the depths of our hearts. We are a royal priesthood (1 Peter 2:9). We do not have to strive to become a people of prayer, we must believe and enter into a walk with God the Father as Jesus enjoyed.

> *"He who says he abides in Him ought himself also to walk just as He walked."* (1 John 2:6)

This is the end of parables because there is nothing to compare with an inner life with God. We may use illustrations, but this is the spectacular reality that defies all metaphors. Jesus then again referred to the cross by describing His coming hours as "returning to the Father". Jesus did not see the next hours as a great end of His life, but rather as a final phase before going back to the Father. Everything He did was for the Father, and beyond the cross He saw the welcoming arms of the Father. Separated for a brief but anguished few hours, Christ kept His eyes firmly on the joy that was set before Him.

> *"Looking unto Jesus, the author and finisher of our faith, who for the joy that was set before Him endured the cross, despising the shame, and has sat down at the right hand of the throne of God."* (Hebrews 12:2)

The disciples assured of His victory

²⁹ His disciples said to him, "Behold, now you are speaking plainly, and using no figures of speech. ³⁰ Now we know that you know all things, and don't need for anyone to question you. By this we believe that you came from God."
³¹ Jesus answered them, "Do you now believe? ³² Behold, the time is coming, yes, and has now come, that you will be scattered, everyone to his own place, and you will leave me alone. Yet I am not alone, because the Father is with me. ³³ I have told you these things, that in me you may have peace. In the world you have trouble; but cheer up! I have overcome the world."

The disciples were no doubt thrilled by the teaching of Jesus, but He brought them back to the reality of their spiritual poverty. Understanding His amazing promises is not the same as experiencing the life-changing power of the Holy Spirit flooding our hearts. He concluded with His reassurance that there is no reason to fear the future, even in the darkest hours of tribulation, because at the bedrock of everything is the victory of Jesus our Captain, over all our enemies: Satan, the flesh, the world, sin and death. Once more Jesus used the past tense for what was still a future event ("*I have overcome the world*"). For Him the cross was done because He and His father had already covenanted to fulfil it.

JOHN 17

THE GREAT HIGH PRIEST PRAYING FOR HIS OWN

John said in chapter 1:14 that the Word dwelt or "tabernacled" (literal translation) among us. The tabernacle of Moses itself was built in approximately nine months, between the giving of the law on Mount Sinai and the second Passover (Numbers 1:1). (This corresponds approximately to the gestation period of a human baby.) The tabernacle speaks first of Christ, then of the church, His body. The elements of the tabernacle are in the gospel of John:

- The tabernacle – *"the Word became flesh and tabernacled amongst us."* (literal translation of John 1:14).
- The golden candlestick or menorah - the light of the world – (John 8:12 and 9:5).
- The shew bread - bread of life (John 6:35).
- The bronze laver – the washing of regeneration – new birth (John 3:5 and 13:8).
- The bronze altar of sacrifice – the cross (John 19).
- The bronze altar of incense – the worship of the Father (John 4:23).
- The Great High Priest – Jesus praying in John 17.

- The Holy of Holies – Christ Himself – John 2:19-21. Jesus used the word "naos" which refers only to the sanctuary consisting of the Holy Place and the Holy of Holies.

The most Holy Place of all is Christ Himself, since He does not merely live in that place, He is that place and defines it. In John 2:19 Jesus refers to Himself as being the temple sanctuary, which was made up of the Holy Place and the Holy of Holies. Astoundingly, He invited them to destroy Him, and then He would rebuild this temple in the resurrection.

In the most Holy place of all, Christ is now interceding for us in heaven itself (Hebrews 9:24). In that place, the innermost being of Christ is being poured out in His prayers. What Jesus prayed in John 17 is without doubt what He is also praying for us now in heaven. This chapter is therefore the Holy of Holies of the gospel of John.

The great prayer that Jesus prayed, was a great welling up of His eternal desires for humanity in relation to God. Prayer itself is always to be an expression of the deepest desires of the heart. God's deepest desires were prayed out here by Jesus. The fulfilment of these prayers was made possible by the cross. they were answered by the outpouring of the Holy Spirit in Acts chapter 2. Jesus was here completing His teaching on the Holy Spirit in the upper room, by praying for the Holy Spirit to be given. For this reason, this prayer contains the essence of the teaching of chapters 13-16, and it also teaches us how we are to pray for the Holy Spirit.

It is a mystery that Jesus, who is God, prayed to God His Father. In the Greek language there are two words for "pray" which are "aiteo" and "erotao." The word "aiteo" generally indicates the attitude of a suppliant praying from a lower position, as in a subject to a king (Acts 12:20), whereas "erotao" is used of a request from an equal, as from one king to another (Luke 14:32).

Jesus never used the word "aiteo" when praying to His father. Throughout John 17 He used the word "erotao". The trinity is a mystery, which was revealed in its fullness through the coming of the Holy Spirit. God is one, yet a family of three in loving relationship. God is not isolated in lofty seclusion. God is love and is in eternal relationship. God has desires and these desires are expressed in the prayers of God the Son and God the Spirit to God the Father. In this respect it is an essential function of the Godhead that there is prayer from one member of the trinity to another. Prayer and priesthood are also written into the essential calling of God's children, who are described by Peter as a royal priesthood (1 Peter 2:9).

In Luke 6:12 it is written that Jesus spent all night on the mountain *"in prayer to God."* A literal translation would be *"in the prayer of God"*. While scholars may argue about these phrases, it must not be forgotten, that the New Testament is wrestling to express something that is unique to Christian thinking. Other Scriptures confirm that there is "a prayer of God". Romans 8:29 affirms that the Spirit is making intercession for us, and Hebrews 7:25 reveals that the only reason we can approach God, is that Jesus *"ever lives to make intercession for us"*. God has longings and these are fulfilled as they are expressed in prayer by the Son of God and by the people of God praying the prayers of God.

The power of the phrase, *"He spent all night in the prayer of God",* should draw the reader into a desire to be absorbed into God's heart, into His yearnings, to pass beyond the consciousness of time and into the eternal courts of God's being.

Prayer is not to be simply battling tiredness in some kind of penitential suffering. It is not a process by which we earn credit with God. It is to pass beyond time, beyond this world and touch the infinite, the eternal, the unlimited, boundless joys of God's abundant being.

Jesus spent a night in bliss, in the wonder of worship, touching God and being touched by God.

The centre of all true ministry: the glory of God.

17 Jesus said these things, then lifting up his eyes to heaven, he said, "Father, the time has come. Glorify your Son, that your Son may also glorify you; ² even as you gave him authority over all flesh, so he will give eternal life to all whom you have given him. ³ This is eternal life, that they should know you, the only true God, and him whom you sent, Jesus Christ. ⁴ I glorified you on the earth. I have accomplished the work which you have given me to do. ⁵ Now, Father, glorify me with your own self with the glory which I had with you before the world existed.

Jesus prayed what may seem to be a selfish prayer, when He prayed that God would glorify Him. However, this prayer is to be understood in the same manner in which a person may ask a head of state: "Please honour me... with your presence." Far from being a selfish prayer, it is a recognition of the greatness of the glory of the Father.

Jonathan Paul was the father of the Pentecostal movement in Germany. He had a very powerful healing ministry. Once, when praying for a man, he asked him: "For whose glory do you want to be healed?" Paul gently led the man to look at his life in the light of the glory of God and he received his healing.

But this prayer is more than just the right motive for life, it is the expression of a longing to know His glory by experience. Moses prayed *"Show me your glory"* (Exodus 33:18) and this is the longing that grips everyone who is ushered into the knowledge of God. We sense that there is something breath-taking, awe-inspiring and overwhelming, deep in the Godhead. We have been blessed, but we long for a sight of the glory of God. Ultimately, it is God's purpose to glorify all His people with Himself. The effect of God's glory is best expressed by the word "bliss", indicating something that is inexpressibly wonderful. Earthly joys are wearying and exhausting, but the joy of being with God, is that His presence is life-imparting, ennobling, uplifting and transforming. A few seconds in God's presence and we are purified, strengthened and equipped. A few seconds in His glory and we are motivated to share this matchless life with a sin-sick, dry and dusty world. A glimpse into glory is to have one's whole character changed forever and brought into line with the divine romance that lies behind God's plan for humanity.

Eternal life is to know God

The Father is to be glorified through the ministry of Jesus. Jesus has been exalted to the highest place in order to give eternal life to fallen human beings. The essential mark of this life is that the recipients are ushered into the personal knowledge of God. This does not mean knowledge about God, but rather knowledge through experience. The difference is similar to seeing a picture of food (which may activate the saliva glands but will never satisfy) as opposed to eating and being nourished by the food.

The gospel is the communication of God in His greatness and in His personality. When eternal life is given to us, qualities are awakened in our souls which can be stirred by nothing else. The knowledge of God is like sunlight to plants, like water to fish, like air to the lungs. When the summer sun reaches the high Arctic, tiny flowers appear and similarly, God's presence causes the human heart to bloom. Beauty unfolds within us, calling forth worship, singing, purpose and hope. It is not that we are half alive without the knowledge of God - we are completely dead. The knowledge of God flicks the switch and the whole life begins to hum with the purpose for which we were created. This is the work for which Christ came into the world.

True ministry – manifesting the Father's name, speaking His words

6 I revealed your name to the people whom you have given me out of the world. They were yours, and you have given them to me. They have kept your word. 7 Now they have known that all things whatever you have given me are from you, 8 for the words which you have given me I have given to them, and they received them, and knew for sure that I came from you. They have believed that you sent me.

Jesus revealed His mission in all its simplicity: to reveal the name of the Father and communicate His words. God was virtually unknown as Father prior to the coming of Jesus. Christ revealed both the name of Father and the nature of Father. There is beauty in the security and peace that Christ exhibited as He lived in the Father's love.

The ministry of Jesus was to listen to the Father, to communicate every word and whisper of the Father's love. Jesus was not merely an impersonal, inanimate channel, as a pipe carrying water. Jesus was a living, breathing revelation of a greater One. This is the heart of all true ministry. The mark of the Spirit's ministry is a sense of wonder at the consciousness of the greater One, who is inspiring and fulfilling His word.

The power of His intercession: to keep His own from evil

9 I pray for them. I don't pray for the world, but for those whom you have given me, for they are yours. 10 All things that are mine are yours, and yours are mine, and I am glorified in them. 11 I am no more in the world, but these are in the world, and I am coming to you. Holy Father, keep them through your name which you have given me, that they may be one, even as we are. 12 While I was with them in the world, I kept them in your name. I have kept those whom you have given me. None of them is lost except the son of destruction, that the Scripture might be fulfilled.

Jesus' prayer was startlingly simple: *"Father! Keep believers from the evil one!"* The wall of protection that surrounds the child of God is the knowledge that we belong to Him. Believers are to be shaped and moulded by God's direct activity, which makes each one belong to the Father and the Son. It is this sense of belonging and personal ownership that is the basis of this prayer. Believers are His, and the life of faith and discipleship is to grow in this consciousness. Belonging to Him removes fear and worry from the heart and breeds the supernatural peace that passes understanding.

His prayer was to keep them in this love, this consciousness. His ministry had been to keep them from wandering, from falling away from this place of love, and this was now His prayer for all His disciples in that generation and in all coming generations.

The power of His intercession: to minister His joy

13 But now I come to you, and I say these things in the world, that they may have my joy made full in themselves. 14 I have given them your word. The world hated them, because they are not of the world, even as I am not of the world. 15 I pray not that you would take them from the world, but that you would keep them from the evil one. 16 They are not of the world even as I am not of the world.

Jesus repeated the phrase *"Now I come to You"*, indicating that His eyes were not fixed on the cross, but on the things following it, most of all His reunion with the Father. The words He prayed in the hearing of His disciples were so that they might have His joy. Joy is the key mark of the Christian who has understood his calling. This joy is rooted in the fact that a believer has left this world and is no longer "of this world".

It is one of the most extraordinary privileges of the Christian "to die before we die" and to live in heaven before we get there. We are enabled now to live with the remarkable capacity to see our life as if it were already over, looking back retrospectively and evaluating how we should live.

The crucial factor in our right thinking is to grasp the significance of our union with Christ through His death and resurrection. If we have anything less than this as the bedrock of our thinking, we will be earth-bound, and will live as the multitudes without faith, merely struggling to survive.

The power of His intercession: to make His own holy

[17] Sanctify them in your truth. Your word is truth. [18] As you sent me into the world, even so I have sent them into the world. [19] For their sakes I sanctify myself, that they themselves also may be sanctified in truth. [20] Not for these only do I pray, but for those also who will believe in me through their word, [21] that they may all be one; even as you, Father, are in me, and I in you, that they also may be one in us; that the world may believe that you sent me. [22] The glory which you have given me, I have given to them; that they may be one, even as we are one;

In these few words Jesus introduced His people to the secret of holiness. Jesus said that He sanctified Himself, but this does not mean that He needed cleansing from impurity. To be washed from sin is to be loosed from the defilement of our inner life. But to be sanctified is much rather the positive work of being set aside for God's delight.

In some circles holiness has been reduced to the avoidance of negative influences, but here Jesus reveals that it is only attainable by entering into the pleasures of God.

God created humanity for His own delight. In the innermost sanctuary of God's being, Christ is the eternal delight of the Father:

"And I was daily His delight, Rejoicing always before Him." (Proverbs 8:30).

Christ is the brightness and centre of the Father's kingdom. The amazing fact is that the story of redemption is the bringing of many sons to this glory of being in the Father's love, of being His delight. To be one with the Father and the Son has of itself nothing to do with the removal of the darkness from our souls. Rather, it has to do with the eternal plan of God to share His being, in loving fellowship with mankind.

The goal of all ministry: to make us one with God

> [23] *I in them, and you in me, that they may be perfected into one; that the world may know that you sent me and loved them, even as you loved me.* [24] *Father, I desire that they also whom you have given me be with me where I am, that they may see my glory, which you have given me, for you loved me before the foundation of the world.* [25] *Righteous Father, the world hasn't known you, but I knew you; and these knew that you sent me.* [26] *I made known to them your name, and will make it known; that the love with which you loved me may be in them, and I in them."*

The goal of all ministry is so that the people of God are swallowed up in the eternal purposes of God, and swallowed up by God Himself. This is to dwell in the eternal fires that make God what He is. Human beings are unaware of the brilliance of light and the power of life that pulsates through God. Those who have had visions of God, such as Isaiah, Moses, Peter, James, John and Paul, all testified to the overwhelming brightness that radiates from the person of God. Jesus revealed that this glory is love in an indescribable dimension. God is an ocean of personal, undying, self-renewing, all-consuming love.

> *"O love of God, how deep and great!*
> *Far deeper than man's deepest hate;*
> *Self-fed, self-kindled, like the light,*
> *Changeless, eternal, infinite."* (H. Bonar).

Jesus is love and dwells in the hidden depths of the Godhead. Through the cross and His passionate intercessions, He has opened a door for each of us to be perfected in love, to be one with God, to dwell in His glory, to be filled with His life. Pentecost is the answer to this prayer, and wherever the Spirit is poured out, believers are taken up and into this unspeakable presence of God beyond time.

JOHN 18

THE KING ON TRIAL

Crossing the Kidron

18 When Jesus had spoken these words, he went out with his disciples over the brook Kidron, where there was a garden, into which he and his disciples entered. ² Now Judas, who betrayed him, also knew the place, for Jesus often met there with his disciples. ³ Judas then, having taken a detachment of soldiers and officers from the chief priests and the Pharisees, came there with lanterns, torches, and weapons. ⁴ Jesus therefore, knowing all the things that were happening to him, went out, and said to them, "Who are you looking for?"

⁵ They answered him, "Jesus of Nazareth."

Jesus said to them, "I am he."

Judas also, who betrayed him, was standing with them. ⁶ When therefore he said to them, "I am he," they went backward, and fell to the ground.

⁷ Again therefore he asked them, "Who are you looking for?"

They said, "Jesus of Nazareth."

⁸ Jesus answered, "I told you that I am he. If therefore you seek me, let these go their way," ⁹ that the word might be fulfilled which he spoke, "Of those whom you have given me, I have lost none."

¹⁰ Simon Peter therefore, having a sword, drew it, struck the high priest's servant, and cut off his right ear. The servant's name was Malchus. ¹¹ Jesus therefore said to Peter, "Put the sword into its sheath. The cup which the Father has given me, shall I not surely drink it?"

¹² So the detachment, the commanding officer, and the officers of the Jews seized Jesus and bound him,

Jesus finished the prayer of chapter 17 at some point on the walk from the upper room to the garden of Gethsemane. Then He crossed the Kidron brook, which separates the mount of Olives from the city of Jerusalem. This marked the point of no return, for He knew what Judas was planning to do. John makes no mention of the hours of prayer in the garden, preparing His soul for the storm that was about to engulf Him. John's narrative passes swiftly to the arrest of Jesus.

The arrival of Judas, leading the band of soldiers, signalled the start of the events that led to His crucifixion. Jesus was ready and stepped forward to meet them, asking them who they were seeking. They answered Jesus' question, saying that they were seeking Jesus of Nazareth. Jesus declared simply *"I am he"*, which is a translation of the phrase "I am". He used yet again the words that identified Him as "Jahwe". Whether it was shock at this declaration, or a reaction to a surge of the divine presence in Christ, the soldiers all fell backwards in spontaneous collapse when faced with the glory and majesty of God. Jesus pressed upon them their opportunity to arrest Him. He stepped forward in conscious surrender to evil men, who were powerless to harm Him without His willing cooperation. Jesus was in control of all the events leading up to His crucifixion, from beginning to end.

Peter's reaction was to rise up in violent defence of his Lord. We are familiar with the fact that he cut off the ear of Malchus, but it must be remembered that he was aiming for the man's head, not his ear. Peter probably remembered this event with deep regret and gratefulness that his aim had been deflected. Peter was still not aware that the unfolding events were the will and plan of God.

Before Annas and Caiaphas

13 and led him to Annas first, for he was father-in-law to Caiaphas, who was high priest that year. 14 Now it was Caiaphas who advised the Jews that it was expedient that one man should perish for the people. 15 Simon Peter followed Jesus, as did another disciple. Now that disciple was known to the high priest, and entered in with Jesus into the court of the high priest; 16 but Peter was standing at the door outside. So the other disciple, who was known to the high priest, went out and spoke to her who kept the door, and brought in Peter. 17 Then the maid who kept the door said to Peter, "Are you also one of this man's disciples?"

He said, "I am not."

18 Now the servants and the officers were standing there, having made a fire of coals, for it was cold. They were warming themselves. Peter was with them, standing and warming himself. 19 The high priest therefore asked Jesus about his disciples and about his teaching. 20 Jesus answered him, "I spoke openly to the world. I always taught in synagogues, and in the temple, where the Jews always meet. I said nothing in secret. 21 Why do you ask me? Ask those who have heard me what I said to them. Behold, they know the things which I said."

22 When he had said this, one of the officers standing by slapped Jesus with his hand, saying, "Do you answer the high priest like that?"

23 Jesus answered him, "If I have spoken evil, testify of the evil; but if well, why do you beat me?"

24 Annas sent him bound to Caiaphas, the high priest. 25 Now Simon Peter was standing and warming himself. They said therefore to him, "You aren't also one of his disciples, are you?"

He denied it and said, "I am not."

26 One of the servants of the high priest, being a relative of him whose ear Peter had cut off, said, "Didn't I see you in the garden with him?"

27 Peter therefore denied it again, and immediately the rooster crowed.

Jesus was led first to Annas. The events described in this section occurred while Annas was interrogating Jesus. The focus was on Peter, who was allowed to slip into the courtyard to be closer to the trial. The "*other disciple*", who knew the High Priest, was certainly John, the author of the gospel, writing with his habitual, self-effacing humility. John was more at risk than Peter, because he was known to the High Priest. But as in the upper room, John was calm and confident in his knowledge of the love of God. He was emboldened by this confidence to risk his life to be close to Jesus.

Peter was soon confronted with the accusation that he was a disciple of Jesus. In answer, he twice used the same phrase that John the Baptist had used in chapter one: "*I am not!*" This stands in stark contrast to the phrase so frequently used by Jesus: "*I am*". By this means the Holy Spirit emphasised the truth that it was Peter's being that needed transformation. His best intentions were not strong enough to carry him through this severe trial. Later Paul said:

> "*by the grace of God I am what I am*" (1 Corinthians 15:10)

God has come to give to us the very life and being that is in God.

It is remarkable that the challenge was about Peter's discipleship. On three occasions in John, Jesus stated the true foundations of Christian discipleship:

1. Abiding in His word: "*Then Jesus said to those Jews who believed Him, "If you abide in My word, you are My disciples indeed."* (John 8:31)
2. Love: "*By this all will know that you are My disciples, if you have love for one another."* (John 13:35)
3. Bearing fruit: "*By this My Father is glorified, that you bear much fruit; so you will be My disciples."* (John 15:8)

These three qualities are only achievable by a fundamental change of being. Peter had the admirable qualities of zeal, commitment and idealism, but could not by these be a consistent disciple of Jesus.

The early morning rooster crowed like an alarm clock, waking Peter as he sleep-walked to disaster. It is remarkable that Peter had to sin three times before he suddenly realised the spiritual weakness of his own heart. So often a person will sin and explain it away with phrases like "that was not the real me", or "the pressure of the moment made me act out of character" or "I promise I'll do better next time."

As much as we may sympathise with Peter, we must also apply the lesson to our own hearts, lest we repeat his mistakes. Peter was to become one of God's greatest servants through his faith in the awesome power of the indwelling Christ combined with a deep realization that without Him, he was nothing.

The section closes with Peter weeping. His heart cracked open at its deepest level, introducing him to the power of healing in a dimension he could never have dreamed possible. We must not cover up our inner lacks through excuses and arguments - we must face ourselves in the cold light of reality, so that we may discover the matchless touch of Jesus to make us whole.

Before Pilate

[28] *They led Jesus therefore from Caiaphas into the Praetorium. It was early, and they themselves didn't enter into the Praetorium, that they might not be defiled, but might eat the Passover.* [29] *Pilate therefore went out to them, and said, "What accusation do you bring against this man?"*

[30] *They answered him, "If this man weren't an evildoer, we wouldn't have delivered him up to you."*

[31] *Pilate therefore said to them, "Take him yourselves, and judge him according to your law."*

Therefore the Jews said to him, "It is illegal for us to put anyone to death," [32] *that the word of Jesus might be fulfilled, which he spoke, signifying by what kind of death he should die.*

[33] *Pilate therefore entered again into the Praetorium, called Jesus, and said to him, "Are you the King of the Jews?"*

[34] *Jesus answered him, "Do you say this by yourself, or did others tell you about me?"*

[35] *Pilate answered, "I'm not a Jew, am I? Your own nation and the chief priests delivered you to me. What have you done?"*

36 Jesus answered, "My Kingdom is not of this world. If my Kingdom were of this world, then my servants would fight, that I wouldn't be delivered to the Jews. But now my Kingdom is not from here."

37 Pilate therefore said to him, "Are you a king then?"

Jesus answered, "You say that I am a king. For this reason I have been born, and for this reason I have come into the world, that I should testify to the truth. Everyone who is of the truth listens to my voice."

38 Pilate said to him, "What is truth?"

When he had said this, he went out again to the Jews, and said to them, "I find no basis for a charge against him. 39 But you have a custom, that I should release someone to you at the Passover. Therefore, do you want me to release to you the King of the Jews?"

40 Then they all shouted again, saying, "Not this man, but Barabbas!" Now Barabbas was a robber.

Pilate is known from sources outside of the Bible to have been a cruel and ambitious man.[12] He had little respect for Jewish authorities and a deep dread of his patron the Roman Emperor. This explains his lack of interest in the trial of Jesus and his reluctance to cooperate with the Jewish leaders. He attempted to hand the case back to the Sanhedrin, who were the religious government of Israel. They had the power to pronounce judgment on religious issues, but they did not have the power to execute anyone (John 18:31). When Stephen was stoned, it was an act of mob violence encouraged by the Sanhedrin, but an act that was illegal all the same. John points out that Jesus had prophesied he would be handed over to the Gentiles for execution (John 18:32).

Pilate asked Jesus directly, whether He was the King of the Jews, to which Jesus replied that He was indeed a king, but not of an earthly kingdom. Jesus was exhibiting that majestic splendour of a true King in full

---

[12] Josephus, Antiquities 18:3:2 and Jewish Wars 2:14:4. Josephus describes a cruel and unnecessary massacre of Jews in Jerusalem during Pilate's rule.

self-control. He was no victim of events, but was ruling in the midst of them. Even now, in the maelstrom of His trial and slow execution, He was calmly passing through, and speaking from an inner peace and serenity. He was witnessing to the truth of an inner kingdom, which cannot be overcome by events in this world.

Jesus' reference to truth kindled a momentary, passing interest by Pilate, who asked *"What is truth?"*, probably with a sceptical tone. Pilate was a believer in the gods of Rome and Greece and was probably deeply disappointed by the earthiness of those gods. There were also many conflicting philosophies, but none of them with a ring of truth. There is a deep, despairing cry in Pilate's question, and that cry is perhaps even stronger in our post-modern, scientific age. Science has led to huge advances in technology, but has provided no answers to the deepest, spiritual yearnings of the human heart. The question Pilate asked of Jesus can be asked in any age, and the answer is still the same. Jesus Christ is the witness to a spiritual kingdom. His matchless teaching and His life, death and resurrection all authenticate His claim to be the truth.

Pilate proclaimed the innocence of Jesus to the Jews, but their minds were made up. The crowd had been primed to ask for Barabbas, who was a murderer (Mark 15:7). Pilate probably expected that, faced with this choice, the Jewish leaders would have backed down. They certainly did not want Barabbas released onto their streets. But forced to choose between good and evil, they chose evil. Evil is irrational and even close to insanity on occasions. Jesus was no danger to anyone except the religious authorities, because He exposed the shallow emptiness of mere religion. Human beings may not wish to choose between God and the devil - they would prefer to choose some middle ground - but this is not possible. Everyone will have to face the consequence of their choices, even if they just wash their hands of Jesus, like Pilate. Not to make a choice is in itself a choice.

JOHN 19

THE KING IS CRUCIFIED

Condemned under Pontius Pilate

19 So Pilate then took Jesus, and flogged him. ² The soldiers twisted thorns into a crown, and put it on his head, and dressed him in a purple garment. ³ They kept saying, "Hail, King of the Jews!" and they kept slapping him.

⁴ Then Pilate went out again, and said to them, "Behold, I bring him out to you, that you may know that I find no basis for a charge against him."

⁵ Jesus therefore came out, wearing the crown of thorns and the purple garment. Pilate said to them, "Behold, the man!"

⁶ When therefore the chief priests and the officers saw him, they shouted, saying, "Crucify! Crucify!"

Pilate said to them, "Take him yourselves, and crucify him, for I find no basis for a charge against him."

⁷ The Jews answered him, "We have a law, and by our law he ought to die, because he made himself the Son of God."

⁸ When therefore Pilate heard this saying, he was more afraid. ⁹ He entered into the Praetorium again, and said to Jesus, "Where are you from?" But Jesus gave him no answer. ¹⁰ Pilate therefore said to him, "Aren't you speaking to me? Don't you know that I have power to release you and have power to crucify you?"

¹¹ Jesus answered, "You would have no power at all against me, unless it were given to you from above. Therefore he who delivered me to you has greater sin."

¹² At this, Pilate was seeking to release him, but the Jews cried out, saying, "If you release this man, you aren't Caesar's

friend! Everyone who makes himself a king speaks against Caesar!"

13 When Pilate therefore heard these words, he brought Jesus out and sat down on the judgment seat at a place called "The Pavement", but in Hebrew, "Gabbatha." 14 Now it was the Preparation Day of the Passover, at about the sixth hour. He said to the Jews, "Behold, your King!"

15 They cried out, "Away with him! Away with him! Crucify him!"

Pilate said to them, "Shall I crucify your King?"

The chief priests answered, "We have no king but Caesar!"

The last act of the unfolding drama began with Pilate having Jesus scourged. There was no reason behind this cruel act, except perhaps, Pilate thought it might satisfy the crowd to see the hated prisoner humiliated and weakened. Scourging could easily cause the death of a weak man, because it often led to the flaying of a man's back and terrible blood loss. Then the soldiers heaped ridicule on Jesus, by scornfully dressing Him as a king. It is in this humiliated condition that Pilate presented him to His accusers and to the crowds.

But the rulers were not satisfied and demanded His death, intensifying their accusation that He had claimed to be the Son of God. Pilate's rush of fear was probably due to a sudden realization that Jesus might be one of the many gods that were directing the fate of humanity. Pilate was undoubtedly superstitious and demanded to hear more from the lips of Jesus. He threatened Jesus with death, reminding Him that he had the authority to decide whether Jesus lived or died. Jesus acknowledged only one authority, namely that of God. In the direst trials of human suffering, each believer finds solace and hope in the certain knowledge that God is in control of everything.

Jesus reminded Pilate that the judicial authority he bore was derived from a higher power. He pointed out that the greatest guilt lay with the Jewish leaders, who were manipulating the power of the judiciary to fulfil their evil plans. From this moment on, Pilate sought to use his authority as judge to release Jesus. It is at this juncture that the High Priests played their master card. They reminded Pilate that the troubles he was facing would ultimately reach the ears of his patron in Rome: Tiberius Caesar. Pilate may have been willing to act righteously, especially because in so doing he could have thwarted the will of the Jews, who he despised. But he was unwilling to risk his standing before his master in Rome. The last cry of the religious authorities was a terrible admission of spiritual failure: the only King they recognised was Caesar: God the Father and His Son were not part of their world.

The King is crucified

16 So then he delivered him to them to be crucified. So they took Jesus and led him away. 17 He went out, bearing his cross, to the place called "The Place of a Skull", which is called in Hebrew, "Golgotha", 18 where they crucified him, and with him two others, on either side one, and Jesus in the middle. 19 Pilate wrote a title also, and put it on the cross. There was written, "JESUS OF NAZARETH, THE KING OF THE JEWS." 20 Therefore many of the Jews read this title, for the place where Jesus was crucified was near the city; and it was written in Hebrew, in Latin, and in Greek. 21 The chief priests of the Jews therefore said to Pilate, "Don't write, 'The King of the Jews,' but, 'he said, "I am King of the Jews."'"

22 Pilate answered, "What I have written, I have written."

23 Then the soldiers, when they had crucified Jesus, took his garments and made four parts, to every soldier a part; and also the coat. Now the coat was without seam, woven from the top throughout. 24 Then they said to one another, "Let's not tear it, but cast lots for it to decide whose it will be," that the Scripture might be fulfilled, which says,

"They parted my garments among them.

For my cloak they cast lots."

Therefore the soldiers did these things.

The King was taken out by hardened soldiers and crucified outside the city walls. The crucifixion probably took place close to a road, in earshot of the passers-by. The purpose of this was to subdue the local population by confronting them with the awful consequences of disobedience to the Roman authorities. The gospel accounts are all restrained in their description of the physical sufferings of Christ. This restraint was surely the will of Christ, who did not die to invoke the pity of the human race. God drew a veil over the deepest pain of His heart and left it for those who love Him to search out and understand how He suffered and why.

Pilate ordered a sign to be fixed above the cross in the three main languages in the Roman province of Judea: Greek, Hebrew and Latin. The chief priests were incensed by this bold declaration that Jesus was the King of the Jews. They were not objecting to the use of the title of King of the Jews, but in the uncompromising way in which Pilate had declared it as fact, not opinion. Mankind has not changed, and today it is permitted to say that Jesus is the only way to the Father if we qualify the statement by inserting "in our opinion". But God is supreme and unaffected by the opinions of those He has created. He caused Pilate to write the simple truth, and however fragile and sinful the vessel was that God used, it was the will of God that these words were written on the sign above the cross.

The soldiers turned to the small heap of clothes, which was the only legacy in worldly goods that Jesus left behind. Most of the garments were quickly dispersed, but the most valuable item remained, which was the seamless robe. This points to two great spiritual legacies that Christ has left on earth: the Bible and His people.

- The Bible is a seamless robe that speaks with unified voice of the person of the Messiah, foretold in the Old Testament in astonishing detail, fulfilled in the gospels, living on in His body, the church, described in the epistles, and coming again as prophesied in the book of Revelation.

- His people are an undivided seamless robe. True, the history of the church is one of schisms and divisions. But through the chaos of Christian institutions calling themselves the church, there shines an unbroken witness of a people who love one another and lay down their lives in love for their King.

The last words of the King

25 But standing by Jesus' cross were his mother, his mother's sister, Mary the wife of Clopas, and Mary Magdalene. 26 Therefore when Jesus saw his mother, and the disciple whom he loved standing there, he said to his mother, "Woman, behold, your son!" 27 Then he said to the disciple, "Behold, your mother!" From that hour, the disciple took her to his own home.

28 After this, Jesus, seeing that all things were now finished, that the Scripture might be fulfilled, said, "I am thirsty." 29 Now a vessel full of vinegar was set there; so they put a sponge full of the vinegar on hyssop, and held it at his mouth. 30 When Jesus therefore had received the vinegar, he said, "It is finished." Then he bowed his head, and gave up his spirit.

The last moments of the crucifixion drew near. Mary means "bitter" in Hebrew, and it is poignant that three Marys stood near the cross, whose hearts were breaking in bitter sorrow at the tragedy and injustice of it all. Like the bitter waters of Marah in Exodus 15:23-25, their bitterness was transformed into sweet water by the power of the words which Jesus now spoke and by the power of the resurrection. All the bitter streams of human experience were absorbed into the person of Christ as He was made to be sin, that we might be transformed into His image.

Jesus looked on His mother Mary and on His beloved apostle John and united them, as He pronounced their adoption, as a decree, not a request. This is of universal significance, in that all who believe in Jesus are adopted into a greater family. Jesus had already taught that obedience to God makes a person closer to Him than blood relatives (Matthew 12:47-50). Now He commanded His followers to adopt one another with a love that is to include all the affection and care that should characterise close family members. Later Paul taught that we have the Spirit of adoption (Romans 8:15 and Galatians 4:5), and that we are heirs of God and joint heirs with Christ. From the moment that Jesus said this, John took Mary to his home and according to one tradition, she stayed with him till she died in Ephesus, where John was serving as an elder many years later.[13] The power of the cross is today revealed in the deep love of God's redeemed people, that reaches out to include the lonely, orphans and the widows. The church is a family where lonely, childless, old people are adopted by young believers, and orphaned youngsters find caring parents. *"God sets the solitary in families"*, (Psalm 68:6 NKJV) as we are adopted into the family of God at the cross.

The hours passed and Jesus was nearing His last breath. He called out for a drink to slake His thirst. This is something that Jesus had mentioned in His teaching, referring to thirst for righteousness in Matthew 5:6, and to raw thirst for God in John 7:37. Jesus was expressing the astonishing fact, that God thirsts for the friendship and fellowship of human beings from the depths of His heart. This was the motive of God in Calvary, to restore human beings to be His companions. Someone gave Him sour wine, symbolic of the tragedy, that human beings have so little to give to God, until they are touched by grace. Jesus drank the cup of bitterness so that we might drink the cup of salvation and be changed. He partook of our sorrows so that we might drink of the cup of joy.

Then came the last great word of the king: *"It is finished."* This word has unfathomable depths of meaning. It is important to catch the joy contained in this cry, as Jesus obtained the goal for which He came into the world. Jesus had fought the battle and won. This was the victor's cry and He alone remained conqueror upon the field of battle.

---

[13] There are two sites that are claimed to be the tomb of Mary. (1) The church of the sepulchre of St Mary at the foot of the Mt of Olives in Jerusalem. (2) The house of the virgin Mary in Ephesus.

When Jesus said *"It is finished"*, He was not observing something, He was making it happen. His word was the expression of absolute authority, speaking into the darkness that had entered the human race through Satan and Adam. Jesus declared that the power of sin and death were destroyed forever. He broke the grip of Satan on Adam's offspring, and released them from the polluting streams of evil. Sin and all its effects were obliterated in that moment, and the message of a new creation could be preached from this time forward, because of what had taken place on the cross.

The word "finished" is also a direct repeat of Genesis 2:1:

"Thus the heavens and the earth, and all the host of them, were finished."

Jesus had not only ended the old man with all his negative tendencies. He had created in Himself a new man, a new creation. In the first creation God began with the heavens and the earth and concluded with the creation of mankind. On the cross, God created a new man in Christ, an act which is the basis of the gospel. He redeemed humanity and prepared it for the creation of new heavens and a new earth after the return of Christ.

Christ ended sin and all its effects, including sickness, curses, addictions and death itself. He then imparted the character and nature of the Son of God to whosoever would believe in Him. He also abolished the need for the law, and declared that the old covenant was finished. He abolished all the rituals of the law and thus broke down the middle wall of partition between Jew and Gentile, making of the two one new man:

"For He Himself is our peace, who has made both one, and has broken down the middle wall of separation, having abolished in His flesh the enmity, that is, the law of commandments contained in

ordinances, so as to create in Himself one new man from the two, thus making peace, and that He might reconcile them both to God in one body through the cross, thereby putting to death the enmity." (Ephesians 2:14-16)

The word Jesus spoke was immediately effective in the invisible world of the Spirit. Satan fled from the scene:

"And you, being dead in your trespasses and the uncircumcision of your flesh, He has made alive together with Him, having forgiven you all trespasses, having wiped out the handwriting of requirements that was against us, which was contrary to us. And He has taken it out of the way, having nailed it to the cross. Having disarmed principalities and powers, He made a public spectacle of them, triumphing over them in it." (Colossians 2:13-15)

In the Spirit Jesus had triumphed over evil. The work He did there was perfectly sufficient and complete to redeem the whole of humanity, if only all would believe the message. *"It is finished"* can also be translated *"It is perfected".* The redemption of humanity was accomplished before Jesus died physically. He was not in the grip of Satan for three days. Jesus' Spirit went into the Father's hands and into paradise:

"And when Jesus had cried out with a loud voice, He said, "Father, into Your hands I commit My spirit.'" Having said this, He breathed His last." (Luke 23:46)

Then, from that place of absolute victory He descended into the place of departed spirits:

"For Christ also suffered once for sins, the just for the unjust, that He might bring us to God, being put to death in the flesh but made alive by the Spirit, by whom also He went and preached to the spirits in

*prison, who formerly were disobedient, when once
the Divine longsuffering waited in the days of Noah,
while the ark was being prepared, in which a few,
that is, eight souls, were saved through water. (1Pe
3:18-20 NKJV)*

Jesus died in triumph and hell trembled at His cry
and collapsed at His entry into their domain.

The cry of Jesus pierced the darkness, but it also
reached the highest throne. It may rightly be wondered
where Satan could hide himself after the spiritual
earthquake of the cross. John had said in his
introduction to the gospel:

*"And the light shines in the darkness, and the
darkness did not comprehend it."* (John 1:5)

This was true of the incarnation, namely that Satan
could not grasp the mystery that God had taken on
human form. But it is even more true of the cross, that
Satan could not grasp the mystery of love incarnate,
that God would love sinners to the point of total
identification. Wisdom is not found in the power of
human intellect, it is found in the matchless love of God
that made a way to bring sinners back to God. Since
the day of Pentecost, the full power of this cry *"It is
finished"* has echoed back and forth across the planet
earth. Wherever this cry has been understood, sinners
have been forgiven, washed and transformed. Satan
hates this word with all its implications, but to those who
have received it in faith, it is the dissolving of every
chain that binds the human spirit. We may turn in our
minds to Revelation 5, thinking that as darkness fled the
scene, heaven erupted in praise to the lamb that had
prevailed.

*"Then I looked, and I heard the voice of many
angels around the throne, the living creatures, and
the elders; and the number of them was ten
thousand times ten thousand, and thousands of
thousands, saying with a loud voice: "Worthy is the*

Lamb who was slain To receive power and riches and wisdom, And strength and honour and glory and blessing!" And every creature which is in heaven and on the earth and under the earth and such as are in the sea, and all that are in them, I heard saying: "Blessing and honour and glory and power Be to Him who sits on the throne, And to the Lamb, forever and ever!" Then the four living creatures said, "Amen!" And the twenty-four elders fell down and worshipped Him who lives forever and ever." (Revelation 5:11-14 NKJV)

The water and the blood

[31] Therefore the Jews, because it was the Preparation Day, so that the bodies wouldn't remain on the cross on the Sabbath (for that Sabbath was a special one), asked of Pilate that their legs might be broken, and that they might be taken away. [32] Therefore the soldiers came, and broke the legs of the first, and of the other who was crucified with him; [33] but when they came to Jesus, and saw that he was already dead, they didn't break his legs. [34] However one of the soldiers pierced his side with a spear, and immediately blood and water came out. [35] He who has seen has testified, and his testimony is true. He knows that he tells the truth, that you may believe. [36] For these things happened that the Scripture might be fulfilled, "A bone of him will not be broken." [37] Again another Scripture says, "They will look on him whom they pierced."

The Sabbath was fast approaching and the Jews did not want the three crucified men to linger on beyond the sunset on Friday that signalled the beginning of the day of rest. A crucified man often died of asphyxiation, as he was unable to breathe with the weight of his body. To prolong the torture, the Romans fitted a wooden support, so that the victims might press upwards with their legs and support their weight, and thus be able to breathe. This explains why the Romans broke the legs of the two others crucified, to hasten their death. But Jesus was already dead. His legs were not broken and this fulfilled the prophecy of Psalm 34:20 and also the prophetic instruction that the Passover lamb was not to have one bone broken (Exodus 12:48). The spiritual meaning of this prophecy was that the Son of God passed through the trauma of the cross, without suffering any damage to the inner integrity of His mind. Such strain on the personality might inflict terrible inner scars, but Jesus passed through the cross and came out unscathed. There was a calm dignity and victory in Christ as He dismissed His spirit.

The soldiers then pierced His side with a spear. This fulfilled yet another prophecy in Zechariah 12:10, that the people of Israel would look on Him whom they had pierced. From Jesus' side flowed blood and water. This is an intriguing and mysterious assertion, and one that John was most eager to affirm as something that he personally witnessed. The explanation lies in the symbolism of the water and the wine that are so foundational to understanding the gospel of John.

The water symbolised the Holy Spirit, and this symbol is abundantly familiar to anyone who reads John's gospel. The wine was also a key symbol, representing the blood of Jesus. The blood is the essence of Jesus in His character and nature. Already in chapter 2, John had presented the miracle of water and wine, a theme which is inherent in the parable of the vine in chapter 15. So, what did it all mean? The answer lies in the uniqueness of the New Testament promise, that Jesus will give us His blood, His very life.

The gift of the Holy Spirit in the Old Testament could be given without changing the nature of the person who received it. Samson was moved by the Spirit but his character was blemished by deep sexual problems. Judas received the anointing of power (Matthew 10:1), but he too was deeply and fatally flawed. This explains the word of Jesus that on judgment day some will claim to have cast out demons and prophesied, yet Jesus will respond with the devastating words:

"And then I will declare to them, I never knew you; depart from Me, you who practice lawlessness!' (Matthew 7:23)

The promise of the New Testament is that when the Holy Spirit is given, He will carry the very life of God Himself. The gift of the New Testament is not just the power of the Spirit, it is the very life-blood of God Himself. That is why the emblems of the new covenant are bread and wine, not bread and water.

Later, in John's first epistle he refers once more to the water and the blood:

> "This is He who came by water and blood - Jesus Christ; not only by water, but by water and blood. And it is the Spirit who bears witness, because the Spirit is truth. For there are three that bear witness in heaven: the Father, the Word, and the Holy Spirit; and these three are one. And there are three that bear witness on earth: the Spirit, the water, and the blood; and these three agree as one. If we receive the witness of men, the witness of God is greater; for this is the witness of God which He has testified of His Son. He who believes in the Son of God has the witness in himself; he who does not believe God has made Him a liar, because he has not believed the testimony that God has given of His Son. And this is the testimony: that God has given us eternal life, and this life is in His Son." (1 John 5:6-11)

John affirmed that the unique testimony of new covenant believers is that God has given them eternal life. At first this may seem to be subjective. But what John is affirming is that the greatest assurance of the believer is the simple fact that he or she was once spiritually dead, and now we have life.

Someone once said that the man with an experience is not at the mercy of the man with an argument. This is the reason why the Jews could not shake the faith of the blind man who had been healed in chapter 9. His final assertion was:

> "One thing I know: that though I was blind, now I see." (John 9:25)

Intellectuals might be able to tear such a man's faith to shreds, but would never be able to destroy it, because it was founded on an unshakeable truth. A Christian is not merely a witness to something he believes, he is an eyewitness to a deep inward change in his nature. The whole Christian message stands on the testimony of witnesses. While there are no living witnesses to the resurrection of Jesus, there are millions of witnesses who will say with disarming simplicity: once I was dead, but Christ gave me life.

When Christ the rock was smitten, there came from Him a river of living water, and in the stream there was also the very life-blood of Christ. We drink His Holy Spirit and His life, and this is the powerful message of the cross: that whoever will believe and receive, will be changed at the very root of their being.

The King is buried

38 After these things, Joseph of Arimathaea, being a disciple of Jesus, but secretly for fear of the Jews, asked of Pilate that he might take away Jesus' body. Pilate gave him permission. He came therefore and took away his body. 39 Nicodemus, who at first came to Jesus by night, also came bringing a mixture of myrrh and aloes, about a hundred Roman pounds. 40 So they took Jesus' body, and bound it in linen cloths with the spices, as the custom of the Jews is to bury. 41 Now in the place where he was crucified there was a garden. In the garden was a new tomb in which no man had ever yet been laid. 42 Then because of the Jews' Preparation Day (for the tomb was near at hand) they laid Jesus there.

The imagery of these verses demands to be connected with other Bible passages. Christ was crucified in a garden, and just as in the midst of the garden of Eden, there was the tree of life, so Christ planted the tree of life on earth. In the same garden there was a freshly-hewn tomb, belonging to Joseph of Arimathea. Joseph and Nicodemus brought a mountain of spices, (about 50kg) which they placed in the tomb. Peter tells us that the body of Jesus did not see any corruption (Acts 2:31). So, there was no smell of death in Jesus's tomb, but rather a sweet-smelling aroma of life. His body rested in the tomb while His spirit was with the Father.

JOHN 20

THE KING IS RISEN

Mary and the disciples at the tomb

20 *Now on the first day of the week, Mary Magdalene went early, while it was still dark, to the tomb, and saw the stone taken away from the tomb.* ² *Therefore she ran and came to Simon Peter and to the other disciple whom Jesus loved, and said to them, "They have taken away the Lord out of the tomb, and we don't know where they have laid him!"*

³ *Therefore Peter and the other disciple went out, and they went toward the tomb.* ⁴ *They both ran together. The other disciple outran Peter, and came to the tomb first.* ⁵ *Stooping and looking in, he saw the linen cloths lying, yet he didn't enter in.* ⁶ *Then Simon Peter came, following him, and entered into the tomb. He saw the linen cloths lying,* ⁷ *and the cloth that had been on his head, not lying with the linen cloths, but rolled up in a place by itself.* ⁸ *So then the other disciple who came first to the tomb also entered in, and he saw and believed.* ⁹ *For as yet they didn't know the Scripture, that he must rise from the dead.* ¹⁰ *So the disciples went away again to their own homes.*

Mary Magdalene was first at the tomb seeking to anoint the body of Jesus (see also Mark 16:1). Finding the stone rolled away, she ran to Peter and John to bring the news to them. It is a beautiful detail that first Mary, and then Peter and John ran, and that John outran Peter. There is passionate love and eagerness in their haste. This was not a matter of passing interest, this was their future, their hope, their very life. Was Mary first at the tomb because she loved Him most? Did John's feet carry him swiftest because he loved Jesus and knew His love more than Peter?

Reaching the tomb, they saw the linen cloths folded as if they had been carefully laid aside. The implication was that no-one had violently grabbed the body of Jesus, but rather that Christ was risen and had carefully laid the grave-clothes aside. It was this detail that impacted John and made him the first to believe that Jesus was indeed risen. It is an important point that, though they had heard the Lord speak of His resurrection on the third day (Mark 10.34), yet they still had not grasped the significance of this prophecy and the stark, practical reality of it.

It is also essential to realise that the fact of the resurrection was not something that had changed their world in the very moment that it took place. It was only as it was revealed to them that their world began to change. Many today believe that Christ rose from the dead, but have not yet received the full impact of this foundational fact which changes everything. Perhaps the disciples had believed it must be some kind of spiritual resurrection, or that it would take place in the dim and distant future. But no, the resurrection of Jesus Christ is the most startling and life-changing fact of all history. Nothing can ever be the same once we grasp this.

Mary saw the Lord first

[11] But Mary was standing outside at the tomb weeping. So as she wept, she stooped and looked into the tomb, [12] and she saw two angels in white sitting, one at the head, and one at the feet, where the body of Jesus had lain. [13] They asked her, "Woman, why are you weeping?"

She said to them, "Because they have taken away my Lord, and I don't know where they have laid him." [14] When she had said this, she turned around and saw Jesus standing, and didn't know that it was Jesus.

[15] Jesus said to her, "Woman, why are you weeping? Who are you looking for?"

She, supposing him to be the gardener, said to him, "Sir, if you have carried him away, tell me where you have laid him, and I will take him away."

16 Jesus said to her, "Mary."

She turned and said to him, "Rabboni!" which is to say, "Teacher!"

17 Jesus said to her, "Don't hold me, for I haven't yet ascended to my Father; but go to my brothers and tell them, 'I am ascending to my Father and your Father, to my God and your God.'"

18 Mary Magdalene came and told the disciples that she had seen the Lord, and that he had said these things to her.

The persistence of Mary is perhaps the most touching aspect of this story. She wept continually as she wondered what had happened to the body of Christ. The details of Mary's life story are not fully known, and it seems safe to presume that she is not the unnamed prostitute mentioned in Luke 7:36-50. Nevertheless, it is certain that her past life had been spiritually darkened, and her mind severely troubled, because Luke tells us that Jesus had delivered her of seven demons (Luke 8:2). Her extravagant love for Jesus was of the same kind as the woman of Luke 7:47, because she had been forgiven much and had experienced deep spiritual transformation. Mary and the unnamed woman had both broken open their treasure of costly perfume (Luke 7:37 and John 12:3), and one at least had washed His feet with her tears, which were even more costly than the perfume (Luke 7:38). Their hair had been their towel (John 12:3 and Luke 7:38). This was the effect of the ministry of Jesus, that their hearts flowed out in abandoned love for Him.

The angels asked why she was weeping. To the angels, human beings must be puzzling creatures. Why so much sorrow since Jesus is risen? Her answer was from a broken heart: she wanted to know where His body lay, so that she might somehow respect His mortal remains, and express her love for Him by a last act of devotion in anointing Him.

Then she turned and saw Jesus and assumed He was the gardener. He asked her two great questions *"Why are you weeping and who are you seeking?"* Mary was weeping because of the unspeakable tragedy of a crucified Messiah. The appearance of God in human form was the most beautiful act of a loving God, reaching out to broken lives with healing and redemption. The response of humanity was appalling. Evil seemed to have triumphed and the light had gone out. For Mary it was even more piercing, since she had looked into that sinless face and met the love and power of God combined in a stream of transforming grace. *"Who was she seeking?"* – she was seeking Jesus, in order that she might pour out her love in a last act of kindness on His corpse.

Her words were remarkable: *"Tell me where you have laid Him and I will take Him away."* Mary was willing to carry that body in her arms and tenderly anoint and bury it. There was no estimation of the barriers that might hinder her from carrying out this task. Her focus was on Him. Her focus was not on some blessing she might receive as a reward for her devotion. She was not calculating whether this might earn her "the baptism with the Holy Spirit" or a "gift of healing". Her heart was directed in disinterested, unselfish love towards Jesus. She loved Him for Himself. There is something so elevated and pure about Mary's act, which challenges all who read of her love so that we in turn might focus our hearts entirely on Him. There was no audience for Mary's words and deeds that morning. She was completely in love with Jesus.

Then Jesus spoke her name and she immediately knew who He was. Her response was to call him "Teacher!" Jesus then gently directed her not to cling to Him by holding on to His body. He was about to ascend to *"My Father and your Father, My God and your God"*.

A new era was about to begin when He would not be known according to the flesh, as Paul said:

"Therefore, from now on, we regard no-one according to the flesh. Even though we have known Christ according to the flesh, yet now we know Him thus no longer." (2 Corinthians 5:16)

Christ would very soon be known only through the person of the Holy Spirit. Believers would no longer see Him physically and follow Him around Galilee. Believers the world over, would know Him intimately and deeply by the power of the indwelling Spirit, revealing Christ in their hearts.

The message that Mary was given was to declare the new covenant adoption of believers into the same relationship with God that Jesus had. It is awe-inspiring that His followers can know God for themselves, and know all the inward life that Jesus knew. The day was dawning when the feeblest believer could call God Father, with full justification.

Christ commissions His disciples

[19] *When therefore it was evening on that day, the first day of the week, and when the doors were locked where the disciples were assembled, for fear of the Jews, Jesus came and stood in the middle, and said to them, "Peace be to you."*
[20] *When he had said this, he showed them his hands and his side. The disciples therefore were glad when they saw the Lord.* [21] *Jesus therefore said to them again, "Peace be to you. As the Father has sent me, even so I send you."* [22] *When he had said this, he breathed on them, and said to them, "Receive the Holy Spirit!* [23] *If you forgive anyone's sins, they have been forgiven them. If you retain anyone's sins, they have been retained."*

The day wore on and the disciples passed the day in amazement at the events unfolding around them. Then in the evening Jesus appeared in the midst of the disciples. His message was *"Peace to you."* Perhaps the greatest robber of blessing among believers is anxiety. When our hearts sink into worry and fear we are paralysed and unable to function spiritually with faith and hope. Fear is by its very nature a negative faith, the belief that bad things are certain to happen. Jesus spoke peace into their souls. It is peace and peace above all that is the very atmosphere in which God dwells, with no fear of any power or form of evil. God's work is to bring confused and bewildered human beings to the throne of God and drink there of the peace that passes understanding.

Jesus then showed them His hands and His side. This was not merely a spirit; this was a human being with a physical body. We may wonder at the nature of His body, and Luke reports He ate with them to bring this truth clearly to their minds:

> ""Behold My hands and My feet, that it is I Myself. Handle Me and see, for a spirit does not have flesh and bones as you see I have." When He had said this, He showed them His hands and His feet. But while they still did not believe for joy, and marvelled, He said to them, "Have you any food here?" So they gave Him a piece of a broiled fish and some honeycomb. And He took it and ate in their presence." (Luke 24:39-43)

The truth of the resurrection can be easily mistaken for the belief in life after death alone. The Bible teaches that after death believers are consciously in the presence of God, as Jesus was in Paradise with the man who died beside Him. Jesus went by the Spirit into the place of departed spirits and preached to them. But this was prior to His resurrection. Now He was risen with a new body, with new faculties, evidently able to pass effortlessly from earth to heaven. By this He was giving demonstration to His disciples of the hope that was now theirs.

Jesus then spoke the foundation of all missionary assurance: *"As the Father has sent Me, so send I you."* God sends His servants with the same promises, the same power and the same intimacy that He gave to Jesus. Every missionary may draw on the same support that Jesus had, the same peace, love and provision.

216

Jesus then breathed upon them and commanded them to *"Receive the Holy Spirit."* This was not a major event in their spiritual lives, because it was never referred to again as a point of reference by any of the apostles. So, what happened? Firstly, it was an act filled with symbolism. The Greek word "emphisao" is only found on this one occasion in the New Testament. It is found moreover on only one occasion in the Greek Old Testament (the Septuagint, translated 250 BC). There it is the word used to translate the Hebrew "Naphah", when God breathed into Adam the breath of life. Jesus was teaching them the vital need to receive the Spirit of God, to live in an attitude of receiving and drawing life and power from Him in the same way we draw breath to live physically. The coming day of Pentecost would be the day when God would breathe from heaven into His body, the church and the result would be life from the dead.

Secondly, it was an act of refreshing and strengthening their souls for the coming days. There are many specific acts of God in our lives, including new birth, the baptism with the Holy Spirit and other critical moments in our spiritual growth and development. But the Holy Spirit is given to us at every stage of our walk to help us through each specific moment. Jesus had promised in Luke 11:9-13 that all who ask will receive the Holy Spirit. If our minds are focused only on the big works of the Holy Spirit, we will miss the fact that God means to give us the Holy Spirit as a constant supply, to help us believe, hope, pray, love and persevere. Every day we are to ask for fresh supply and receive the answer in faith, as easily as breathing.

The final part of this commissioning of the disciples was the authority to confirm the forgiveness of sins. It is true that only God can forgive sins (Mark 2:7 and 10). But God has given it to the church to represent Him. It is for this reason that leaders must take great care in their handling of spiritual discipline. For the flock, the church leadership is the main interpreter of the mind and will of God. When individuals get into difficulty, their personal relationship with God is compromised, and their spiritual witness is clouded. They need faithful men and women who will speak truth to them. Pastors and leaders are to study to show themselves approved of God by prayerful reading of the Bible, by waiting on God for understanding, and by cultivating a heart of love for those who fail and fall into sin. It is one of the most solemn burdens of elders and leaders to lead sinners to true repentance and salvation.

Thomas and the great confession

[24] *But Thomas, one of the twelve, called Didymus, wasn't with them when Jesus came.* [25] *The other disciples therefore said to him, "We have seen the Lord!"*
But he said to them, "Unless I see in his hands the print of the nails, put my finger into the print of the nails, and put my hand into his side, I will not believe."
[26] *After eight days again his disciples were inside and Thomas was with them. Jesus came, the doors being locked, and stood in the middle, and said, "Peace be to you."* [27] *Then he said to Thomas, "Reach here your finger, and see my hands. Reach here your hand, and put it into my side. Don't be unbelieving, but believing."*
[28] *Thomas answered him, "My Lord and my God!"*
[29] *Jesus said to him, "Because you have seen me, you have believed. Blessed are those who have not seen, and have believed."*
[30] *Therefore Jesus did many other signs in the presence of his disciples, which are not written in this book;* [31] *but these are written, that you may believe that Jesus is the Christ, the Son of God, and that believing you may have life in his name.*

Thomas has unfairly been named "doubting Thomas", because of the moment described by John, when he declared he would not believe unless he saw and touched the risen Christ. It is true that he could have simply believed the testimony of the other 10 apostles. But the question is: what was it that he was struggling to believe? He knew that Jesus was the Messiah, and that He had power to raise the dead. But there was one last step that Thomas was struggling with: the deity of Christ.

Thomas made his stand, not knowing that Jesus was invisibly present. It is sometimes asserted that Jesus passed through locked doors, and while that is unquestionably true, it is also true that He never left the disciples. He was present with them from this point onwards, wherever they went. He was hidden from their sight, but they were being led to believe in His presence without any sensation of it. This was a short phase when He was revealed physically, but it was only an interim period preceding the outpouring of the Holy Spirit.

Jesus now came once more and revealed Himself. He answered the words spoken by Thomas eight days earlier and invited him to put his finger in His wounds, and his hand in Jesus' side. This is the constant invitation of Jesus to His followers. Imagine the nuclear furnace that burns in the being of Christ. He is resplendent in light unapproachable and majestic in dazzling glory that causes Cherubim and Seraphim to cry "Holy, Holy, Holy" day and night without ceasing. Now He invited Thomas to put his hand into that inner nuclear furnace of the living God. When we are brought into Christ and Christ into us, it is one of the most mysterious and powerful facts of the New Testament.

Thomas had no need to stretch forth his hand, but found himself believing with all his heart, and he burst out with the great confession of who Jesus was, that no human being had ever uttered before:

"My Lord and my God!"

After the resurrection, the awareness of the divinity of Jesus was further unfolded to the apostles, and became the bedrock of the preaching and teaching of the early church. Over the centuries, Arius and other theologians have rejected the divinity of Christ, as have the Jews, the Muslims, the Jehovah Witnesses and many other religious groups and sects. It is remarkable that John himself at this point gave his main reason for writing this gospel, that his readers should believe that

Jesus is indeed the Messiah and by believing this should have life from God.

The belief that the Messiah would be God in human form is based on texts such as:

> *"Therefore the Lord Himself will give you a sign: Behold, the virgin shall conceive and bear a Son, and shall call His name Immanuel." (Immanuel – literally translated: God with us).* (Isaiah 7:14)

> *"For unto us a Child is born, Unto us a Son is given; And the government will be upon His shoulder. And His name will be called Wonderful, Counsellor, Mighty God, Everlasting Father, Prince of Peace."* (Isaiah 9:6)

This belief in the divinity of Jesus is the foundation of the New Testament. He is the perfect expression of God, having stepped onto the world stage out of eternity, to redeem a fallen humanity and give them life.

JOHN 21

BREAKFAST BY THE SEA

The Maker of all things makes breakfast

21 After these things, Jesus revealed himself again to the disciples at the sea of Tiberias. He revealed himself this way. ² Simon Peter, Thomas called Didymus, Nathanael of Cana in Galilee, and the sons of Zebedee, and two others of his disciples were together. ³ Simon Peter said to them, "I'm going fishing."

They told him, "We are also coming with you." They immediately went out, and entered into the boat. That night, they caught nothing. ⁴ But when day had already come, Jesus stood on the beach, yet the disciples didn't know that it was Jesus. ⁵ Jesus therefore said to them, "Children, have you anything to eat?"

They answered him, "No."

⁶ He said to them, "Cast the net on the right side of the boat, and you will find some."

They cast it therefore, and now they weren't able to draw it in for the multitude of fish. ⁷ That disciple therefore whom Jesus loved said to Peter, "It's the Lord!"

So when Simon Peter heard that it was the Lord, he wrapped his coat around himself (for he was naked), and threw himself into the sea. ⁸ But the other disciples came in the little boat (for they were not far from the land, but about two hundred cubits away), dragging the net full of fish. ⁹ So when they got out on the land, they saw a fire of coals there, with fish and bread laid on it. ¹⁰ Jesus said to them, "Bring some of the fish which you have just caught."

¹¹ Simon Peter went up, and drew the net to land, full of one hundred fifty-three great fish. Even though there were so many, the net wasn't torn.
¹² Jesus said to them, "Come and eat breakfast!"
None of the disciples dared inquire of him, "Who are you?" knowing that it was the Lord.
¹³ Then Jesus came and took the bread, gave it to them, and the fish likewise. ¹⁴ This is now the third time that Jesus was revealed to his disciples after he had risen from the dead.

Jesus had commanded his disciples to go to Galilee, and the scene now switched from Jerusalem to the shores of the sea of Galilee. John begins his description of this event by the simple statement of God's method: Jesus showed Himself. This is the remarkable, simple method of the Holy Spirit in the conversion of sinners and the edification and strengthening of disciples. God reveals His Son through preaching and lives are changed.

The scene is described so simply and with all the artless authority of eye-witness detail. There were seven disciples together in all and suddenly, Peter announced that he was going fishing. This was so typical of the man we have come to know through the Scriptures. He spoke and acted from a deep spontaneity that is perhaps the reason he was chosen as the chief spokesman on the day of Pentecost. Peter didn't think everything through before he jumped in. He confessed Jesus was Messiah (Matthew 16:16), he stepped out of the boat when he saw Jesus walking on the water (Matthew 14:28) and he denied Christ in the heat of the moment (Matthew 26:69-75). The reason he suddenly embarked on this expedition is unknown, but was probably quite simple: he was hungry and had nothing to eat. Peter had not yet fully grasped that Jesus would provide for his every need. In fact, this was the third time that Peter would hear the call of Jesus while fishing. Jesus saw Peter casting a net into the sea of Galilee and called him to follow him (Mark 1:16-17). Peter had then left his nets and followed Jesus. But he had gone back to fishing in Luke 5 when we read that he had passed the whole night fishing without success (Luke 5:5).

Again, he left all to follow Jesus. Now Peter had gone back a third time to fishing, to his familiar territory, where he felt secure and knew he could provide for himself. And again, he had spent a fruitless night out on the lake.

Now Jesus stood on the shore and called out *"Children have you any food?"* Their tired, discouraged answer echoed back that they had caught nothing. Jesus then advised them to cast their nets on the right side of the boat and suddenly their nets were filled. John was the first to recognise Jesus: *"It is the Lord."* At many points in our lives, we may have not noticed the hand of God. We may have thought it was luck or circumstances, but it was truly the hand of God.

John paused to reflect, but spontaneous Peter didn't waste time thinking about things. He grabbed his garment and flung himself into the sea, leaving the others to handle the catch. As he drew near to the Lord, he saw a fire of coals and some fish with bread ready to eat. The risen Christ had stooped to making a fire and preparing breakfast. The humility of Jesus Christ is so breath-taking, mainly because it is in contrast to his elevated character and position. Human beings should be humble because they are so small, so weak, so sinful. But Christ has nothing to be humble about, for He is God and Lord and full of infinite power and authority. Yet His humility is an integral part of His greatness and His perfection. He was at home in the commonplace things of life, and His glory is revealed in the most ordinary situations.

The searching question: do you love Me?

15 So when they had eaten their breakfast, Jesus said to Simon Peter, "Simon, son of Jonah, do you love me more than these?"

He said to him, "Yes, Lord; you know that I have affection for you."

He said to him, "Feed my lambs." 16 He said to him again a second time, "Simon, son of Jonah, do you love me?"

He said to him, "Yes, Lord; you know that I have affection for you."

He said to him, "Tend my sheep." *17* He said to him the third time, "Simon, son of Jonah, do you have affection for me?"

Peter was grieved because he asked him the third time, "Do you have affection for me?" He said to him, "Lord, you know everything. You know that I have affection for you."

Jesus said to him, "Feed my sheep. *18* Most certainly I tell you, when you were young, you dressed yourself and walked where you wanted to. But when you are old, you will stretch out your hands, and another will dress you and carry you where you don't want to go."

19 Now he said this, signifying by what kind of death he would glorify God. When he had said this, he said to him, "Follow me."

20 Then Peter, turning around, saw a disciple following. This was the disciple whom Jesus loved, the one who had also leaned on Jesus' breast at the supper and asked, "Lord, who is going to betray you?" *21* Peter seeing him, said to Jesus, "Lord, what about this man?"

22 Jesus said to him, "If I desire that he stay until I come, what is that to you? You follow me." *23* This saying therefore went out among the brothers, that this disciple wouldn't die. Yet Jesus didn't say to him that he wouldn't die, but, "If I desire that he stay until I come, what is that to you?" *24* This is the disciple who testifies about these things, and wrote these things. We know that his witness is true. *25* There are also many other things which Jesus did, which if they would all be written, I suppose that even the world itself wouldn't have room for the books that would be written.

Jesus then asked Peter the most searching question: "*Do you love me more than these others do?*" Jesus used the Greek word "agape", which is the pure, unbiased love of God. Peter answered with the word "phileo", which Kenneth Taylor translated: "I am your friend", while J.N. Darby translated it: "I am attached to You." There is a difference of degree between "agape" and "phileo". The inference is that Peter was finding it hard to say "I love you". Perhaps it was the chastening experience of denying the Lord that made him hesitate. On the third occasion Jesus used the same word as Peter, and Peter was grieved because it highlighted the weakness of his love.

The conversation is still probing for any pastor or leader today. Jesus was confirming his choice of Peter as the leading apostle. One of the qualities which made him an outstanding leader was his artless honesty. Peter was transparent and sincere. He was also weak and flawed. Jesus challenged Peter to recognise the weakness of his affection for Jesus. Jesus also affirmed to Peter and to all the disciples that this love was the main requirement for their place and ministry in His kingdom. Love is the chief qualification to serve God and shepherd His people. Preachers may give the flock the word every Sunday, but the word has no life without love as the motive. The need of the flock is for love, to be fed the food of loving words from God, and to be sheltered by loving oversight and generous provision. No-one, from the most charismatic preacher to the cleverest theologian, is qualified to understand and handle God's word without love in their hearts.

Jesus then prophesied the death of Peter by cruel execution (vv 18-19). From this it may be assumed that this gospel was written after Peter's death in around AD 64, since John gives no further clarification of this word of Jesus, assuming the readers knew what had transpired.

Peter was curious about the future of John the beloved disciple, and asked Jesus about him. Jesus gently directed Peter not to be concerned about the future of others, but to keep his eyes on following Him.

In the closing lines, John identified himself as the beloved disciple. He corrected the mistaken idea that he would not die before the return of Christ. He affirmed that he, John, the author of these lines heard those words and that Jesus did not say he would not die, but rather that if Jesus wanted it, he would not die.

The closing words admit that John's gospel is only a flavour of the matchless life of Christ. If everything Jesus did were written down, then the world would not contain the books. This may seem hyperbole, but John was not referring merely to miracles that Jesus did, but to the way He did things: His tones, His inflections, His prayers, His sighs, His commands, His joys. Those who love Him would capture every second of that life because of their unashamed belief that this was no ordinary life. This was a life full of meaning and revelation so powerful, life-changing and pure that every moment had an infinite depth of meaning, every glance a power to reach the despairing with infinite hope and surging love.

The message and the challenge

John's gospel has a depth and clarity about its message. It is a declaration of the character and identity of Christ as the eternal Son of God the Father. He was God come to dwell among us and to redeem us. The challenge is in the unusual use of language. The great I am seeks access to our hearts. The challenge is to let Jesus be Himself to us, in purging our hearts from the awful power of sin, and regenerating our life. Christ will be to us a door to life abundant and full of joy. The challenge is simple: we are to open our hearts and allow Him to swallow us up and make us one with God.

Study Guide

John's gospel and the flying eagle

1. Why might someone be tempted to worship the Bible?
2. What are the remarkable qualities of an eagle?
3. In what way might Jesus be compared to an eagle?
4. Give some examples of how the Bible gives several descriptions of the same event from different perspectives?
5. Can you think of any verse(s) that describe believers as eagles? Why is this such an important thing to understand?
6. Why do you think we need 4 gospels?
7. What did Jesus mean when He said He is from above and unregenerate people are from beneath?
8. How can we have this life from above?
9. Does Jesus expect believers to walk on water?
10. What was the inner attitude of Jesus to the Father? Give some quotes from the gospel of John.
11. What are the key aspects of Jesus' inner life?

John 1: The Word Became Flesh

1. Compare the meaning of *"In the beginning"* in Genesis 1:1, 1 John 1:1 and John 1:1. Do you agree with the author that John 1:1 is the earliest point in the whole Bible, even before Genesis 1?
2. What was not in the beginning? This is a long list, so just focus on the main things you can think of.
3. What was in the beginning?
4. What kind of atmosphere surrounds the place of the beginning? Has this ever changed? Was this the inward life of Jesus?

5. What can we learn about the effect of Christ on our hearts by comparing Him with the light of the sun?
6. What does John mean by calling Jesus the "logos"?
7. The author exchanges the word "logos" with the word "love". What does this explain?
8. What does John say about the "Logos" in relationship to God?
9. In what way does John 1 make it clear that the "logos" is a person?
10. What is the role of "logos" in the creation of the physical universe?
11. What does the prologue teach us about the "logos" in relation to humanity?
12. What did John the Baptist mean when he said: "I did not know Him" (John 1:31)?
13. John said "I am not" (1:21). What might this mean in the context of the whole gospel?
14. What is "life" in the understanding of the Bible?
15. What do you think drew the disciples of John the Baptist to begin following Jesus?
16. What was so striking about the way Jesus spoke to the first little group of His disciples?
17. What did the supernatural knowledge of Jesus convey to the first disciples?

John 2: The six stone waterpots

1. Why is it significant that Jesus began His ministry at a wedding?
2. What does it mean that the wine ran out?
3. Why do you think Mary believed Jesus had the answer to the problem?
4. Why do you think Jesus thought of the cross when Mary told Him the wine had run out?
5. What do the 6 waterpots represent?
6. Name the six waterpots of John's gospel. How does this help you understand the message of John's gospel?
7. What do the water and the wine symbolise?
8. What do you learn about the ministry of Jesus

in the new covenant that contrasts with the old covenant?

9. How is the vine of chapter 15 connected with the transformation of water to wine?
10. What are the three steps that led to the miracle and what can we learn from them?
11. Who was the first to receive the best wine at the wedding in Cana and what might this mean?
12. Where is the visit to the temple by Jesus prophesied?
13. How would you describe the state of things in the temple?
14. What do you learn from the fact that Jesus cleansed the temple twice, at the beginning and end of His ministry?
15. What do we learn from the cleansing of the temple about the will of God for our lives?
16. What did Jesus mean when He said *"Destroy this temple, and in three days I will raise it up again"* (John 2:19)?
17. Why was Jesus reserved in His relationship to the many who believed in Him?

John 3: Nicodemus – the first waterpot

1. What is the material that is unique to John's gospel?
2. Why does the teaching of Jesus begin with the subject of new birth?
3. How is new birth connected with Passover?
4. Who was Nicodemus?
5. Why might you think Nicodemus might not need to be born again?
6. What is the great problem of each individual?
7. What are the marks of sin in a person whose life is relatively upright?
8. What is God's answer to the problem of the human race?
9. Do you agree with the author that the miracle of new birth takes place in three major steps?
10. What is the mark of a new nature?
11. How do we see and enter the kingdom?

12. Why is the cross the answer to receiving a new nature?
13. How does Numbers 21:5-9, when the serpent was lifted up, help you understand the work of the cross?
14. Why does Jesus speak of the cross as having already taken place in John 3:16?
15. What did Jesus mean by the "world" in John 3:16?
16. Is there any evidence in John's gospel that Nicodemus swam against the tide of sin?
17. What were the remarkable characteristics of the person of John the Baptist?
18. What did John the Baptist say that indicated he understood the greatness of Jesus?
19. What are the four great declarations made by John the Baptist at the end of chapter 3?

John 4: The 2nd waterpot – the woman of Samaria

1. Who were the Samaritans?
2. Why is it remarkable that Jesus chose to visit this part of Israel?
3. How do we know that the woman of Samaria was a moral failure?
4. Describe the kind of pain and hurt she was feeling.
5. Why did the request of Jesus for water touch her heart so deeply?
6. What are the two things that Jesus said the woman needed to know?
7. Do you think these two things could be used to summarise the message of the New Testament?
8. Who is Jesus?
9. What is His gift?
10. How does the gift of God fit in with the waterpots of chapter 2?
11. What does Jesus mean by saying that whoever drinks of this water shall never thirst again?
12. Why does this gift lead to worship?

13. What do you think the woman experienced as she listened to Jesus and believed that He was the Messiah?
14. Why were the disciples so out of step with Jesus at this point? Do you think they would have got in the way of Jesus reaching the woman?
15. If the fields were white for harvest, why did the disciples not realise this? How do we apply this truth to our own lives?
16. What does the second sign of John's gospel (the healing of the nobleman's son) teach us? In answering this question, think of the power of Jesus to heal over a long distance.
17. This miracle speaks of a father's love for his son. How is this theme central to the Godhead and particularly to the main themes of John's gospel?

John 5: The 3rd waterpot – the man by the pool of Bethesda

1. In what way was the scene by the pool a picture of Israel in the Old Testament?
2. How is a stagnant pool to be understood, in contrast to the theme of living water in chapter 4?
3. Why should the church not be stagnant?
4. Why did Jesus ask the man if he wanted to be made whole?
5. What are the implications of being made spiritually whole?
6. What does the man's answer tell you about the spiritual condition of the crowd of sick people?
7. What spiritual significance do you see in the command of Jesus to "rise, take up your bed and walk!"
8. Why is the reaction of the Pharisees so sad?
9. Why is the further command of Jesus to "sin no more" so important if we are to lead people to full spiritual health.

10. What significance do you see in the claim of Jesus that He and His father were working on the sabbath?
11. Why was John Baptist such an important witness to the identity of Jesus as Messiah?
12. Do you know personally of any recent miracles that might make people think about the claims of Jesus?
13. What did Jesus mean that the Father was witnessing to His identity? (John 5:37).
14. In what way does the whole Bible point to Jesus? (John 5:39).
15. Why did Jesus emphasise that Moses spoke of Him?

John 6: The kingdom, the bread and the wine

1. How does this chapter link the Passover with the communion?
2. Why is broken bread the centre of the kingdom of God?
3. Define what is meant by brokenness?
4. Why did the crowds want Jesus to be their king?
5. What does it do for your faith to know that the number 8 is woven into the gospel of John?
6. What is the significance of the number 8?
7. Why is it important that Jesus is the I am?
8. Jesus is the bread of life: what does this mean?
9. What is the difference between the "I do" and the "I am"? What does this teach you about the importance of relationship with Jesus?
10. What does it mean to drink His blood?
11. What is the essence of God?
12. What do we do to eat and drink the body and blood of Jesus?
13. Jesus said that we can only come to Him with the help of the Father. How does this change our attitude to coming?
14. Why is it impossible to come to Jesus without the Father's help?
15. What are the two Hebrew words for the shewbread and what do you learn from them?

16. Why is the teaching of Jesus so offensive?

John 7: Rivers of Living Water

1. How many chapters in John cover the days that Jesus was at the Feast of Tabernacles?
2. Jesus said to His brothers that His time was not ready to go up to Jerusalem. What does this teach you about the way He lived?
3. What are the implications of the first great cry of Jesus, that people knew who He was?
4. Read Jeremiah 8:7 and Romans 1:18-19. What do you conclude about human responsibility from these verses?
5. Why do you think Jesus would not engage with the people about the fact that He was born in Bethlehem, while many assumed He was born in Nazareth.
6. What is the connection between the pool of Siloam and the great cry of Jesus in John 7:37?
7. What Old Testament events can you think of that can be connected with the cry of Jesus to come to Him and drink?
8. How do we connect John 7:37 with John 19:34 and Exodus 17:1-7?
9. What does John 7:37-9 teach us about the gift with the Holy Spirit?
10. How do we drink of the Holy Spirit?
11. What will be the manifestation of the Holy Spirit?
12. Why did this great cry of Jesus impact the crowds and make many believe that He was the Messiah?
13. Why did the guards sent to arrest Him seem so overcome at the words of Jesus? Can you think of moments when you have been amazed at the presence of God and His word?
14. Why is the attitude of the rulers to Nicodemus so surprising, given what we know about him?

John 8: The 4th waterpot – The woman taken in adultery

1. Where was Jesus' home according to the last verse of Ch. 7 and the first verse of Ch. 8?
2. Why is this "home" such a key to being anointed?
3. Describe in your own words the trap that the Pharisees set for Jesus.
4. What do you think it meant that Jesus wrote on the ground with His finger? Do you agree with the author in his reference to Moses and Daniel?
5. How did Jesus reverse the trap they set for Him?
6. What is the first great need of every person?
7. What do you think was the effect on the woman when Jesus told her to sin no more?
8. Why is the friendship of Jesus so important to us, after we have been forgiven and set free?
9. What problems did the woman still face after she had experienced salvation?
10. What does it tell you about the work of God, that the Father is bringing people to know who Jesus is?
11. Jesus said He knew where He was from and where He was going. What did He mean?
12. What does it mean that Jesus is the "I am"?
13. How would Jesus be able to draw all people to Himself after He was crucified?
14. Why is Jesus' oneness with the Father a key to His life?
15. What was the sin of the Pharisees? Why is it such a dreadful sin?
16. Why was it absurd of the Jews to claim they had never been in bondage to anyone (8:33)?
17. What does freedom look like? Is it freedom to do my own thing?
18. What does it mean that those who commit sins are slaves to sin?
19. What is the difference between being a spiritual son of Abraham and a natural one? (8:37-40)

20. What did Jesus mean by saying that the Pharisees were children of the devil?
21. How do we cease to have this affinity with darkness?
22. Is our choice ultimately between God and the devil? Is there really no middle ground?
23. The riddle that the Pharisees posed to Jesus is not answered in this passage. It was answered at the cross. Sum up the lesson of the story of James and Henry.

John 9: The 5th waterpot – the blind man

1. What was so strange about the question of the disciples about the origin of the man's blindness?
2. How can it be true that everything will be for the glory of God in the end?
3. Why do you think Jesus so rarely looks at the past of the people He ministered to?
4. What lessons do you draw from the action of Jesus in smearing mud on the man's eyes?
5. In what way do the eyes represent the heart?
6. Jesus sent the man to wash in the pool of Siloam. In what way is this a symbol of going to the cross?
7. Reflect on the reaction of the man to being healed from a lifetime of blindness. What should our reaction be when our eyes are opened to know the Lord?
8. What is the two-fold work of the Holy Spirit on our spiritual eyes?
9. Why did Jesus choose to do miracles on the Sabbath?
10. What was the problem with the Sabbath day observance of the Jews at this time?
11. Why did the Pharisees not become believers when they received the proof that the healing was genuine?
12. Why was this man's faith unshakable?

THE EAGLE AND THE WATERPOTS

13. In what way was the blind man healed of spiritual blindness?
14. Why is true faith so hard for some religious people to attain?
15. Why were the religious leaders doubly guilty after these events?

John 10: The Good Shepherd

1. Why are the chapter divisions sometimes misleading?
2. Explain the parable of the sheepfold. Who was the doorkeeper who opened the door to Jesus?
3. Who/what faculty is the doorkeeper of your life?
4. Why did the rulers of the Jews find it so hard to accept that Jesus was the Messiah?
5. Jesus said that they were unfaithful shepherds. What is the characteristic of such leaders?
6. What is the main characteristic of a true shepherd?
7. What is the connection between being "the door" and "the good shepherd"? Why might a familiarity with the role of shepherds in 1st century Judea help us understand this connection?
8. In what way can Jesus be described as the beautiful shepherd?
9. Think about other doors mentioned in the Bible. How do they help you understand what Jesus is the door to? (See for example Exodus 12:7, Hebrews 10:19-20 and Luke 9-13).
10. If Jesus is the Good Shepherd, what will happen if we stay close to Him? (Think of Psalm 23).
11. What was the Feast of Dedication?
12. Where were the deeds of the Maccabees prophesied in the Old Testament?
13. Why is it so paradoxical that the Jews tried to kill Jesus at the feast of dedication?
14. What does it mean that no-one can pluck us from the hand of God the Father?
15. Does this statement mean that Christians can never lose their salvation?

16. Do the warnings of Scripture strengthen or weaken our salvation?
17. What did Jesus mean by quoting *"You are gods!"* (Psalm 82:6)?
18. Is it right to think that this is connected with other themes in John's gospel?

John 11: The 6th waterpot - Lazarus

1. Describe the relationship between Jesus and the family in Bethany.
2. What was Mary's attitude to Jesus?
3. In what way was Martha different to Mary?
4. Why would they have expected Jesus to heal Lazarus?
5. Why do you think Jesus didn't heal Lazarus straight away?
6. List the four definitions of death in the Bible.
7. How could it be true that Lazarus was not dead?
8. Is there a good death, a death that makes God glad? (Think of Good Friday)?
9. What did the death of Jesus accomplish?
10. Why was Martha's attitude so good in a crisis?
11. When did Martha believe she would see Lazarus again?
12. Why was Martha's faith in the prayers of Jesus so important? What do learn from this?
13. What did Jesus mean when He said that believers shall never die?
14. Describe the dark place that Mary was in.
15. Why did Jesus weep?
16. In what way are we saved by the prayers and faith of Jesus?
17. What does the power of Jesus to raise the dead tell us about the power of the gospel to help sinners?
18. Do some believers still wear grave clothes? What would this look like?
19. What effect did this miracle have on the lives of Lazarus, Martha and Mary?
20. What effect should the fact of resurrection have on believers?

21. What was so strange about the reaction of the rulers?
22. What were their motives?
23. What does the prophecy of Caiaphas teach us about the way God uses people?

John 12: The calm before the storm

1. Can you think of any verses that tell us that believers have died and risen with Christ?
2. What are the five elements that characterise the church in resurrection life, but still living in this world?
3. Why is it so helpful to realise that there are still enemies like Judas, despite the victory of the cross?
4. Read Zechariah 9:9-10 and comment on the implications of Jesus riding into Jerusalem on a donkey.
5. How will Jesus come at the end of the age?
6. Why did Jesus decline to see the Greeks?
7. Why could Jesus not send His disciples into all the world until He had died and risen again?
8. In what way does the image of the seed dying apply to all believers?
9. In what way does the cry of Jesus in verse 28 sum up His whole purpose in life?
10. A voice came from heaven. This is the 3rd occasion in the life of Jesus. What do these 3 words from heaven teach us about God's message to the world?
11. Why do you think the voice of the Father was not understood or even heard clearly by so many?
12. What did it mean that the devil was to be cast out through the cross?
13. How would Jesus draw multitudes to Himself if He were lifted up on a cross? What does this teach us about our message to the world?
14. What did Jesus say would happen if we do not walk in the light we have received?

15. Why do you think walking with God is so important?
16. What was the warning that Isaiah gave to Israel (quoted by Jesus in verse 40)?
17. Does God make people dull so that they may be lost? How might the loss of free will awaken souls to their desperate need for God?

John 13: The washing of the disciples' feet

1. How did John know what Jesus was thinking? What do you learn from this?
2. What did John see in the face of Jesus?
3. Why was it such a surprise when Jesus dressed Himself like a slave?
4. Why would the disciples have been convicted by this action?
5. Jesus washed the feet of all the disciples. What does this teach you about the way we should serve in the church?
6. Why is continual washing a key element of being a Christian? Why must it be a regular experience to be washed by Jesus (See Psalm 24:3-4)?
7. What does it meant that only our feet need washing?
8. God doesn't wash us with water, so with what does He wash us?
9. Can you link this with the theme of water and washing in other chapters of John?
10. Why was John different in his response to the statement of Jesus that one of them would betray Him?
11. Why did Peter ask John to ask Jesus? What can we learn from this?
12. Why do you think Peter believed he might be the one to betray Jesus?
13. What did it mean that Jesus gave the bread dipped in wine to Judas?
14. Why did this provoke Him to a negative reaction?
15. What was the new commandment that Jesus now gave them?

16. Why did He wait till this point to announce it? Is it related to the teaching of the next chapters on the person and work of the Holy Spirit?
17. Why was Peter so vulnerable? What did he believe about his own powers of devotion?
18. How do you see comfort in the words of Jesus to Peter?
19. Why do you think we have to pass through such deep waters to discover the power of Jesus to change us?

John 14: The water explained

1. Do you agree that this section of the Bible contains the most profound teaching on the person and work of the Holy Spirit?
2. How do the opening words of Ch. 14 relate to the last words of Ch. 13?
3. Jesus said that we must not let our hearts be troubled. Do we have a choice not to let worry enter our hearts?
4. The word "many abiding places" is based on the word abide, which occurs many times in this section. Do you agree that this is not referring solely to the second coming? What does it refer to?
5. Where else is the Father's house mentioned in the New Testament?
6. Where is the home of the believer in a troubled world? Why should believers never feel abandoned?
7. What do you conclude from the way that Thomas felt free to contradict the Lord?
8. Jesus said He is the way, the truth and the life. Where does the way lead?
9. Why do you think Jesus was surprised that they claimed not to know the Father?
10. Do you agree that the coming of the Holy Spirit is an introduction to the Father, not just the Spirit?
11. How does the coming of the Holy Spirit change our prayer life?

12. What does it mean to pray in the name of Jesus?
13. In what way do believers do greater works that Jesus through the Holy Spirit?
14. Why can only believers receive the Holy Spirit?
15. What is the key condition for receiving the Holy Spirit according to Jesus?
16. What are the implications of this for understanding the work of the Holy Spirit?
17. What are the stages by which we can know the indwelling of the Holy Spirit?
18. How does the Holy Spirit enable the church to continue knowing Jesus, while the world does not see Him or know Him?
19. In what way do only believers have life?
20. What does the Holy Spirit teach us?
21. What does it mean that Jesus said the Father is greater than He?
22. Why is it so important that Jesus said He was going to the cross to show He loved the Father?

John 15: The water turned to wine

1. How does the theme of the vine connect with the miracle at Cana in chapter 2?
2. What do you learn from the teaching that believers are branches of Jesus the vine?
3. How do we abide in the vine?
4. Why could it be said that to abide in Jesus is to abide in love?
5. What does 'entering into the Holy of Holies' have to do with abiding in Christ?
6. What is the fruit of abiding in Christ?
7. How does this lead to soul-winning?
8. Do you agree that God cannot create love?
9. Why is Christ the key to everyone's life?
10. What will happen to the life of the believer who does not abide in Christ?
11. What does it mean to abide in the words of Jesus?
12. Why is joy a key element of our witness?

13. What does Jesus teach that is new in the Bible and can be described as central to the new covenant?
14. How is this new covenant linked with the coming of the Holy Spirit
15. Do you agree that friendship with Jesus is the highest attainment of any person?
16. What does it mean that Jesus chose us?
17. How can abiding in the love of God lead to persecution?
18. How do you explain the hatred for people who are filled with the love of Jesus?
19. What is the key work of the Holy Spirit that makes us effective witnesses of Jesus?

John 16: The end of parables

1. Why is it important that believers be mentally prepared for trouble in their Christian lives?
2. Where did Jesus teach that the church age would not be one of perfection?
3. In church history, is it true that much persecution has come from religious sources? Give examples.
4. Give examples from the New Testament.
5. What does it mean that Jesus had to go away so that the Holy Spirit would come?
6. In what way must believers make sacrifices if the Holy Spirit is to be poured out?
7. Why do we need the Holy Spirit to teach us about sin?
8. What is the heart of righteousness?
9. What will be the effect on unbelievers if they are convicted of coming judgment?
10. What does it mean that the Holy Spirit will teach us all truth? (See verse 13).
11. Are there things that the Holy Spirit will not teach us supernaturally?
12. List some of the things that we can only know through the power of the Holy Spirit.
13. Why is a listening heart to be associated with the Holy Spirit?

14. What are the deepest things we can ever know?
15. What did it mean that they would not see Jesus for a while but then they would see Him?
16. Jesus is known only by the Holy Spirit. So what does this teach you about His chief work?
17. What does this mean about our relationship with God now?
18. What did Jesus mean when He said that there would come a time when He would not need to pray for us?
19. Why do you think that this section is without parables?
20. Why do the final words of this section remove fear from the hearts of the disciples?

John17: The great High Priest praying for His own

1. List some parallels between the tabernacle and the gospel of John.
2. Where is the most holy place for the Christian? There are different ways in which we might address this question.
3. How might the prayer of John 17 be related to the teaching that precedes it in chapters 14-16?
4. What insights do you have into the relationship between God the Father and God the Son through this prayer? How does this illuminate the truth that God is love?
5. Where else in the Bible do we read about the prayers of God to God? What does this teach you about prayer?
6. Jesus prayed that God would glorify Him. Why was this not a selfish prayer?
7. Try and define the word "glory"?
8. What might it mean to experience the glory of God?
9. What does it mean that eternal life is to know the Father and Jesus?
10. What was the mission of Jesus in the world? There are many answers to this question, but relate your answer to His motives revealed in this chapter.

11. Summarise what Jesus was praying for us His disciples.
12. How is the unity of believers related to knowing the love of the Father?
13. What do you think the author means by saying, believers can die before they die?
14. What does it mean to be sanctified?
15. Do you agree that the goal of all ministry is to make us one with God?
16. God is holy, God is full of glory, God is love. Reflect on the wonder of God living in us.
17. Do you agree that this prayer was answered on the day of Pentecost? What does this teach you about the baptism with the Holy Spirit?

John 18: The King on trial

1. Why do you think Judas and the soldiers fell back when Jesus said I AM?
2. What does it teach us that Jesus had to help the soldiers to arrest Him?
3. Why was Peter's defence of Jesus with a sword so wrong on so many levels?
4. Who was the "other" disciple? Why was he in greater danger than Peter?
5. Peter answered the questions put to him with the words "I am not". What is the significance of this in the context of John's gospel? Contrast this with 1 Corinthians 15:10.
6. What are the three key statements in John on being true disciples?
7. Do you think these keys are based on our commitment? If not, what are they based on?
8. What does Peter's triple denial of the Lord deny us? How might we hear the cock crowing?
9. Do you think Peter needed this experience to prepare him to be used by God? Explain your answer.
10. Why did the Jews need Pilate to help them fulfil their plan to murder Christ?
11. What do you think Pilate meant when he asked Jesus "What is truth?" Your answer will involve

speculation because the answer is not clear from the Bible.

12. What do people believe today about truth?
13. What do you conclude from the way God made the people choose between Barabbas and Jesus?
14. Why is it not an option to wash one's hands when it comes to the claims of Jesus Christ?

John 19: The King is crucified

1. Why did Pilate scourge Jesus?
2. The scourging was prophesied in Isaiah 53:5. What was God's purpose in allowing Jesus to be scourged?
3. Who gave Pilate the power to decide the execution of Jesus? What effect should this have on our trust in the permissive will of God?
4. What was the master card that the High Priests used to make Pilate kill Jesus?
5. Why was it such a tragic statement when they said they had no king but Caesar?
6. What does it tell us that the description of Christ' sufferings is so restrained?
7. Why did the Jewish authorities object to the sign above the cross?
8. What is the similar objection by people today who want Christians to be politically correct?
9. What are the possible symbolic meanings of the seamless robe of Christ?
10. Why do you think that God arranged to have three women named Mary at the cross? (Read Exodus 15:23-25).
11. What is the universal significance of the words of Jesus to His mother and John? How should these words change our attitude to one another?
12. What does the cry "I thirst" mean?
13. Explore the different meanings of the great cry "It is finished!"
14. How does this cry echo the statement of Genesis 2:1?

15. How do we know that Jesus finished our redemption on the cross?
16. What was Jesus doing between His death and resurrection, according to the scriptures?
17. Why was it significant that the soldiers did not break the legs of Jesus?
18. What was the significance of the flow of water and blood from the side of Christ?
19. Why do you think the Bible mentions that Jesus was crucified and buried in a garden? Relate this to other scriptures especially in Genesis 2.
20. What was the smell in the tomb of Jesus and why?

John 20: The King is risen

1. What made Mary, Peter and John run?
2. What was it about the folded grave clothes that made John believe in the resurrection of Jesus?
3. Why do you think the disciples were so slow to believe that Jesus was risen?
4. Why do you think Mary Magdala loved Jesus more than anyone else?
5. Why were the angels puzzled that Mary was weeping?
6. Why was Mary weeping and what was she seeking?
7. Name anything beautiful you see in the love of Mary for Jesus.
8. What was so amazing about the message that Jesus gave Mary for the disciples?
9. Jesus first words to the disciples were: "Peace to you". Do you think this is still our greatest need?
10. Why does God dwell in perfect peace?
11. What is the difference between life after death and the resurrection from the dead?
12. What will a new body be like for us judging from the new body of Jesus?
13. What are the implications of the words of Jesus: "As My Father has sent Me, so send I you."?

14. What happened when Jesus breathed on His disciples and told them to receive the Holy Spirit?
15. How many times do we need to receive strengthening and refreshing from the Holy Spirit?
16. What do you think it means that Jesus gave the apostles power to forgive sins?
17. What was the great issue with which Thomas was wrestling?
18. What is so startling about the confession of Thomas when he saw the Lord?
19. Why is the invitation of Jesus to put a finger in His wounds and our hand in His side relevant to us?
20. John wrote to bring people to faith that Jesus is Messiah. What texts in the Old Testament prepare us to realise that the Messiah would be God in human form?

John 21: Breakfast by the sea

1. What is God's method for the conversion of sinners and the edification of believers?
2. Why do you think Peter went back to fishing?
3. Why do you think God prevented them from catching fish all night? What was He teaching them and us?
4. Contrast the reactions of Peter to the presence of Jesus. Are our reactions to Jesus conditioned by our character? Does this help you to accept yourself and be yourself?
5. It was John who first noticed that "it was the Lord." Why are believers sometimes so slow to see His hand in our difficulties?
6. Why is Jesus glorified by the fact that He made breakfast for the disciples? What can we learn from this about how we should behave?
7. Do you agree that Peter's love was weak? Why is confessing our weaknesses so important if we are to go deeper?

8. What do you learn from the fact that Jesus first called Peter to be an evangelist and then called him to be a pastor also?

9. From this conversation, what is the most important qualification for serving Jesus?

10. Peter died by crucifixion in around 65AD in Rome. How can this fact help us to date the gospel of John?

11. Peter was curious about John's future ministry. Why is it so important not to compare ourselves with other Christians and ministers?

12. What has impacted you most in studying the gospel of John?

13. John said the world could not contain the books that could be written about Jesus. What does this comment tell you about John's attitude to Jesus?

Printed in Great Britain
by Amazon